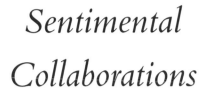

Sentimental Collaborations

MOURNING

AND

MIDDLE-CLASS

IDENTITY

IN

NINETEENTH-CENTURY

AMERICA

Mary Louise Kete

DUKE UNIVERSITY PRESS

DURHAM AND LONDON

2000

© 1999 Duke University Press

All rights reserved

Printed in the United States of America on acid-free paper ⊗

Typeset in Bembo by Tseng Information Systems, Inc.

Library of Congress Cataloging-in-Publication Data appear

on the last printed page of this book.

This work is dedicated

to the memory of my parents,

JOAN WALSH KETE *and* LOUIS JOSEPH KETE,

and to the future with my daughter,

MADELINE ELOISE KETE HOWE,

and my husband,

JOHN HAROLD HOWE

CONTENTS

Should dearest friends some kind memento trace,

Along the unwritten columns of this book

When distance or the grave hides form and face

Into this volume sweet t'will be to look.

Each fond remembrance oft will speak to you

In language which may never be forgot

Of those who ever constant were and true

And gently whisper O forget me not.

—Lois Gould, Dover, Vermont, March 1837

At the 1992 Democratic Convention, I talked about a personal event that fundamentally changed the way I viewed the world: an accident that almost killed our son. I will not repeat the story here except to say that the most important lesson for me was that people I didn't even know reached out to me and my family to lift us up in their hearts and in their prayers, with compassion of such intensity that I felt it as a palpable force, a healing, reaching out of those multitudes of caring souls and falling on us like a mantle of divine grace.

—Albert Gore, 1994 Harvard Commencement

Several years ago when I was in graduate school, my mother-in-law (a professor of environmental studies) showed me a manuscript from the last century. I might be interested in it, she thought, because it was full of poetry that reminded her of Mark Twain's Emmeline Grangerford and she knew of my interest in nineteenth-century American women's writing. "Look at this! What do you think of these?" she said, as she passed me a piece of pale blue paper covered with a long poem beginning: "Oh can it be that Wayland's dead / My lovely darling son." She was right. These pages did seem to be the prototypes of Emmeline Grangerford's "tributes." Sitting together on the sofa we were, at first, confident in our shared taste and shared cultural knowledge: recognizing these as like Twain's poem, we could safely classify them as the silly, naive, sentimental effusions of pretentious backwoods denizens. "How could anyone have thought these were beautiful?" we knowingly said to each other. Recognizing these poems this way reinforced our mutual recognition of ourselves as knowing, tasteful, and sophisticated readers. Daughter-in-law to mother-in-law, graduate student to professor, we bonded (as Oprah Winfrey might put it) over our shared perception of the ugliness of this poetry.

Yet, we continued to read and as we did a strange thing happened. We began to exchange looks with each other that did not convey a shared knowingness but an interrogatory wariness. I wondered what my mother-in-law would think if I confessed to being genuinely moved and intrigued by some of these poems. She, it turns out, wondered the same. "You know," she said, "when I first read through them, I cried. I know they're bad poems but . . . ?" These poems were different from Twain's. They were not so easy to laugh at. Or, maybe, they were too similar. Like Huck responding to Emmeline's "crayons," my mother-in-law and I experienced a mild case of the "fantods" on reading these accounts of lost love and ancient griefs. Despite the really alien aesthetic and across the distance of years, we were both moved to sympathy with the efforts of these frontier women to give voice to their loss.

The graduate student in me recognized that these were traces of what Ann Douglas had called the "feminization of American culture." The topics were clearly sentimental (dying children, domesticated heaven, gentle Jesus), yet neither my mother-in-law nor I could quite consign these poems to the status of bad copies of things not understood or devolutions of a once rigorous Christianity. Our experience seemed a clear example of the one described by Jane Tompkins at the beginning of her now classic essay on *Uncle Tom's Cabin* in *Sensational Designs.* Although these poems clearly did not easily fit the parameters of either the Romantic or modernist aesthetics, they did seem to be guided by some notion of what was beautiful. But, what was it? At first glance most of the poems seemed to be by and to women, all were about domestic issues. Could these be the traces of a "feminine" poetic practice that has been disregarded because of the patriarchal and modernist bias of twentieth-century literary history?

This project began, then, as a straightforward contribution to the feminist revision of American literary history. Here was evidence that would help flesh out our understanding of the distinctly feminine aesthetic of sentimentalism. Or, so I thought. Given this set of assumptions, I posed the following questions. What were the operative, and obviously now forgotten, poetics of this practice? Who were these people and what did they think they were doing? What were their literary models? As I pursued the answers to this project it became less "straightforward." First of all, I soon realized that many of the writers in this and comparable manuscripts were men, and on further research I found that some of the published models used by these amateur poets had been written by men. This poetry, then, seemed to qualify the "separate spheres" model of American literary history that had enabled so much of the feminist recovery of nineteenth-century American women's writing. Instead, it called for a much more subtle understanding of gender construction in the nineteenth century, one that would take class into account as well.

Although all the writers didn't happen to be women, they did all happen to be of the generation that was inventing what it would mean to be middle class in America. I also realized that conventional literary histories wouldn't be much help because for the most part this poetry has been dismissed without serious formal or cultural analysis. For all intents and purposes, Twain's parody had fully replaced the original. While the "Ode to Stephen Dowling Bots Dec'd" might be easily found in college anthologies, Longfellow and Whittier (much less Lydia Sigourney or Fanny Osgood) were hardly represented.

To answer my questions I began to patch together a methodology as much informed by anthropology and sociology as by literary history and theory. Like Claude Lévi-Strauss's bricolage, when I picked up certain ideas from these social sciences I turned them to my own uses and perhaps they are now unrecognizable. But throughout the project I drew much encouragement from the field of anthropology. My original question, "What did these people think they were doing?" became "How did this poetry help its writers make sense of the world?" I began to pay attention to the set of "artifacts," literary and nonliterary, that was associated with the poetry and as I did I came to several important realizations. Most important, I realized that all these poems were, first and foremost, gifts. And again, borrowing from anthropology, I began to wonder if whether, in addition to understanding them as a examples of a particular literary genre, they might also be gestures of signification in a symbology that I didn't quite understand. Of course, Lewis Hyde's wide-ranging and evocative interrogation of gift giving and creativity in *The Gift: Imagination and the Erotic Life of Property* provided a good example of someone else who seemed to be going down the same road. Like him I went to the library and wrestled with the tradition of anthropological discussions of the gift, beginning with Marcel Mauss's 1924 essay on the gift and the discussions of Mary Douglas. These were terrifically helpful, except that they all talk about gift economies as if they are in clear opposition to market economies. Only recently have anthropologists (such as David Cheal and Annette Weiner) begun to complicate this idea by investigating the role that gift economies play in market economies. These have been much more helpful to me and have led me to depart significantly from Hyde's reification of the difference between the "two spheres" of market and gift exchange. I also ended up drawing quite a bit on the field of sociology, especially the work of Pierre Bourdieu, whose conceptualization of the way that the various, simultaneous, and interrelating "habitus" of culture can be constructed and maintained has helped me to reconceptualize American Romanticism. In this model sentimentalism plays an important role in the dissemination of Romanticism throughout American culture during the antebellum era. My research supports British sociologist Colin Campbell's suggestion that the "ethos of Romanticism" is not as antithetical to "the spirit of modern consumerism" as has been supposed. I suggest that, in fact, these two terms are not only mutually dependent but also that the mode of sentimentality forms the link between consumerism and Romanticism in American culture.

I realize that I am not alone in turning to the social sciences to wrestle with the problem of sentimentality in American culture. However, hardly any of the growing number of studies concerning this issue pay much attention to formal rhetorical or literary analysis at all. Throughout my project I have felt that the broad strokes of "cultural studies," as it is often practiced, need to be and can be refined and supported by the techniques and vocabulary of close textual analysis. What I began to realize is that sentimentality is not a genre, nor has it been, even in the eighteenth and nineteenth centuries, the peculiar provenance of women. Neither is it a sham display of emotion for the self-interested manipulations of others. It is not "bad" Romanticism. I would like to suggest, instead, that sentimentality is best understood, in formal literary terms, as a mode akin to irony, tragedy, or comedy, in that it can inflect any genre and in that it has some small set of shared, identifiable characteristics. The peculiar and contradictory work of sentiment in our culture stems from these formal characteristics. Literary sentimentality is just the written trace of a broad cultural discourse that I call "sentimental collaboration": the exchange of sympathy establishing the ground for participation in a common cultural or intellectual project.

Before concluding this preface, I'd like to give a brief example from recent history of the ongoing consequences of sentimental collaboration. Two years into his term as vice president, Al Gore turned the opportunity to address the alumni of Harvard University during the 1994 commencement exercises into an occasion to deliver a jeremiad, or political sermon, entitled "The Cynics Are Wrong." Announcing his rejection of what he described as the prevailing and dangerous attitude of cynicism about the possibilities of American democracy, Gore "affirms his faith in America's future" (*Harvard Magazine* 28). Cynicism, according to Gore, "represents now a secession from society, a dissolution of the bonds be-

tween people and families and communities, an indifference to the fate
of anything or anyone beyond the self" (31). The antidote to such antisocial, antidemocratic cynicism, posits Gore, is what I would describe
as "sentimental collaboration"—the exchange of sympathy which establishes the ground for participation in a common cultural or intellectual
project. In offering an exemplum drawn from his own life, Gore explains
how his involuntary entry into sentimental collaboration saved his own
political faith. But it was the telling and retelling of this story in the public arena of the 1992 presidential campaign, I would argue, that was the
salvation of his own political career.

During this Harvard commencement speech, as at the 1992 Democratic national convention, Gore sought to engage his listeners with the
gift of his own story about the effect of sentiment in his life. Gore's story
told of the time when his young son had been hit by a car in the parking
lot of a shopping mall and of the crisis of faith and redemption which
followed. This gift of sentiment—to his former college classmates and to
his own graduating daughter and her classmates at Harvard—continues
the economy of sympathy that, for Gore, had played such a crucial role
in the recovery of his son's health and in the recovery of Gore's own faith
in the liberal project of democracy.

When, in front of millions of American viewers of the 1992 Democratic National convention, Gore had deployed this anecdote, it dropped
on him the "mantle" of representative—ordinary, common—American.
This particular mantle had been harder for Gore to claim than it had
been for his running mate, presidential candidate Bill Clinton, who more
easily fit into preestablished presidential iconographies. Clinton's campaign biography easily updated the log cabin–to–White House story that
has been familiar, honored and repeated since Andrew Jackson's era. But
Gore is, and has been seen as, one of the most privileged of Americans.
The story Gore told during those campaign years was an attempt to replace the image of Gore as scion of one of the wealthiest families in
America and Harvard-educated son of a senator with this one: a man
looking down at his wife, who is kneeling on the tarmac of the wasteland
of a shopping mall parking lot while holding the broken, unconscious
body of a boy. In this story, Gore is a man who shops at malls, a man
who must traverse the disorientating ground of the parking lot—child in
tow—to get to the twentieth-century agora. There he might find enter-

tainment and there he might be able to participate in American culture by buying something. He is a man who might worry that his child might demand something the man can't afford; and finally, he is a man who has suffered a loss that many others either have also suffered or have imagined suffering. As a narrative interpolation within a campaign speech, this story attempted to reconstitute Gore as one of the many, one of the "regular," middle-class Americans, and established, thereby, his claim to compete for the second highest office in American politics.

Quite interesting, I think, is the fact that the rhetorical function of Gore's story during the convention was not undercut by the presence of his recovered son. The child did not have to be dead to be successfully turned into an image for circulation within an economy of sentiment. Perhaps the boy's live presence actually served as a testament to the restorative power Gore was claiming for sympathy. For the story of the power of sympathy, at the 1992 convention, was both a retelling and a plea for more of the same. See me, the candidate was saying through this story, as a man who feels as you do, who will act as you would, because we all are defined by our relationships to our children and are threatened by the possibility of the loss of those children.

Through the help of strangers, as Gore tells it, the parking lot was transformed from a scene of family destruction to a scene of family salvation, a salvation that could not have been achieved without a loosening of the boundaries surrounding the unit of that family and the boundaries surrounding the individual subjectivities of persons involved. "I don't know," Gore speculates, "what barriers in my soul had prevented me from understanding emotionally that basic connection to others until after they reached me in the dark of my family's sorrow. But I suppose it was a form of cynicism on my part." Even the margin land of America, the parking lot where we leave our cars (the extensions of our homes) before crossing into the familiar site of the exchange of cultural and commodity capital which is the mall, becomes subjected to domestification by the forces of sympathy within Gore's narration.

But the real gift Gore offered his Harvard audience two years later was his exegetical analysis of his personal story of grief and solace. "Having felt this power in my own life," Gore explained to his fellow graduates of the Harvard class of 1969, "I believe that sympathy and compassion are revolutionary forces in the world at large and that they are work-ing now" (32). Making his own life an allegorical type of America and the world at large, Gore testifies to the ability of sentimental collabora-tion. As sympathy restored his family and himself, so sympathy might restore the nation. Such reconstruction for Gore himself—Gore uses the term "healing"—came in the wake of the twin alienating experiences of his generation: he is both the betrayed American son (having soldiered in Vietnam) and the individually helpless father (unable to protect his own son from harm). The sympathy, which in Gore's conversion nar-rative envelops him "like a mantle of divine grace" under which "we are all astonishingly similar in the most important parts of existence," becomes within Gore's political sermon the single most important as-sumption undergirding the American "credo" he offers. Sympathy is the ground of his newly reaffirmed belief in America as "the model to which the world aspires." In his Harvard commencement speech, Gore extended the analogy of self, voters, and nation he had established in his Demo-cratic convention speech to include the world. As sympathy cured Gore personally, so sympathy, he avers, will cure the present ills of America and so it will cure the political despair of the world.

Coming from an American politician speaking to an audience of po-tential voters on the cusp of the twenty-first century, Gore's reitera-tion of mid-nineteenth-century American sentimental discourse has an almost uncanny quality to it. It seems to deny the distance separating the American political experience of then and now. Although, if any-thing, I want to insist upon the distance between (and the particularity of) different historical moments in American society, Gore's speech raises the question of the ongoing yet under-theorized role of the mode of sentimentality in American literary and cultural life. The too numer-ous examples of the deployment of sentiment by American politicians of the so-called left and the so-called right, and by the media on behalf of socially "progressive" or "conservative" causes, leaves little room to doubt that sentimentality is one of what we might (with Shirley Samuels) call the "structuring structures" of American life. Most examples of the on-going force of sentimentality in American political experience—be they Richard Nixon's "Checkers Speech," the AIDS Quilt Project, Clarence Thomas's Supreme Court nomination testimony, the AT&T television commercials of the 1980s, or Newt Gingrich's offer of a Contract with America and the current right-to-life movement—deploy the same logic of sentimentalism as Gore did in this Harvard speech.

The particular example of Gore's speeches gives some indication of why sentimentalism is such a strong current in today's culture. Although it has been more fashionable to point out and to decry the negative ideological aspects of sentimentalism—that is, the aspects of sentimentalism that seem to manipulate individual emotional responses in the service of another's class or cultural interests—my goal has been to excavate the utopian aspects of sentimentality. Surely it is easy to see Gore's "The Cynics are Wrong" speech as itself a cynical political gesture, one composed by a bevy of speech writers to manage a problem of perception. But does it—and, more accurately, did his 1992 stump speeches—do the real, actual political work of contributing to the election of the Clinton/Gore platform because of its clever, "inauthentic" manipulation of emotional tropes and affects? Or does some of the real political power of sentimentality come from its less acknowledged utopian force, a force that operates to express what Fredric Jameson describes as "the unity of a collectivity" (291)? It seems to me that Gore's speech models the way that sentimentality performs its ideological work specifically through its (and here I'm quoting Jameson again) "symbolic affirmation of a specific historical and class form of collective unity" (291): a symbolic affirmation of the "collective unity" of American identity.

Or, more precisely, Gore's speeches show the way that sentimentality facilitates the constitution and perpetuation of that seemingly boundless and affirming category of "ordinary," common Americans who are neither rich, poor, black, white male, female. The utopian self, which operates ideologically to elide those very differences, is defined, rather, by what it does: it loves and it shops. This self, the self Gore lost and found, is essentially economic. It exists only in and through the circulation or exchange of emotions through an economy of sentiment such as Gore described, and only in and through the circulation of money and goods in a market economy. Remove yourself from either and you remove yourself from the category of "American"; you certainly lose any claim to representative American-ness. Gore's story shows the intersection of these economies in the parking lot of the mall where the dystopic and utopic possibilities of American identity have the most chance of becoming real. His successful use of this story shows the degree to which late-twentieth-century American culture still depends on the form of discourse, sentimentality, that emerged along with its most distinctive speakers in the nineteenth century: the American middle class.

I have received many gifts over the course of this project and though I know they were given without thought of return, I feel I must make some effort, however inadequate, to thank those to whom I owe so much. First, I want to thank Sacvan Bercovitch; the idea for this project began in a graduate seminar he taught on the problems of American literary history. Professor Bercovitch's generous enthusiasm, early and late, has been a constant source of support. Second, I want to thank Robyn Warhol. She continues to provide a model for understanding the ways that gender and genre inform each other. Without her guidance at critical moments, this work would have remained an idea.

I also want to thank Lawrence Buell, Philip Fisher, and Lynn Wardley, who read numerous early versions of this, for their generous attention and insightful criticisms. Stanley Cavell, Stephen Greenblatt, Barbara Johnson, Kathryne Lundberg, Derek Pearsall, Werner Sollars, Susan Suleiman, and Helen Vendler also read various parts of this early on. Their feedback helped me more, perhaps, than they were aware of and certainly more than I can express here. Although graduate school can be a lonely place, I was lucky in friendships and I would like to thank Kathleen Kete, Anita Goldman, Cheryl Nixon, and James Mendelssohn who made the writing much more fun than I had any right to expect. I would especially like to thank Laura Korabkin with whom I have continued a seemingly endless conversation about sentiment and nineteenth-century American culture. Since coming to the University of Vermont, I have been graced with many supportive colleagues and friends. I would particularly like to thank Philip Baruth, Tony Bradley, Irene Kacandes, Huck Gutman, Lisa Schnell, Mike Stanton, Nancy Welch, and Kari Winter who have all listened and advised most patiently as I transformed the dissertation into a book. Generous suggestions came from Donald Pease and Michelle Burnham who read the manuscript for Duke University Press.

I also want to thank the institutions who provided the material conditions for undertaking the task of research and writing. These include the American Antiquarian Society, the Schlesinger Library, Bailey-Howe

Library's Special Collections, the Vermont Historical Society, and the New Hampshire Historical Society. While at Harvard I received two fellowships that enabled me to research and write the dissertation on which *Sentimental Collaborations* is based. I would like to thank the Harvard English Department for the Graduate Research Fellowship that let me rummage profitably in libraries, attics, and archives, and I would like to thank the Mellon Foundation for the fellowship that allowed me to devote myself full time to the task of writing. The work of transforming a dissertation into a book would have been much more difficult without the support of grants from the University of Vermont's Dean Fund and the College Research and Scholarship Fund.

This book also owes much to persons outside of academia, especially Ralph and Verne Howe who shared not only their extensive private collection of nineteenth-century Americana with me but also their rich knowledge of local New England culture. Early on in this project, through the help of the Howes, I was able to interview two elderly women who were directly related to contributors to the *Harriet Gould's Book*. Though they are now memories, I would like to express my thanks to Mrs. Ruby Howe Jones and Mrs. Helen Gould Upton who helped me think about what it might have meant for the women of their grandparent's generation to write, read, and exchange poetry as they evidently did. I would also like to thank Phillip Kete, who read the whole manuscript in a heroic act of brotherly affection, and Cynthya Spencer, who has raised the practice of the gift economy to a high art.

Most of all, I owe my husband, John Howe, more than I can ever repay for his patience and love as this book developed.

The Forgotten Language
of Sentimentality

For as it is dis-location and detachment from the life of God that
makes things ugly, the poet, who re-attaches things to nature and
the Whole, — re-attaching even artificial things and violation of nature, to nature, by a deeper insight, — disposes very easily of the
most disagreeable facts. — Emerson, "The Poet," 1844

Unlike most recent attempts to come to terms with the American sentimental tradition which focus on narrative and the novel, I have become
convinced that the poetry of the nineteenth century, as a practice and as
a product, deserves closer attention. After all, when Ralph Waldo Emerson in 1837 addressed the Harvard Phi Beta Kappa Society with an appeal
for and description of "The American Scholar," he began by making a
millennial claim for poetry: "Who can doubt that poetry will revive and
lead in a new age, as the star in the constellation Harp, which now flames
in our zenith, astronomers announce, shall one day be the pole star for a
thousand years" (64). To those who were not familiar with the most recent astronomical theories, it might have been possible to doubt that out
of the plethora of stars crowding the zenith of the sky, one would eventually move into the lonely, fixed position of the pole star around which
the rest of the galaxy revolves and by which earthly observers navigate.
But it was hardly possible to "doubt that poetry will revive and lead in
a new age," because Emerson was only describing what many people felt
and were enacting in villages and farmsteads across New England.

Although Emerson's poet is insistently gendered male, numerous
women as well as men attested to their faith in the capacity of poetry
to correct the threatening "dislocation of and detachment from the life

of God" ("The Poet" 229). They did this by writing poetry in what Lois Gould of Dover, Vermont, called the "language which may never be forgot" (*Harriet Gould's Book* 2). This language, whose rules and usages have become obscured in the present century, governed more than literary expressions. In fact, as the popular sentimental poet Lydia Sigourney averred, it was understood as a fundamentally supra-verbal mode of expression.[1] The best model of what Sigourney considered the "unspoken language" of the soul occurs in the time of infancy: "The mother speaks it well / To the unfolding spirit of her babe" ("Unspoken Language" 19–20). Verbal and material expressions of the language of sentiment, such as poetry or embroidery, were seen as imperfect but useful approximations of this originary language. For us, they may serve as traces of a fundamental construct through which nineteenth-century Americans made sense of themselves.[2] If, as Emerson explains in "The Poet," "words are also actions, and actions are a kind of words," then the popular poetry of nineteenth-century America should provide a decipherable index to the dynamics of American culture (225).[3]

The poetry that "flamed at the zenith" of America's literary culture in the years between the War of 1812 and the end of the Reconstruction period forces a confrontation between conventional notions of sentimentalism and conventional notions of the history of American literature. The many poets writing what has been dismissed as "sentimental" and inconsequential poetry were engaged in what Emerson considered the urgent work of "reattaching even artificial things and violation of nature, to nature" and thereby healing the "dislocation and detachment" of man from God ("The Poet" 229).[4] Their engagement deserves reevaluation, as it both affected the cultural parameters of the nineteenth-century American world and shaped the aesthetic expectations of later Americans.[5] Just as much as Emerson, the readers, writers, buyers, and givers of sentimental poetry were actively calling into being "the pole star" to a "new age" of America. The new age of nineteenth-century America became the age for themselves, the American middle class. "Events, actions arise," claims Emerson, "that must be sung, that will be sung" ("American Scholar" 64). I will be arguing that the events and actions shaping what it meant to be an American were being sung in a key set by the poetics of sentimentality. The nature of this poetics has remained elusive despite much excellent recent work on the sentimental or domestic novel. The poetics of sentimentality is best revealed by attention to quotidian verse that celebrates not the sublime, the individual, and the possibility of dissent, but the domestic, the familial, and the possibility of consent.

In this way the sentimental mode can be seen as the functional aspect of the American Romantic movement, the aspect that enables the widespread diffusion of Romantic sensibilities through a culture invested in imagining itself as a cohesive, integral whole.[6] Imagine, for a moment, the exclusion of Wordsworth's Lucy poems from considerations of the British Romantic period because of their focus on the ordinary, the domestic, or on loss, and you have imagined the nature of the gap that currently exists in conventional studies of American Romanticism.[7] A manuscript album of poetry that my mother-in-law shared with me several years ago offers an occasion to begin to address this problem. Taken as a whole this manuscript (*Harriet Gould's Book*) is one of the fullest examples of the give and take, the circulation, of affections that characterizes, for me, the culture-building power of sentimental discourse. It provides a model for reexamining some of the key assumptions of American studies, including the role of women and other marginal individuals in the creation of what it means to be an American. In the first part of this study, I derive a theoretical and formal understanding of the language of sentiment from a close examination of this manuscript and its provenance. Sentiment, I argue, structures a collaboration through which individuals can join together in solving the seemingly local problem of grief in the face of death. The poems in *Harriet Gould's Book* trace the way that hardscrabble farmers deployed poetry in an economy of sentimental artifacts through which they were able to define and claim the center of cultural power as they defined and laid claim to a revolutionary, new sense of self.

But these poems also suggest the degree to which this collaborated American subject must betray itself. The successful, utopian solutions of certain problems of loss, themselves, lead to violent disintegrations of the very structures they have set into place. For, after all, the term "collaboration" is uncanny. As the *American Heritage Dictionary* explains, it means both "to join together in a joint intellectual project" and "to cooperate with the enemy." Sentimental collaboration works, I show in the three remaining parts of the book, to construct a particularly American form of personal subjectivity, national subjectivity, and aesthetic subjectivity. These forms of subjectivity, I argue, result from the simultaneous participation in joint intellectual projects and in treasonous cooperations. To understand the contradictory aspects of sentimentality is to understand the contradictory aspects of American consciousness.

Before going on to introduce the chapters of this book in any detail, I'd like to offer a brief discussion of one of the untitled mourning poems of *Harriet Gould's Book:* [8]

> Oh can it be that Wayland's dead
> My lovely darling son
> Oh can it be his soul has fled
> To its eternal home.
>
> How sad how very sad the hour
> That bore him far away
> Oh ne'er while memory holds her seat
> Shall I forget that day.
>
> But deeper sadder is the gloom
> That rests on all around
> As one by one the days move on
> In their appointed rounds,
>
> And still my babe returns no more
> To cheer my aching heart
> The silken ties that bound him there
> Have all been torn apart.
>
> How can I check the falling tear
> How can I hush the sigh
> Dear Savior let me ever feel
> Thy grace and presence nigh
>
> I know my boy though lost to me
> Has reached the blissful shore
> The soul divested of its clay
> Can sing its suffering o'er

He's safely housed from every storm,
Secure on Jesus' breast.
O may we strive to meet him there
And share his blissful rest.

And while we tread the toilsome way,
Which oft is dark and drear
We know that both our darling boys
Are safe from grief and fear.

And if to God we faithful prove,
And act the Christian part
We'll join them in that world above
Where we shall never part.

(Abigail Gould Howe III)

To those in the midst of Emerson's "shop, the plough, and the ledger"
or, in the case of women poets such as Abigail Howe, the kitchen, the
farmyard, and the nursery, the mode of sentimentality provided a means
of confronting the philosophical problem of skepticism posed by the experience of loss. Grief drives such characteristically sentimental asser-
tions of hope and benevolence as: "I know my boy though lost to me /
Has reached the blissful shore." This claim made by Abigail Gould Howe
in a poem written on the death of one of her sons is really an answer
to a repeatedly posed spiritual skepticism, an answer she comes to only
with difficulty. The dominant mood of Abigail Howe's mourning poem
is interrogative. She begins with an exclamation of bereftness:

Oh can it be that Wayland's dead
My lovely darling son
Oh can it be his soul has fled
To its eternal home.

In the middle of the poem she describes the physical manifestations of
her continued grief as she seeks a method to achieve solace: "How can I
check the falling tear / How can I hush the sigh."

The solution to her grief is posited in a vision of the reunification of
the family after death:

He's safely housed from every storm,
Secure on Jesus' breast.
O may we strive to meet him there
And share his blissful rest.

Abigail Howe's mourning poem for her son Wayland suggests that the distinguishing function of the poetics of sentimentality is the same as that claimed by Emerson for the poet: to reattach symbolic connections that have been severed by the contingencies of human existence. This is the utopian promise that wielded great ideological effect. Her poem, an imaginative construction, is a medium for the restoration of "the silken ties that bound him" to her heart that had "all been torn apart." It is also a chance to imagine the bonds between herself and her child as different than they really were: as eternal, not temporary; as necessary, not arbitrary. This act of conservation is essentially generative; the symbolic work of imagining a replacement also provides for the symbolic re-production of that which is considered original or authentic.[9]

The replacement family that Abigail Howe imagines for her dead child and for herself is superior to the one that has been actually lost. Wayland shall be "housed from every storm" upon "Jesus' breast." The "world above / Where we shall never part" is a world in which the earthly hierarchy between parent and child will be subsumed if Abigail should be able to join her son within the heavenly domestic space dominated by the parental Jesus. Abigail Howe's use of conditionals, "*may* we strive," "*if* to God," "*We'll* join them," at the close of this poem undercuts the confidence she has expressed in the middle of the poem when she claims: "I know my boy though lost to me / Has reached the blissful shore" or "We know that both our darling boys / Are safe from grief and fear." The subjunctive leaves open the possibility that the conditions of loss might continue, that there will be no reconstitution of the family or healing of the loss and that Abigail will never find a way "to check the falling tear" or "hush the sigh." In the process of addressing the problem of grief in this poem, one of eight dealing directly with infant death by several women from the Dover community, Abigail is able to displace the "I" whose isolated pain dominates the first twenty-six lines of the poem with the "we" of the concluding ten lines. It is in the voice of this "we," a joint self composed of herself and her husband, that Abigail is able to imagine (if only conditionally) a utopian resolution to her personal doubts. In other words, Abigail Gould Howe's poem for Wayland addresses the challenge of her own experience of grief in the language of sentiment.

In part I of what follows, I lay out the formal components of this "language which may never be forgot" in terms of its grammar and lexicon. Writers such as Abigail Gould Howe used these formal elements as a means of transforming their grief into restorative mourning, skepticism into optimism. My readings of this manuscript are meant to provide a theoretical foundation for my overall treatment of sentimental culture, which moves from vernacular texts, as here, to works of former and present canonical status and a historical foundation for a study that spans across the years from the formation of antebellum American culture through the aftermath of the Civil War. The first chapter, "*Harriet Gould's Book:* Description and Provenance," introduces the reader to the widespread cultural practice of sentimental collaboration in the early nineteenth century through a "thick description" of *Harriet Gould's Book,* which situates the manuscript at the nexus of several contexts: historical, political, and aesthetic. The second chapter, "We Shore These Fragments against Our Ruin," provides a close analysis of the poetics governing the individual poems and the manuscript as a whole. I lay the ground work, here, for understanding sentimentality as a discursive mode that transcends the boundaries of genre and performs its specific cultural work through a shared set of formal features.

The second part, "Sentimental Collaborations: Mourning and the American Self," focuses on sentimentality's role in the construction of a personal subjectivity that was not at odds with, but a necessary condition of, community. Both chapters depend on an interdisciplinary framework that harnesses the methodology of anthropology and sociology to the interpretative power of formal literary analysis. Both are concerned with the paradoxical way that the mode of sentimentality inflects particular genres in different ways; where the lyric gains the novel-like capacity to move through time and to encompass multiple voices, the novel gains the lyric-like capacity to open up one moment of time and to collapse heteroglossia into monologia. In chapter 3, " 'And Sister Sing the Song I Love': The Economy of Self and Other in the Stasis of Lyric," I continue my discussion of *Harriet Gould's Book* to argue that these lyrics are the traces of a symbolic economy. Through the circulation of these traces, the participants in this economy construct and maintain a collaborative sense of personal identity. Such collaborative individualism (for want of a better term) is the necessary correlative to the more commonly studied possessive individual often thought to be at the heart of liberal society. Chapter 4 turns to the novel to find more fully rendered descriptions of what this economy of sentiment might have looked like. In "Circulation of the Dead and the Making of the Self in the Novel" I use a model of reading suggested by the archival poems of *Harriet Gould's Book* to explore two paradigmatically sentimental novels: Harriet Beecher Stowe's *Uncle Tom's Cabin* and Elizabeth Stuart Phelps's *The Gates Ajar*. Each depicts the formation of sentimental collaborations between characters, and each seeks to engage its readers in collaborations through the deployment of sentiment. In *Uncle Tom's Cabin,* the collaborative subject results from the circulation of dead children; in *The Gates Ajar* this subject derives from the circulation of dead men.

The third part, "The Competition of Sentimental Nationalisms: Lydia Sigourney and Henry Wadsworth Longfellow," describes the way that these two seemingly very different poets used the collaborative potential of sentimentality to formulate definitions of "America" and "Americans" in sentimental terms. I contrast the success of these typically sentimental poets to define these concepts with the effort of earlier poet Joel Barlow, who had offered a neo-classic vision of America in the form of an epic. In chapter 5, "The Competition of Sentimental Nationalisms," I describe the way that each of these nineteenth-century poets relied on the increasingly popular aesthetics of sentimentality to carve out a new career path as a professional poet that was part of their effort to define the American subject. However, the different sentimental Americas generated by each reveals the critical inflections of gender carried by an ubiquitous American sentimentality. In Chapter 6, "The Other American Poets," I argue that, having secured themselves as American poets, Sigourney and Longfellow anticipate and try to counter the threats to the integrity of their sentimental Americas. Both poets inoculate their nationalist projects against what they imagined is the worst threat—the threat of disunion—by using the rhetorical strategies of sentimentality to coerce their readers into joining with them in the articulation of a shared vision of America. Neither they, nor the political figures such as Abraham Lincoln who shared their vision of a sentimental America, could have realized the degree to which sentimental solutions to the problems facing the nation were not only inadequate but were actually partaking of the same structures generating this strife.

This was, however, clear to many after the war. Mark Twain, nostalgically celebrating the antebellum culture of his youth during the politically traumatic but personally triumphant Reconstruction years, suggests this connection in his two reconstruction era "boys' books," *The Adventures of Tom Sawyer* and *The Adventures of Huckleberry Finn*. In the final part, "Mourning Sentimentality in Reconstruction-Era America: Mark Twain's Nostalgic Realism," I argue for a reevaluation of Twain's relationship both to the culture of sentiment and to its aesthetic expressions. In chapter 7, "Invoking the Bonds of Affection: *Tom Sawyer* and America's Morning," I contextualize Twain's vexed relationship to sentimentality within a broader contemporary cultural debate about the efficacy of sentimentality as a mode of rhetoric. Twain's *Tom Sawyer,* like Abraham Lincoln's Second Inaugural Address, bespeaks a continued faith in the ability of sentiment to solve the political problems of the perpetuation and reproduction of the promises of America. Yet, I go on to suggest in chapter 8, "Mourning America's Morning: *The Adventures of Huckleberry Finn*," that *Huck Finn* interrogates the degree to which sentimentality undermines its own promises while refusing to repudiate those promises. Seen in this light, both Twain's continued reliance on sentimentality and his role in the development of what have come to seem as the counterstrategies of realism are part of a lifelong effort to solve the problems of a sentimental culture. Twain's "realism," then, is a reformative gesture meant to restore the potential of literature as a vehicle for the construction of the necessary connections among people through the circulation of authentic affections.

Each of the last three parts is concerned with a particular function of sentimental collaboration: what kind of self, what kind of nation, and what kind of art was called into being through the efficacy of the "language which may never be forgot"? Working together on these questions, as a joint project, was itself one of the ways that a cohesive group identity encompassing and defining the American middle class began to emerge during this era. Each of the parts of this book examines the way that the ideological force of sentimental discourse in American culture arises from the promise of utopian community as an answer to particular threats of loss and alienation. The members of Harriet Gould's rural community model this ideological force as they address the seemingly local and individual problem of parental grief by forging closer reciprocal ties among the larger group of the community. They left traces of this in the form of poetry, memoirs, gravestones, and mourning art. But so did many more famous Americans, such as Emerson, Stowe, Phelps, Sigourney, Longfellow, Lincoln, and Twain, when they used the radically conserving power of sentimental collaboration to reconfigure loss as gain in their own lives and work.

PART ONE

The "Language Which May Never Be Forgot"

GRAVE OF WARREN GOULD,
DOVER COMMON CEMETERY, DOVER, VERMONT.
"John Warren / Son of / John P. & Harriet /
A. Gould, Died / April 6, 1843. / Æ 6 y'rs 7 mo. / & 29 days. /
Jesus said suffer little / children to come unto me / and forbid
them not for of / such is the kingdom of heaven."

Should dearest friends some kind memento trace,
Along the unwritten columns of this book
When distance or the grave hides form and face
Into this volume sweet t'will be to look.

Each fond remembrance oft will speak to you
In language which may never be forgot
Of those who ever constant were and true
And gently whisper O forget me not.

—Lois Gould, *Harriet Gould's Book,* 1837

In 1930, when Gordon Haight began the last critical biography of the popular and prolific nineteenth-century poet Lydia Huntley Sigourney, he explained that he had searched in vain for "some few pieces that would establish her right to the reputation she enjoyed for a half a century as America's leading poetess" (preface). Sigourney posed a critical problem to Haight, who, like others interested in the problem of literary history during the early years of the modernist movement, sought to understand its roots and impulses.[1] The three hundred or so pages of his biography testify to the earnestness of his effort, but, like Huck, he "couldn't make it go some how;" he couldn't make sense of what had seemed so obvious just fifty years before. Sigourney, Haight avers, had been the female equivalent of Henry Wadsworth Longfellow: beloved, anthologized, recited, celebrated, and copied. She had been a model American poet. But why? What had Haight's grandparents seen in her?

If, in the wake of "The Wasteland" and "The Cantos," Longfellow was becoming more and more irrelevant, how much more so was Sigourney. Both her poetry and her way of practicing poetry were ugly, earnest, commercial—irredeemable from the vantage point of modernism. She was too "unprofessional" because she wrote only from inspiration with little revision and less craft; she often gave her poems away as gifts (Haight). Yet more damning, she was too commercial in that she courted the literary marketplace with an obvious aim to make money (Haight).

Worst of all, where Longfellow's problem seems to have been that his poetics was too "feminine," Sigourney's problem was compounded by the fact that she was, in fact, female.[2] Haight was disturbed by the evidence that Sigourney was given to using "paint," or makeup, and that her sons resented the emasculating effect her financial success had upon their father (Haight xx). Having searched the forty or so volumes of her poetry for some evidence of literary merit, Haight had to admit defeat because he found not one poem that was not "sentimental, false or flawed" (Haight xx).

All in all Sigourney was a mystery to Haight. By 1930, the language she wrote in seems to have been forgotten; hers had become an alien culture. What vestiges remained could only be repudiated. Nothing seemed to account for her previous reputation as "America's leading poetess" except the generally poor taste of nineteenth-century Americans against whom the post-Victorians imagined themselves. Haight could only make sense of her as an antitype to the modern poet, and his book can be read as an excellent demonstration, in the negative, of modernist poetics. Her poetry is earnest, not ironic; didactic, not ambiguous; rhyming, not free; conventional, not innovative; accessible, not esoteric. Nevertheless, it continued to be taught in schools and elocution classes, so, no doubt, Haight and members of his generation were surprised at the degree to which their new poetics had successfully supplanted the old by the mid-twentieth century. In 1930 it must have seemed unfathomable that by the 1970s the poetry of Longfellow and Whittier would fall so completely below the critical horizon. The measure of modernism's success was its triumph over what many saw as one of the most characteristic expressions of a bankrupt culture.[3]

The poetics of sentiment—who can say what, to whom, and in what manner—came to be so completely elided that its recovery has been one of the most challenging tasks for recent literary historians.[4] To say, however, that the poetics of sentiment has been elided is not to say that it has not continued to perform important work in American culture. While an abstract or critical understanding of the language has been lost (to academics in particular), Americans have continued to speak and to be shaped by it. But why? In addition, the "bad taste" of earlier Americans no longer seems an adequate explanation for the force and prevalence of sentimentality in the mid–nineteenth century as faith in the "good taste" (even the possibility of good as bad taste) of our own grandparents and even of ourselves has been shaken. Perhaps the answer to Haight's question—what accounts for Sigourney's reputation as "America's leading poetess"?—has less to do with aesthetic judgments and more to do with purpose or function. What was it that poetry such as Sigourney's and Longfellow's did for its writers and its readers in the nineteenth century? Perhaps the answer to this question reveals something important about the nature and continuing function of sentimentality in today's America.

At least part of the answer, surely, has begun to be formulated by students of feminist literary history and by students of the novel who have looked in detail at the published works of authors such as Harriet Beecher Stowe or Susan Warner. Feminist literary historians began the reevaluation of sentimentality as part of rediscovery of the rich trove of women's writings in the nineteenth century. Nina Baym, for example, in her groundbreaking study *Woman's Fiction* (1978), set about the task of remembering women's literary work of the nineteenth century through an author-based survey that focuses on fictions "by and about women in America, 1820s–70." It had been twenty or more years since serious attention had been paid to women's contributions to American culture.[5] While bringing these authors and their stories into critical view, Baym also proffered an explicitly feminist challenge to conventional views of the ideological work of literary history in naming, evaluating, and reproducing values. As Baym herself remarks in her bibliographical notes to her revised edition of *Woman's Fiction,* the 1970s saw the establishment of a new historical context for understanding nineteenth-century American culture in the work of Nancy Cott, Ann Douglas, Barbara Welter. Since that time attention to the contribution of women to American culture has not diminished and the problem of sentimentality has remained central.

By the mid-1980s sentimentality was agreed to have been a powerful force in the literary lives and works of nineteenth-century women authors. But what was it? A subgenre of the novel or an aesthetic? Most definitions that considered sentimentality as a species of the American novel followed the one provided by Baym for what she called women's fictions. These might be summarized this way: a protagonist who is generally weak, vulnerable, and female (or equivalent) devotes herself to attaining heart, hearth, and home through the exercise of self-sacrifice and moral devotion. Beginning as either orphaned or inadequately mothered, the protagonist is provided with several alternative models of womanhood from which she is to draw on in her development into what Barbara Welter famously codified as the "true woman."[6] Most definitions that considered sentimentality as an aesthetic mode stressed the centrality of representations of the pathetic as a means to manipulate the emotions of the reader. Most aesthetic definitions through the 1980s engaged in the question of whether and to what degree such an aesthetic was bound by time or gender. Such discussions took issue with the opinion that texts dominated by the sentimental were, by definition, ugly or flawed. The most influential of these was Jane Tompkins's 1985 argument in *Sensational Designs* that *Uncle Tom's Cabin* typified a specifically feminine, if not feminist, aesthetic devoted to the values of American women in opposition to the dysfunctional values of American men. Such an aesthetic celebrated the emotions as a privileged form of knowledge, and women (particularly as mothers) as privileged knowers. By the end of the 1980s feminist literary historians had become stalled as the debate about sentimentality calcified around the issues of whether and to what degree sentimentality was or was not ideologically salutary for those women who read and wrote it.

But the 1980s had also seen the beginning of more formalist attention to the questions of how sentimentality functioned. Philip Fisher, for one, in his study *Hard Facts: Setting and Form in the American Novel,* argued that the typically sentimental move of Stowe's *Uncle Tom's Cabin* was the extension of the mantle of recognition or subjectivity to those from whom it had conventionally been withheld. Sentimentality, Fisher suggests, is a rhetorical device within novels dependent on the establishment of equations between the known and the unknown so that the differences between these categories collapse into familiarity. Like Fisher, Robyn Warhol in *Gendered Interventions* focuses on the rhetorical effect of one of the common devices of sentimental novels: the direct address of the reader by the narrator. Warhol's strict attention to this narratological crux points out that the direct appeal of the narrator to the reader serves to break down differences between categories of experience: the experiences of the reader in his or her own remembered life and those of the characters in the life being represented on the pages of the book and those of the persona of the narrator in the world outside of the story.

All these critics focus primarily on the novel; yet a fuller answer to Haight's question is suggested by Shirley Samuels in her brief introduction to a collection of essays called *The Culture of Sentiment*. Here she expresses what is perhaps the new critical commonplace when she explains that sentimentality "is literally at the heart of nineteenth-century American culture" (4). And the heart of nineteenth-century American culture was inhabited by many, of whom Lydia Sigourney is but one prominent example. The goal of this part is to remember in a formal, particular, and historicized manner, the "language which may never be forgot": the language of American culture.

To do this I have turned away from the works of those who considered themselves "authors" to consider the works of those who didn't: those who read, wrote, and exchanged sentimental literature as part of what they did as farmers, housekeepers, shopkeepers, or mill workers. This is not to say that professional artists or authors have less legitimacy as actors in their culture but only to recognize that their cultural roles are specific and that their published writings give few clues to the full circuit of communication within which they functioned. The writing of nonprofessionals provides unique clues to what and how ordinary people were reading, as well as clues to what and why they themselves wrote. These writings complicate, in important ways, many of our common understandings about nineteenth-century American literary culture.[7] Some traces of these practices remain on gravestones, in memorial portraiture, in hair "remembrancers," in newspapers, in magazines, in books, and in manuscript albums. These "ordinary" expressions of a now uncommon practice provide a key into the grammar—into the possibilities and probabilities—of the language; for they point to how the language was received as well as to how and to what end it was produced.

These unpolished examples of a popular practice expose, more clearly than the work of self-conscious authors, the raw elements of a complex cultural code. Most important, this poetry allows for the clarification and expansion of our understanding of what, exactly, are the definitive elements of sentimentality. Work on the nineteenth-century novel has underscored the importance of the topoi of home and family and on the presence of the rhetorical gesture of direct address. As the poems of *Harriet Gould's Book* show, the set of topoi should be expanded to include the subject of bonds. All three should be understood as always under the condition of loss. The three signal concerns of the sentimental mode, then, are *lost* homes, *lost* families, and *broken* bonds. But these subjects of representation do not, themselves, suffice. Warhol's suggestion that direct address is a defining characteristic of the sentimental novel should also be expanded and qualified. What these poems show is that the sentimental mode depends on a distinctive rhetoric and diction. As I'll explain more fully below, the essential rhetorical trope of sentimentalism is the apostrophe, which, in both its common forms, allows for the marked violation and reconstitution of distinct planes of representation. The defining diction of sentimentality is a bricolage of highly embellished "poetic" tag-lines appropriated from recognized sources mortared together with the vernacular diction of everyday and ordinary language. While it is easiest for me to use a literary vocabulary to describe this set of the least common denominators of sentimentality, this set is also present in nonliterary expressions, such as gravestones and the embroideries made of human hair called "hair-wreaths." My main concern in the following chapters, is not merely with generating a formal description of sentimentality, but to use this better understanding of form to improve our understanding of the cultural whys and wherefores of sentiment.[8] In the following two chapters I offer a close reading of a book of manuscript poetry written by non-elite New Englanders over the first half of the nineteenth century to suggest a new paradigm for understanding sentimentality as a discourse generated by the need to counteract — to nullify — the effect of loss. Each of the formal aspects of the discourse works to facilitate, even enforce, a collaborative effort against loss by engaging the subject and the object of sentiment in a constitutive economy of presentation and re-presentation. Because of the rich context within which it is embedded, *Harriet Gould's Book* suggests what kind of person could and did enunciate sentiment and what kind of person could and did receive it and on what occasions. *Harriet Gould's Book,* more clearly than many a more skillfully executed or famously named text, exposes the structuring armature of American culture.

CHAPTER I

Harriet Gould's Book:
Description and Provenance

Let me begin at the beginning, on March 18, 1837, when a woman named Lois Gould gave her new sister-in-law, Harriet Lazell Gould, a book of blank pages bound in cardboard covered with ornamental, marbled paper and an embossed leather spine.[1] Similar books were used for diaries, recipe books, housekeeping records, or household accounts, but Lois Gould seemed to have a specific use in mind. In a large, bold hand she titled it "Harriet Gould's Book, Dover, Vermont, March 18th, 1837" and went on to write the inscription that serves as an epigraph to this part of the present study.[2] It is this inscription that transforms the limitless potential of the blank book into what it is: a keepsake album filled with verbal "remembrances." More important, the inscription provides directions for when, how, and why the book should be used. If it had been slightly later in the century and if Lois had been slightly better off financially, Harriet might have been given an album printed especially for a keepsake with engravings and gilt. But as it was, Harriet and her friends *did* turn the pages of this ordinary book to the extraordinary use of remembering. Together they wrote down forty different poems as "fond remembrances" of themselves. Almost every page of the album is written on, and eight additional poems were kept in an envelope between the cover and the pages of the book. The poems that are dated do not follow in chronological order—the majority of the poems are from the late 1830s and 1840s—and the dated entries suggest the album was more or less active through the early 1860s. Writers apparently chose the placement of their contributions with some degree of care, just as they used obvious care in their handwriting. Few of the texts have scratch-outs or corrections—all seem to be "clean" copies. All of the verse is didactic; all of it is to some degree influenced by the influx of British and Continental Romantic verse that was beginning to be featured in the poetry columns of the local papers.[3] The subjects of the poems in the album range from political and religious credos, to elegies on friends and ministers, to meditations on death. All of the poems touch on loss. All of the poems are gifts.

The provenance and contents of *Harriet Gould's Book* prove it to be, in many ways, typical. From the period of the early republic through the Reconstruction era it was common for a woman or girl (less frequently a man or boy) to keep such an album. The owner of the album would ask her friends to write in it and they would respond in one of the following ways: (1) copy something composed by someone else and attribute it to that person, (2) write something original, or (3) alter a poem composed by someone else to fit the present circumstances better. Sometimes the owner would do all the actual writing in her own hand; but usually albums contain evidence of several autographs. Often the owner would also write her own favorites in her album. Less frequently, the owner would fill the album with extracts or verses chosen solely by and for herself. *Harriet Gould's Book* is consistent with this description, but in other ways, this manuscript is atypical and therefore of more interest than many other examples. For one thing, the degree of its completion—almost every page is written on—shows that Harriet Gould apparently kept up her interest in the practice over the course of several decades as she matured from bride to widow. Many similar examples bespeak an initial enthusiasm that fails to be maintained.[4] Second, it is part of a rich collection of associated items—diaries, other albums, hair-remembrancers, weavings, genealogies—owned by related individuals and providing an unusually deep context for unraveling the various personal relationships of the writers.

As can be seen by leafing through the appendixes, where these poems are transcribed, Harriet herself was a significant contributor to her own book. Following the directions embodied in Lois's epigraph, Harriet copied favorite poems and experimented with original verse as a means of memorializing her own losses as they occurred. Her contributions testify to (as they supplement) the memorializing power of the "remembrances" written by others.[5] The other writers in the *Book* lived in the town of Dover or nearby; most, like Harriet and her husband, John, belonged to the Baptist church. Many were related, either by blood or marriage, to Harriet. Whether written by others or by herself, these remembrances exhibit a high degree of intertextuality. They talk *to* each other, quoting each other or appropriating and redeploying lines, fragments, images, from shared sources. They talk *with* each other, to the extent that the manuscript as a whole seems the product of a corporate author despite the signatures that mark the writers of some, though not all, of the pieces. Though the products of numerous separate writers, these poems bespeak an effort to work together on the common projects of their lives. It is for this reason that I have come to understand the main function of sentimentality to be collaboration.

Although Harriet Gould wrote in her own album, *Harriet Gould's Book* itself is a composite created by many authors whose works are unified under her direction. Harriet, as owner, is both author and compiler, not unlike the medieval owners of manuscripts.[6] As an artifact, the album seems to have circulated to some degree after the death of Harriet Gould and then to have come into the possession of the Howes of Wilmington, Vermont, through Harriet's sister-in-law Abigail Gould Howe. Family lore has it that the *Book* had been transferred to Eva Parmelee Howe on the occasion of the death of her four-year-old son in the 1920s, then later came into the possession of Florence Fox Howe before being given to its present owners, Ralph and Verne Howe.[7] (With the collection is a much later example kept by Florence Fox Howe at the turn of the last century and a later example kept by Abigail Gould Howe, herself.) The loose poems tucked into the pages of the book, which I consider an integral part of the album, were all written by or to Harriet and by or to her sister-in-law Abigail on the occasions of the loss of their children.

Harriet Gould's Book, like the many albums it typifies, offers a view of nineteenth-century life that is, in many respects, inconsistent with the popular view of that time. It insists upon the omnipresence of loss and dislocation while, for the late twentieth century, the antebellum years have tended to be constructed as the locus of longings for stable homes and families. This nostalgic view of the past conveniently allows us to see our present moment as one of decline and to define the present America as in a state of perdition.[8] Because we are invested in picturing the past as a time of utopian fulfillment, the expressions of anxiety, fear, and loss that are contained in much antebellum poetry have tended to be read and dismissed as suspect, inauthentic, or self-indulgent. In other words, these anxieties have been seen as "sentimental," in the derogatory sense of displaying a disproportionate amount of emotion for the occasion.[9] They have also been seen as morbid since many of the themes and subjects deal either directly or indirectly with death and grief.

But, as historians such as Phillipe Ariès suggest, the cultural role of death as a node of social organization has shifted to such a degree in the past century that it is hard to unpack the meaning and the function of such seemingly excessive attention to death and grief. In the conclusion of his survey of Western attitudes toward death, Ariès argues that the "beginning of the twentieth century saw the completion of the psychological mechanism that removed death from society, eliminated its character of public ceremony, and made it a private act" (575). Quoting Geoffrey Gorer, Ariès further argues that by mid 20th century "death had become as shameful and unmentionable as sex was in the Victorian era. One taboo had been substituted for another" (575).[10] This historical shift has been particularly dramatic in America. As Martha Pike and Janice Armstrong argue in the introduction to their collection of essays *A Time to Mourn: Expressions of Grief in Nineteenth-Century America,* mourning was one of the few and first acceptable occasions for the purchase and display of nonessential commodities.[11] In the twentieth century, only marriage comes close to the role mourning once held in terms of the production and reproduction of social status. *Harriet Gould's Book* corroborates these findings. More than that, it shows that mourning was a technology for the reorganization of the self that demanded and enforced the collaborative participation of more than one person.

Despite the fact that the people who left their traces in *Harriet Gould's Book* made no particular claim to fame, it is possible to learn quite a bit about them. Much of the provenance of this particular manuscript can be established from evidence in the album itself combined with evidence from local histories, graveyards, genealogies, church records, and the personal memories of the descendants of these writers.[12] For the most part, the parents of the generation that dominates this book were some of the first settlers of this area; the Goulds, Howes, and Lazells had all migrated from the lower Connecticut River valley or from the greater Boston area in the final years of the eighteenth century. Vermont, of course, has an indisputable place in New England culture, but it was not one of the original thirteen states and much of the area was not settled until after the Revolution.[13] Except for the fertile and more temperate Connecticut River valley and the coastline of Lake Champlain, most of Vermont is mountainous and inhospitable to farming. Population expansion in lower New England and the legal barriers to geographical expansion west drove settlers north to take up small farming, sheep raising, and, principally, tree harvesting and wood processing.

Harriet Gould (1807–92) lived and died in the southern Vermont county of Windham, which lies halfway between the Connecticut River valley town of Brattleboro and the Hoosetonic valley town of Bennington.[14] As part of the land contested in colonial days by the holders of the New York and New Hampshire grants, Dover was not incorporated until just after the turn of the nineteenth century, in 1803. Only in the 1830s, around the time when this blank book was put into service as a poetry album by the second- and third-generation settlers, did the distinctive Vermont frame houses completely replace the original log structures.[15] With the introduction of sheep farming in the 1820s, the forest cover of most of the Green Mountains and valleys was removed except for occasional groves and in the most inaccessible gores. Photographs from mid- and late century show a Vermont landscape that was much more pastoral, less forested, than today.[16] Brattleboro and Bennington thrived under these conditions. But each had been established towns with literary aspirations from prerevolutionary days. It was to Brattleboro, for example, that Royall Tyler had retired and at Bennington that Ethan Allen had written his polemical diatribes and from which he organized the Green Mountain Boys. Numerous antebellum literary figures (such as Harriet Beecher Stowe) came to Brattleboro in the years before the Civil War to take the water cure at one of the first hydrotherapy sanatoriums in the country.[17] On the other side of the Green Mountain watershed lay Bennington with its strong tradition of revolutionary ferment and its complementary connections to both southern New England and New York culture.[18]

As William Gilmore has argued in his study of the same Vermont region, the culture of rural New England during the early republic was strikingly different from the rural culture of Europe. Whereas in Europe rural geography corresponded to traditional culture (which Gilmore defines as innately conservative, transmitted orally, and stressing relationships with the past), Vermont typified a new and distinctly American phenomenon.[19] Although geographically distant from the large urban centers, these communities were not culturally insular but connected via the rivers with older more established communities with whom they continued to identify. Most important, even during the earliest frontier efforts, settlers were tied into regional, national, and international cultural events through the media of newspapers and books (Gilmore). The mass media of print culture enabled American settlers to maintain strong connections with contemporary life in distant places. Although far from Boston or Hartford and although hardly well off financially, Dover residents were never far from what V. L. Parrington famously described as the "main currents of American culture." In 1840, for example, ten to fifteen thousand people heard Daniel Webster speak only a few miles from Dover on Stratton Mountain (Doyle 120).[20] Brattleboro and Bennington both had had presses and publishers early in the century which produced newspapers taken by residents of the hill towns such as Dover. For these reasons, the settlement of Vermont provides a type for the settlement of other American frontiers later in the century. When, for example, Henry Ward Beecher described the settlers of the Western Reserve as driving their churches, schools, and presses along with them like cattle he might have been speaking of the early settlement of Vermont as well.

Print media, as recent research on reading in early America has shown, played a new and important role in the formation of a national "American" culture.[21] It worked, as mass culture tends to do, to homogenize culture through the widespread and promiscuous dispersion of information, opinions, and tastes. One somewhat familiar example of the way that print culture in America affected the way that early nineteenth-century Americans thought about themselves is the American Antiquarian Society's edition of *The Diary of an Apprentice Cabinetmaker: Edward Jenner Carpenter's "Journal," 1844–45*. Edward Carpenter's *Journal* recounts what Carpenter was reading, what lectures he attended, and how these practices fit into his life as an apprentice in western Massachusetts. Similarly, *Harriet Gould's Book* provides some evidence of *what* rural New Englanders were reading. But, more important, it provides evidence of *how* they were reading; how readers re-deployed what they had read for their own purposes.

Harriet and her neighbors didn't have to expend much money or effort to read poetry. A major feature of nineteenth-century New England newspapers was the poetry column that was prominently featured on the first page of publications serving Dover, such as the *Brattleboro Reformer,* the *Vermont Gazette,* and the *Spooner's Vermont Journal.* Although the poems tend to have pride of place on the left-hand column of the front page, they share the page with news items, editorials, and advertisements. Editors of these local papers chose their selections from various sources, including their readers, other newspapers, magazines, and books. Later in the century, Mark Twain was to make much fun of the contents of these "original poetry columns" even as he contributed his own serious and satiric verse.[22] But in the early nineteenth century, before the disputed split arose between the culture of the many (low) and the culture of the few (high), New England poetry columns might well feature a poem by Lord Byron, one by Felicia Hemans, one by the Rev. Mr. So and So of Hartford, and a remembrance of one's neighbor down the hill.[23] So, when Harriet Gould's neighbors and family members turned to her book, they had a wide variety of models to refer to beyond the small set of texts (such as the poetry of Shakespeare, the Bible, *Pilgrim's Progress,* the prose of sermons, and the verse of Protestant hymns) common to nineteenth-century household libraries.

In fact, the importance of verse in early nineteenth-century America qualifies the critical commonplace holding the novel as the peculiar and distinctive expression of middle-class culture and poetry as a province of the elite. Verse, in early nineteenth-century America, existed in a curious and under-theorized cultural space where it was both widely revered and widely practiced. Narrative and lyric verse were privileged literary genres that differed significantly from both sanctioned and nonsanctioned prose forms. Verse aroused neither the suspicion of the novel (conspicuously not sanctioned in early America) nor the respect of the sermon or prose history.[24] As Lawrence Levine and Paul DiMaggio (among others) have argued, the clear distinction between "high" or elite and "low" or popular arts is a late-nineteenth-century phenomenon. Poetry was no exception. It served as a way of sharing stories, both entertaining and admonitory, as well as a vehicle for prayer or meditation. Neither the production nor the consumption of poetry was the exclusive activity of specially trained experts. Despite the respect in which it was held, poetry was something anyone could practice, and thus it provides us with unique insight into the "habitus" (as Pierre Bourdieu would say) of nineteenth-century America than other more specialized, more professional, literary practices. One did not have to claim special status as an artist in order to write poetry of value. After all, the singing and recitation of hymns was not only a part of Christian worship practice but also a popular form of household entertainment.[25] Unlike sermon writing, which necessitated special training and a special place in the community, and unlike novel writing which necessitated extended amounts of time, poetry writing could be (and was) practiced by anyone in a very short time. Inspiration, not skill, was the key; and function, not beauty, was the standard of judgment.

This is not to say that aesthetic distinctions were not recognized. Rather, I mean to stress that poetry occupied a place closer to that of prayer, and so, like prayer, its aesthetic dimension was subordinate to its pragmatic dimension. Like prayer, poetry was a vehicle for the examination of one's spiritual status and a means of addressing God. It dealt with reality, not fiction, even as it called on its writers to represent themselves imaginatively. In addition, the shift in taste that had occurred over the course of the eighteenth century in Britain away from the neo-Augustan dictates of Pope and Dryden and toward an embrace of spontaneity and inspiration had just begun to register in America. The American colonies had been slow to embrace what we now call Romanticism. Even at the turn of the century the major poets in America, such as the Connecticut wit Joel Barlow, the Vermont poet Royall Tyler, or Boston's Mercy Warren, continued to deploy neo-Augustan forms and criteria of taste. The fully realized Romanticism of *Harriet Gould's Book* suggests that ordinary people participated inordinantly in the articulation of a particularly American expression of Romanticism.

Harriet Gould's Book came into existence (its presentation date is 1837) at the confluence of several cultural traditions, and it bespeaks the formation of what comes to be recognized as the American Romantic movement.[26] They may not have read Coleridge (although it was a Vermonter, James Marsh, who introduced the *Biographia Literaria* to Emerson), but they were reading Felicia Hemans, William Wordsworth, and Lord Byron as well as Hannah More, Thomas Gray, and Edward Young. Joining the stream of British literary influences was the stream of religious verse featuring the emotionally effusive hymns of Isaac Watts and John Wesley. Just as the canons of secular taste were being revised to sanction inspiration and spontaneity over intellectualism and wit, hymnals were being revised to embrace better a newly gentled Jesus.[27] These two streams met via the print media in the person of Harriet Gould, who was both a Vermonter and a Baptist. Being a Vermonter meant that the new literary and religious movements met with a political stream that was, in many ways, radically liberal. After all, Vermont had both forbidden slavery and dis-established religion in its constitution (Doyle 102). Political and religious affiliations resonate against one another throughout Harriet's *Book,* for the time covered by the album was marked by the schism separating the American Baptist Church from the Southern Baptist Church over the issue of slavery (Ahlstrom 665).[28] Living on the geographic frontier, writers such as Gould seemed, nevertheless, to serve in the vanguard of literary, political, and religious movements of their day.

Some of the range of topics and references characteristic of the book as a whole are illustrated by the contributions of Alvin Gould, Harriet's brother-in-law, on page 3 of the manuscript. These three contributions expressing the writer's stance on abolition, motherhood, and happiness are matched by four epigraphs at the close of the book from such figures as Lavater, Socrates, and William Penn. But one of Alvin Gould's contributions to *Harriet Gould's Book* particularly typifies what I earlier called the confluence of influences producing American Romanticism. Here he blends the discourse of Christian Providence with the discourse of a rights-based Enlightenment discourse in an antislavery verse:

New England's fruitful soil
Requires no culture from a servile toil;
No master's torturing lash offends the ear,
No slave is now or ever shall be here;
Whene'er he treads upon our sacred fields,
Their guardian genius an asylum yields;
His chains drop from him; and on Reason's plan
He claims the gift of God—the Rights of Man—

Celebrating his own home, "New England's fruitful soil," Gould emphasizes its salutary effect on the "chains" of a slavery. Alvin Gould is the most conspicuously political of the writers in Harriet's circle in taking on the issue of slavery. He also takes on another issue of great and explicit concern during this era: the role of women. The following prose passage, also written by Alvin Gould, describes the power ascribed to women by the ideology of republican motherhood, which was at this time transforming into that of "true womanhood." The mother's celebrated power over the child is by virtue of her superior bond with him:

> Who but a mother can so form and temper the infant mind, that the man, like the fabled demi-god, whom his mother plunged into the Styx, shall be invulnerable in every part. Blessed privilege! to train up the child of one's heart, in the way of truth and soberness having the guarantee of heaven that when he is old he will not depart from it.[29]

Where Alvin Gould builds a pedestal for women out of their roles as mothers, Harriet herself offers a no less idealized but more self-deprecating description of woman's place. In a twenty-line explication of the biblical story of Genesis that begins, "When Adam was created he dealt in Eden's Shade / As Moses has related and soon a bride was made," Harriet describes the other component of the "true woman" she no doubt aspired to be. As Elizabeth Oakes Smith would argue in her 1841 poem entitled "The Sinless Child," a woman's authentic self could only be found in union—relation—with a lover who would recognize, and be recognized by, her.[30] Harriet's poem goes on to specify and authorize the subservient position of women relative to men in this way:

> So Adam he rejoiced to see his lovely bride
> A part of his own body the product of his side
> The woman was not taken from Adam's head you know
> So she must never rule him tis evidently so
> The woman was not taken from Adam's feet you see.
> So he must not abuse her, the meaning seems to be
> The woman she was taken from under Adam's arm
> So she must be protected from injury and harm
> The woman she was taken from near to Adam's heart
> By which you are directed that they must never part.
>
> (page 16)

Neither Alvin nor his sister-in-law Harriet are more or less progressive in terms of gender relations than the other; each is voicing a different yet complementary aspect of the construct of gender solidifying at this historical juncture. These are the most obviously "political" topics of the poems in Harriet's *Book*. However, while most of the other writers ostensibly eschew politics in favor of the conserving, preserving task prescribed by Lois Gould, their work is no less political. Each participates in the effort to call into being a notion of self able to meet the new demands of nineteenth-century America. In the following pages I will be discussing the way that the poetry these and many New Englanders left behind is one of tools that carved out what it means to be middle class in America.

Unlike most of the residents of southern Vermont and western New England towns who were mostly Congregationalists (if they had any church affiliation), those who wrote in Harriet's *Book* were predominantly affiliated with the Baptist church, and this, more than anything else, distinguishes this album from other New England examples. Ann Douglas and Sidney Ahlstrom both suggest that the Baptists represented the forefront of American religious culture.[31] According to both Douglas and Alhstrom, Baptists were on the cultural vanguard due to their commitment to and participation in the Second Great Awakening and thus to the belief in an emotionalized and personalized relation to the Holy Spirit as well as to the Bible. In other words, they were on the vanguard of a fully sentimental culture whose effect is most visibly registered in popular religion.

As might be expected, this enthusiastic Christianity is expressed consistently throughout their verse. The very first poem of the album, in Harriet Gould's hand (but attributed to Mansfield Bruce, who was minister of the Dover Baptist Church for a short time in the 1830s), testifies to the role and nature of the community's Christianity:

> Through all the life let virtue Shine,
> And by the Lord be led.
> Then shall his blessings all divine,
> Still cluster round thy head.
> Thy days shall glide along in peace
> And Jesus be thy friend
> Thy death shall be a sweet release
> Thy days shall never end—

Rejecting the doctrine of predetermination for a belief in inner and essential virtue (which has only to be "let" to shine), these Baptists follow their God (who is more friend than master) to a death which promises only "sweet release" and eternal life. Their Christianity, however, was also expressed in the way they understood their geographical location. On today's maps of the area, the mountain overshadowing the area is designated as Mount Snow, a popular ski and golf resort. Until the 1950s, this mountain was known as Mount Pisgah, suggesting a carryover of the colonial Protestant tendency to incorporate the literal landscape into a biblical and providential one (Kull 1). Viewed from the top of Mount Pisgah, Dover—their own town—becomes a type of Canaan, the promised land.[32] This framing of the local environment on a biblical template is reflected in one of John Gould's contributions to his wife's album that begins:

> Farewell unto this wilderness
> Of dismal foes and sad distress
> Now from the top of Pisgah I
> The Heavenly Canaan do espy
>   (page 32)

If taken literally, Dover, an earthly instance of Canaan, will be replaced by the true or "Heavenly Canaan" after death. The equation linking Dover, Canaan, and Heaven both domesticates heaven and sacralizes home so that "sad distress" may be replaced by joy.

Harriet Gould's Book testifies to a culture almost as far from ours as that which produced medieval devotional literature, and it challenges us to reconsider our ideas of authoriality and authority and literary value almost as much. Is sentimentality, then, the discursive expression of the collapse of the spiritual iconoclasm of New England's Calvinism and its transformation into the necessarily representable domesticated cosmology of nineteenth-century enthusiasm?[33] If so, what does this mean? The question I am asking is answered neither by the school of thought represented by Gordon Haight (that sentimentality represents the bad taste of nineteenth-century Americans) nor by the school of thought initiated by Ann Douglas (that sentimentality represents the moral degradation of the American character).

CHAPTER 2

"We Shore These Fragments
against Our Ruin"

Most recent attempts at describing sentimentality have agreed that it is a discursive mode informing and shaping culture as well as literature and that it can be most easily identified by its heavy use of tropes of the home and family.[1] For the most part, recent definitions of American sentimentalism have arisen in response to novels such as *Uncle Tom's Cabin* or to nonfiction narratives such as the black slave narratives of Frederick Douglass or Harriet Jacobs. The two most important of these are Jane Tompkins's 1985 *Sensational Designs: The Cultural Work of American Fiction 1790–1860* and Philip Fisher's 1987 *Hard Facts: Setting and Form in the American Novel,* both of which examine nineteenth-century popular fiction. Although there are significant differences in their arguments, both Tompkins and Fisher identify sentimental fiction by its heavy reliance on tropes of domesticity to perform didactic work. Character and thematics, two of the most important issues for the novel, dominate in each account. Tompkins, for example, argues that Stowe's novel offers a utopian vision of a political world reorganized on a template of a mother-centered domestic space. Sentimentalism, then, is a feminist poetics. Fisher argues in a different way; he claims that the deployment of images of home and family forces a reclassification of Uncle Tom's status from that of property to that of human being. Sentimentalism, then, is a liberal poetics.

Such recent work on the problem of sentiment has begun to erode the perception that sentimentality is characterized by a saccharine or false celebration of home and family. Instead, these two topics have come to be seen as crucial and savvy devices in a rhetoric of significant cultural import. Home and family are, indisputably, among the signal topoi of the sentimental mode. However, it is more precise to say that two of the three fundamental subjects of sentiment are homes and families under the condition of loss. *Harriet Gould's Book* allows us to see that in Stowe's novel it is Uncle Tom's empty cabin that comes to symbolize all that was lost under slavery. Of the over forty poems written on the pages of *Harriet Gould's Book* itself and the eight separate poems that comprise an addenda to the bound pages, almost all signal loss of some kind.

But to what end? The poetry in *Harriet Gould's Book,* like much of the popular poetry of the years just before the war, expresses a belief in the need to establish and maintain connections to one another and to God in the face of loss.[2] Albums such as this one suggest not only that New Englanders seemed to experience their lives as fraught with the risk of loss, but that they also used loss to generate their sense of themselves as beings related to, and contingent on, others. If this is typical, then sentimentality might best be understood as a specific kind of mourning. To grieve was to experience cynicism, discontinuity, isolation. To mourn was to break down the borders of distance or death and to establish the connections through which one could understand and identify oneself. The alternative was, if not ruin, to have to begin again the process of establishing the kind of connections which allowed the self to exist. The threat of loss spanned the continuum of experience, from loss within the home of one's children, parents, siblings, or spouse, to loss within the local community of neighbors, to loss of cultural integrity due to the influx of heterogeneous immigrant groups and to the exodus of emigrants from New England to distant regions.

Numerous poems from *Harriet Gould's Book* demonstrate the role of loss in the constitution of a self that exists only by and through others. On page 4 of *Harriet Gould's Book,* for example, Olive S. Gould begins with a quatrain celebrating her ideal home:

> How sweet to dwell where all is peace
> Where calm delight ensues
> How sweet to feel superior bliss
> And have our souls renewed.

Where Olive Gould "dwell[s]" is a product of her relationship with others. Olive Gould, here, could be referring to how she is presently experiencing her relationship with Harriet, with the broader community of Dover, or perhaps with her specific religious community. Each of these overlapping spaces is characterized by feelings of "peace," "delight," "bliss," and renewal. The positive or "sweet" quality of such a dwelling is not intrinsic to the physical place, but lasts only as long as the mutual perception of delight "ensues." If the previous quatrain has described how home could be, the first two lines of the next describe a more likely alternative: to wander, forgotten, on thorn-strewn path far from the sweetness of home or the sweetness of heaven:

> Or should our path with thorns be strewed
> And we by all forgot
> How sweet in heaven a friend to view
> That will forget us not.

The conditional structure of this stanza—emphasized by the use of "should"—clarifies how much the sweetness of heaven depends on the deprivation of Olive's prior existence. In particular, this sweetness derives from the contrast between a state of being forgotten and a state of being remembered. Olive closes by invoking the power of memory to embody her own and Harriet's affections and so to help maintain an ongoing, if not immortal, sense of self. The sweetness of heaven, like the sometime sweetness of home, will come from the reestablishment of a prior friendship—a friendship sealed by mutual remembrance.

It is the threat of loss that makes the declaration of presences—of the presence of and in affection—necessary. For, these poems suggest, it is freely given affection, not blood, that holds families together.[3] In Harriet's circle, the friendships that reinforce the ties of blood between siblings and that form the basis for a community, where otherwise there would be none, are themselves fragile and threatened with disruption: the characteristically sentimental utopian reconstitution of the family is driven by an initial representation of that family as threatened by loss. One paradigmatic example was written by Abigail M. Lazell, Harriet's sister. Many of the assumptions underscoring the sentimental mode, particularly the importance of the experience of loss as the authorizing catalyst for understanding and communication, are contained in this ode, beginning:

> Ah! none but those who feel can tell
> The sorrow which the bosom swells,

> The pangs which rend the bursting heart
> When called from those we love to part.
>
> (page 10)

Empathy born of a shared experience is the authorization of speech. Only those "who feel can tell" the only thing that is important to tell, that is, "the sorrow which the bosom swells." The expression of sorrow is not the end point of sentimental representation, but rather the beginning. It is sorrow that drives the utopian image of solace which closes the poem:

> He'll take thee to that deathless shore
> Where friend with friend shall glory give
> To Him that died that we might live.

Successful communication—successful telling of sorrow—yields the transformation of that sorrow into a permanent joy. Abigail M. Lazell seems to subscribe to a model of heaven that reflects her ideal of earthly friendship. Heaven is a place where one will be in close community with one's friends, where one will participate in the shared project of worship and in the shared project of continued existence. As in many poems from the album, Lazell's hope for what the experience of her God would be is described in quite homely and physical terms. Jesus is a "dearest Friend," who, despite the fact that he whom "he loves he chasteneth," also sees "thee in thy loneliness, / And closely to his side he'll press / The heart that rests on him alone" (lines 7, 5, 8–10).

Repeatedly in *Harriet Gould's Book,* writers describe their God as a superlative figure of homely affection, for the imaginary family is modeled on the actual one only to replace it. These poems certainly trace the transformation of the Calvinist iconoclastic concepts of God into the sentimentalized God of nineteenth-century evangelism. Ann Douglas's powerful reintroduction of sentiment to the field of American studies argues that this was an attempt at the co-optation of cultural power by women and ministers. But as the many poems by the men of Dover show, nonclerical men as well as women shared the language of sentiment and used it for similar ends. This is not to say that sentimentality does not carry clear gender valences, but that its practice did not, of itself, mark one as feminine as much as it marked one with class identity.[4] The practice of sentimentality was a strategy for claiming a cultural status independent of one's financial or birth status.[5]

Harriet Gould's Book suggests that neither the bonds of law nor the bonds of blood were able to withstand the stress of loss without the active intervention of family members. Family, in this way, is not unlike the more obviously constructed community of the church. Both are voluntary. In both instances that which holds the family together are bonds of affection which can be given and received but not bought or legislated.[6] For Harriet, as presumably for her friends and neighbors,

> The longest run of earthly bliss
> Is short and hangs upon a breath
> The strongest tie of nature is
> But weak and soon dissolv'd by death.
>
> (page 13)

The ideal image of family created over and over by writers in Harriet's *Book* is distinctly uncanny, in the sense of *unheimlich* or unhomely, because of its superior ability to resist the dissolving power of death and distance. Death and distance are resisted and immortality achieved through the active, voluntary exchange and circulation of affections embodied tangibly in vehicles such as these poems.

For Abigail Lazell and her brother Curtis, Jesus is a kind of superlative member of the family; a family constituted by voluntary (friend-like) relationships among the members. Jesus is superior due to his innate freedom from death and his therefore unlimited ability to suffer, give, and receive. In the poem copied onto page 33 of Harriet's *Book,* Curtis Lazell's description of Jesus is not simply feminized (as arguments such as the one made by David Reynolds or Ann Douglas would lead us to expect). Instead, Jesus becomes the model of an ideal sibling. The speaker's trust in Jesus is based on the assumption of a similarity between Jesus and humanity. Jesus has experienced not only "very human pain," but also "the sickning anguish of despair" (4, 22). Sharing pain, loss, and despair elicits the voluntary ("shall") gesture of solace which seeks to "sweetly sooth" to "gently dry / The throbbing heart the streaming eye" (23–24). But more, sharing pain, elicits a bond of reciprocal responsibility and care.

Jesus' experience of the common human condition is the ground for divine compassion. This exemplary characteristic—compassion—is expressed by the gestures of nurturing care. Likewise, it is not blood that forms ideal relationships between people but a common experience. Curtis Lazell's idea of Jesus is of someone who "allays" fears, "guards" him from temptation, and bestows pity (5, 12). In other words, it is action not blood that binds individuals together. All these are actions the writers of Harriet's *Book* try to emulate as they promise Harriet that present woes will be replaced by eternal joys, warn her against despair, and condole her sorrows.

In the concluding stanza, Curtis describes his greatest hope. He hopes that on his deathbed, "when I have safely past / Through every conflict but the last," he will be watched by his "Savior" who will "wipe the latest tear away" (31–36). The perfect "unchanging" (33) friend will watch beside the speaker's deathbed to perform the last services of friendship by taking care of the final tokens—the latest tear—of the speaker's earthly affections. Jesus, Curtis's poem suggests, will know that this is important because he, too, "hast died" and knows the worth of tears to the speaker, who has mentioned them five times in six stanzas. The action that Curtis hopes Jesus will perform for him on his deathbed is not unlike that which another of Harriet's brothers, Isaac, hopes she will perform for him. In the poem on page 14, which I discuss more fully in chapter 3, Isaac hopes that,

> When sleeping in my grass grown bed
> Shouldst thou still linger here above
> Wilt thou not kneel beside my head
> And Sister sing the song I love.
>   (lines 13–16)

Isaac, Harriet, Curtis, and Jesus are bound together by feeling—compassion—into a family that is impervious to death.

In the fifth stanza of the poem on page 33 Curtis reinforces his account of Jesus' nature by referring to the New Testament story of Jesus' grief for Lazarus. The shortest sentence of the *New Testament*, "Jesus Wept" (John 11.35), was often invoked by sentimentalists, for whom Jesus' susceptibility to the power of grief almost equals his act of redemption. In response to his own grief over the loss of his friend and in sympathy for

Lazarus's sisters' grief for their brother, Jesus violates the boundaries between life and death to restore his friend to himself. In this fifth stanza
Curtis reinforces the emotional thrust of his poem by shifting from a
third-person description of Jesus to a second-person appeal to "Thou
Savior." Jesus' grief both authorizes the speaker's own grief and promises the speaker spiritual relief. As Curtis's sister Abigail claimed in the
same album, "only those who feel can tell." The domestic space of the
home and family is, like the family, often celebrated as both a promise of
what is to come and remembrance of what is lost. Home, in these ren-
derings, is a necessarily constructed space held together through active,
not passive, resistance to the entropic forces of loss and forgetting.

If home and family under the conditions of loss are inarguably two of
the fundamental topoi of sentiment, the third is equally important. This
third topic is that which holds homes together, holds families together,
and holds the self together: that is, bonds. The poems of *Harriet Gould's
Book* repeatedly demonstrate that sentimentality depends as much on the
representation of the vitiation of the boundaries of "distance and death"
by the deployment of salutary "bonds" between individuals as on representations of lost homes and families. Once this is noticed it becomes
clear that it is the bond of friendship which transcends the boundary of
class in Maria Cummins's *The Lamplighter,* as it is the bond of love that
transcends the boundary of death in *Uncle Tom's Cabin.* The great promise of sentiment, after all, is that it will force the gates (boundaries) of
heaven ajar as in the ultimate sentimental novel of the 1860s, Elizabeth
Oakes Smith's *The Gates Ajar.*[7]

Of the nearly fifty poems comprising the whole of *Harriet Gould's
Book,* some thirty refer directly to partings, ties, bands, or bonds. These
"bonds" (which figure both as promissory notes and as ties) are formed
through an exchange of tokens of affection in an economy not of capital
but of emotions. When Harriet's Dover neighbor, L. C. Burr, writes of
the dominant place of loss in her life (page 35), she represents this loss as
a disruption of connections:

> The broken ties of happier days
> How often do they seem
> To come before the mental gaze.
>
> (lines 1–3)

She restates, at the conclusion to her poem, the primary challenge met by sentimentality: "how sadly death / Can sever human ties" (15–16). Here Lucy Burr is only reiterating a sentiment copied into Harriet's book by Hannah F. Gould and many others:[8]

> How oft the tendrest ties are broken
> How oft the parting tear must flow
> The words of friendship scarce are spoken
> Ere those are gone we love below
> Like suns they rose and all was bright
> Like suns they set and all is night.
>
> (page 15)

If this is the given perception of reality—a reality that falls short of what is ideal—then the problem comes to be one of reattaching human ties through the active deployment of affections lodged and represented in these poems.

And this project, of course, comes very close to Emerson's definition of the work of poetry:

> For as it is the dis-location and detachment from the life of God that makes things ugly, the poet, who re-attaches things to nature and the Whole,—re-attaching even artificial things and violation of nature, to nature, by a deeper insight,—disposes very easily of the most disagreeable facts. ("The Poet," 229)

As Curtis Lazell's poem indicates, the main model for how to do this was biblical. "Jesus wept," not at learning of Lazarus's death (for he had known this earlier), but when confronted with the grief of his friend Mary (Lazarus's sister): "When Jesus therefore saw her weeping, and the Jews also weeping which came with her, he groaned in the spirit, and was troubled" (John 11.33). Joining his grief with the grief of his friends Mary and Martha, Jesus performs the miracle that, by John's account, precipitates Caiaphas's prophecy that "Jesus should die for that nation" (John 11.51). Sympathy, compassion, leads Jesus to defy the boundaries of death by raising his friend, their brother, from the dead. In this reading, the transformation of grief into mourning, wherein the occasion for grief is obviated, precipitates the key transformative event of Christian mythology. A similarly collaborative mourning by ordinary Americans in the nineteenth century becomes the transformative experience for them as well.

A poem by Lucy Lazell (page 17), another sister of Harriet, also celebrates a relationship that is at once voluntary (friendship) and inherent (familial), at once historical and predictive. Most important, this poem shows the degree to which both the problem addressed by sentiment and the answer provided by sentiment is encompassed by the concept of bonds.

Addressing her newly married sister and her new brother-in-law and the larger group of "Christian friends both old and young" who might have access to Harriet's *Book,* Lucy Lazell describes her feelings for them as a bond of love forged by shared emotional experiences: "My dearest friends in bonds of love / Whose hearts in sweetest friendship prove" (lines 28, 1–2). But this expression of "union dear" is occasioned by the threat of, as the refrain of the poem puts it, "the parting hand" (5, 4). The emotional relationship among the friends is described in quiet and everyday detail as Lucy Lazell recounts the past: "How sweet the hours have pass'd away / When we have met to sing and pray" (9–10). Lucy has enjoyed their "company sweet" and witnessed the "flowing tears" and other expressions of their "hopes and fears" (5, 20–21). The heaven that Lucy Lazell imagines in this poem, her version of "Canaan's shore," (31, 27) is defined as a place where "we'll no more take the parting hand." The main characteristic of Lucy Lazell's "happy happy land" is that it will be a place where "we may meet beyond the grave" (38, 35).

Lucy Lazell not only depicts the violation of the boundaries of "distance and death" through the institution of salutary, voluntary "bonds" between individuals, she is also attempting to do just that for herself and her sister Harriet.[9] Her effort at achieving a state of mutual transcendence depends, as in many other poems of this volume, on the collaborative formation of ideal bonds through an exchange of tokens of affection, and the mechanism for this is the rhetorical trope of apostrophe. Apostrophe, most simply defined as a "digression in discourse, a turning away from an audience to address an absent or imaginary person," is, of course, a traditional poetic device.[10] This turning of address facilitates a breakdown of the boundaries between reader, writer, and represented object. But this apostrophe is also key to the reconstruction of the new and salutary bonds fixing the realignment of emotional alliances and ontological categories which is the object of sentimental discourse. As both Jonathan Culler, in his 1981 *The Pursuit of Signs: Semiotics, Literature, Deconstruction,* and Barbara Johnson, in her 1986 essay "Apostrophe, Animation, and Abortion," agree, the effect of apostrophe is constitutive rather than mimetic. For Culler, "apostrophe is not the representation of an event; if it works, it produces a fictive, discursive event" (153). For Johnson, apostrophe is the "direct address of an absent, dead, or inanimate being by a first person speaker. . . . The absent, dead, or inanimate entity addressed is thereby made present, animate, and anthropomorphic" (30). Both critics emphasize that the creation of this fictive being, this fictive subject able to receive such address, remains always an imaginary construct of the speaking subject. But what happens when apostrophe is deployed in such a way as to demand a reciprocal act from whoever or whatever is addressed? *Harriet Gould's Book* raises the question of the interrelationship and interdependence between the two imagined subjectivities which are constructed through the means of a voluntary system of gift exchange.

Both of the main variations of the trope of apostrophe operate in Lucy Lazell's poem and in the sentimental mode in general. The opening direct address to the reader, "My dearest friends," and the conventional apostrophe or the address of an abstraction, "O glorious day O blessed hope" (line 36) do more than complement each other; they multiply each other's force. The role of second-person direct address in the sentimental novel of the nineteenth century has been the subject of interesting recent work by narratologists such as Robyn Warhol in her study *Gendered Interventions* and in Irene Kacandes' forthcoming study of what she calls *Talkfictions.*[11] Warhol, whose interest has been in the valences carried by authorial interventions into prose narratives, theorizes a gendered subjectivity for both the persona of the narrator and the persona of the reader. Direct address of the reader by the persona of the narrator is an attempt, Warhol argues, to define and position that reader relative to the represented characters and scenes in the book. In the case of the sentimental novelists, this address of the imagined reader is supposed to increase the emotional affinity between the actual reader and the fictional subject of the representation.

With the exception of Johnson's important article on apostrophe and animation, the question of direct address within the lyric has been less studied in recent years. But direct address of an explicit reader is ubiquitous in *Harriet Gould's Book*. As in the novels described by Warhol, one of the goals seems to be to create an analogy between the speaker's description of his or her own state of being and the reader's. However, unlike in the nineteenth-century novel, the poems of *Harriet Gould's Book* have a specific historical reader: each poem is, de facto, directly addressed to Harriet Gould, whose *Book* it was and at whose request each poem was written. Each "kind memento" or "fond remembrance" serves as a letter carrying a message between Harriet and the writer. In other words, the initial plane of reference and representation is explicitly formed by the direct address of one known individual to another. Some particular poems, however, redundantly name their intended reader in a way that underscores the power of direct address to impose the writer's idea of the reader upon her. For example, above the verse written by Hannah S. Jones in Harriet Gould's album on "June 11th 1838" she wrote "For Mrs Harriet A. Gould" (page 37). Such clear direction is not really needed in the context of the album. After all, the whole collection was formally addressed to its owner by the giver of the book. But, written as it was only a year after Harriet's marriage Hannah emphasizes Harriet's relatively new state. More frequently, as in the poem by Lucy Lazell, writers direct efforts to a reader—in this case Harriet—who is defined by the nature of the affective relationship between reader and writer. Harriet, herself, is most often positioned as a "dear sister" or as a "friend" by those who address her.

In Lucy Lazell's poem and other examples from the album, the speaker uses direct address to subject the reader to a didactic process through which the lessons known, or learned by the persona of the poem, are experientially shared by the persona of the reader. In the body of Lucy's poem, for example, the speaker twice describes her own emotional state: "And when I see that we must part / You draw like cords around my heart"; and "O could I stay with friends so kind / How would it cheer my drooping mind" (page 17, lines 7–8, 13–14). Lucy then describes what she sees as her friend's current emotional state: "How oft I've seen your flowing tears / And heard you tell your hopes and fears" (20–21). After having marked the distinctions between her reader's wonted state and their shared wished-for state, Lucy reinforces the analogy by embracing her addressed readers in an important "we": "Ye mourning souls in sad surprise / *We* seek for mansions in the skies" (24–25; emphasis added).

Those souls mourning in sad surprise are distinct in their separation from the "we" of Harriet, John, and Lucy who are together—one plural subject—in their search for heaven. Lucy Lazell speaks for, or rather to, both herself and the Goulds with the simultaneous hope and imperative "O trust his grace in all that land / We'll no more take the parting hand" (26–27).

For, as the poems of two of Harriet's brothers show, the physical gesture of the "parting hand" would be made unnecessary by the verbal gesture of apostrophe. Curtis Lazell's poem on page 12, "At Parting," begins, "Sister quickly we must part," while his brother Isaac's poem (page 14) builds toward the direct address of his reader, "Oh Sister, sing the song I love." In the poem on page 19 another male member of Harriet's cohort, J. H. Bright, intensifies the force of the direct address in his use of the second-person informal "thee and thy," which by 1838 had already become archaic.[12] But Bright also relies heavily on the conditionals "should" and "if" as a means to specify the conditions under which Harriet, the specified reader of the poem, will best benefit from its message: "Should sorrow o'er thy brow" (line 1), "If ever life should seem" (9), "If like the wearied dove" (13), "If thoughtless flowers" (17), "When sickness pales thy cheek" (25). Bright's message to a future Harriet who might be experiencing sorrow or death is a promise:

> Sweet hope from earth shall whisper then
> Tho' thou from earth be riven
> There's bliss beyond thy ken
> There's rest for thee in heaven.
>
> (29–32)

Even in poems written by Harriet, she is often explicitly addressing (if not admonishing) herself, speaking to, not for, herself as reader in a form of apostrophe. The self Harriet addresses is a self that she hopes to call into being through these acts of writing. (Sixteen out of the poems written in the bound pages of the book are written by Harriet and addressed to herself.) One of the poems that Harriet wrote in her book, dated May 20 of an unknown year (page 29), begins with a question:

> When in childhood's sunny morning
> Gaily bounds the heart and high

If the dark and stormy future
All were spread before the eye
Who would wish to live and meet it
Who would not sooner die.

(lines 1–6)

She goes on in a similar vein, emphasizing how distressing and alienating is a life characterized by grief and loneliness:

When the waves of disappointment
O'er hopes brightest scenery roll
When the loved in death are sleeping
When the anguish sinks the soul
Who without a friend to share it
Could drink all life's bitter bowl.

(7–12)

Speaking to herself, Harriet affirms to this self that "It is meet that scorn and scandal / Toil and strife should wait *us* here" (13–14; emphasis added). The self Harriet addresses, this "us," is a collective self composed of the speaker (Harriet in the present) and the reader (Harriet in the future) of this poem. The self addressed in this way transcends the boundaries of physical reality because it is neither free nor individuated from the rest of humanity. Harriet concludes with a statement of faith:

Cloud and storm will only fit *us*
For a holier happier sphere
Sorrow flings no poisoned arrow
Where affection wipes the tear.

(15–18; emphasis added)

Harriet's poem, written in her own album for her own perusal, apostrophizes the reader in the first-person plural. Writing this assertion to herself serves, like Benjamin Franklin's tally of virtues and vices, to help her indoctrinate herself. Or, to put it another way, these poems are vehicles for the internalization of a set of values which are, as the poem recognizes, counter to what is represented as the "natural" response to the impermanence of the world. The natural response, depicted by Harriet in the first two stanzas as not informed by Christian insight, would be one of despair and isolation. But as a form of apostrophe or direct address, this verse "credimus" of salvation calls a particular self into being through a practice consistent with the Protestant tradition of self-examination and self-constitution.

In contrast to direct address, the classic form of apostrophe—prayer-like invocation to an absent abstraction—disavows and turns away from the ordinary as it appeals to the transcendent, extraordinary ideal. In this way it performs the opposite but complementary action of direct address, which appeals to and attempts to constitute the reader, a reader who exists in the "ordinary world." If, as I have argued, all of the poems in the book can be read as already addressed to the known reader, Harriet Gould, then the poems of *Harriet Gould's Book* are already apostrophes or divergences from the ordinary experience of the writer's lives. They are specialized communications. Thus, when the poems of *Harriet Gould's Book* redundantly mark their addressee or employ the classic form of apostrophe to an absent person or to an abstract concept, they are making a turn within a turn.

One of these, "Lines on the Death of Warren S. Gould who died April 6th 1843," is composed of fifteen stanzas beginning

> Oh can it be a year has fled
> Its scenes of grief and joy
> Since we were bending o'er the bed
> Of thow my sainted boy?
> (I.1–4)

Harriet Gould's use of the second-person familiar "thow" directly addresses the dead child. As in her "On the Late Elder Jonathan Huntley" (page 5), this direct address of the dead belies any essential, as opposed to temporary, difference between the dead child and the living parents. In contrast, in the thirteenth stanza, Harriet Gould turns her words away from her boy and addresses God with a formulaic periphrasis: "Oh thow that smitest but to heal" (I.49). She then, again formulaically (which is not to say insincerely), asks that since "I have felt thy chastening rod / Assist me now to do thy will / And put my trust in God" (50, 52). The difference between the status of Harriet Gould and her God is underscored, but not diminished, by this prayer-like address. The address is inserted into what is predominantly a verse epistle directed to one whom the speaker of the poem prefers to consider as only temporarily separated from her present self:

> That when I've trod life's journey o'er
> And at death's portal stand
> My Warren at the opening door
> May wave his little hand.
>
> (I.53–56)

The combination of these two distinct forms of apostrophe within the poems of Harriet Gould's album is typical of much of the discourse characterized by the term sentimental. It is one of the ways that the writer is able to force or aid a realignment of the reader's spiritual expectations. On the one hand, direct address collapses the distance between the writer and the reader. The classic form of apostrophe, on the other hand, bridges the gap between temporality and eternity. It is a way of claiming affinity with an eternal, transcendent, and ideal subjectivity.

The difference between and the importance of the two forms of apostrophe can perhaps be seen more clearly in the interplay between two poems in the album. The first (page 8), written in April of 1837, one month after Harriet had been given the album, is by Lucy Howard. The second Harriet Gould wrote after Lucy Howard's death (page 25).

Lucy Howard's poem typifies the role of classic apostrophe within the tradition of the sentimental lyric. Celebrating that the welcomed springtime has finally arrived at the high, close valley of Vermont in late April, Lucy Howard closes by turning her local landscape into an allegorical and eternal one. The conventional celebration of spring becomes an act of interpretative transformation. The literal spring is translated into an allegory: after death "the bright, eternal spring" replaces the transient springtime (line 15). This becomes wholly "emblem of heaven above" (13). Nature and the normal progression of the seasons is a language that can be deciphered. The welcomed springtime of April 1837 foretold a time when "we" (13; meaning herself, Lucy Howard, Harriet, and whoever else shared in their intimate community), should share an eternal community together. When Lucy Howard shifts the object of her address from spring to a "we" that will be established in the future, she is continuing the trope of apostrophe, since the true, ideal "we," like the "eternal" versus the present spring, is an equal abstraction. Her use of apostrophe here is an authorizing strategy for her vision of a utopian re-unification of her present community, which is made up of friends as well as family. Lucy Howard professes in this poem to look forward not only to her own death but also to Harriet's, when the present actual spring would come to seem like the "night" before an "everlasting day" (16).

After Lucy dies, only four years after writing her poem in Harriet's *Book,* her friend closes her own mourning poem (page 25) with the hope that after her own death "I [may] meet you above the skies" (line 12). In "To the Memory of Mrs. Lucy Howard who died Feb. 3rd 1841," Harriet Gould celebrates her friendship with Lucy Howard, whom she addresses as a "Dear Sister" (1). Where in Lucy Howard's poem the natural world is invoked as a hieroglyphic, a sign or an "emblem" of the sacred only to be displaced as less real than that which it signifies, Harriet invokes the literal body of her "Dear Sister" to assert the value and permanence of their relationship, which will transcend the temporary separation of death. The rubric or title of Harriet Gould's mourning poem suggests that it should be read as a letter to the dead. The object of this direct address is Lucy Howard's memory, for it is in memory that both she and Harriet exist. The rest of the poem continues in this epistolary vein as the writer describes for her addressee, Memory, the occasion upon which she is writing. Having "left you and bade you adieu," Harriet explains that "Your body is laid in the cold grave to rest," (1, 3) as if, perhaps, Lucy's memory may not be conscious of this fact. Harriet Gould's every-day, matter-of-fact tone is qualified by her use of the conjunction "but" to begin the closing line of this quatrain: "But I trust your soul is among the blest" (4). The "but" points to her sense of the contrast between the state of the physical body after death and that of the spiritual body or "soul." The second quatrain moves from the past into the present, de-scribing how Harriet envisions herself, grimly "journeying in this world of sin," and her friend who is singing and "freed from the cares and sor-rows of life" (5, 7). The final quatrain, separated graphically from the ini-tial octet, acts as a closing by offering this word of advice, "Rest sweetly my friend." Harriet hopes further that "nothing disturb" her friend "till awaken'd by God" and, more important (as signaled by her use of the interjection "O"), she hopes that "then may I meet you above the skies" (9, 10, 12).

Harriet and Lucy can be seen to have joined together in this album on the creation, the calling into being, of a heaven that was at least partially defined as that place where their friendship would not be interrupted. Lucy Howard wrote her hopes for the future in a gift to her friend; her hopes shape those of Harriet, which are returned after Lucy's death. They share, in this desire, some of the values of Mark Twain's Huckleberry Finn, who rejects an idea of heaven that would preclude his ongoing friendship with Tom Sawyer. They also share with each other, and with the many writers of the book, the assumption that the imminence, as well as the occurrence, of loss or death is the best subject and the most legitimate occasion for the expenditure of the energy and the creativity necessary to create art. Like almost all the poems in this manuscript, these are predicated upon the transience and vulnerability of relationships, and almost all position themselves as bulwarks against this transience, or as mediums through which communication can continue to occur despite it. The literary postmortem conversation between Lucy Howard and her friend Harriet shows these expectations being met and countered by a shared belief in an intransigent, eternal afterworld where the important, self-constituting relationships of a collaborative self will be not impeded.

Apostrophe creates the site in which the important utopian promise of sentimentality—of nonviolated community, of restored losses, of healed wounds—can be offered to its writers and readers. It is the method by which obstructions are removed and salutary bonds instituted and protected. This association between the rhetorical strategies of direct address to the reader and apostrophic appeal to an abstraction calls together both the symbolic self of the present and the past subject with a symbolic representation of a future more perfect self. Though in the conservative service of mourning a felt loss, apostrophe allows sentiment to be generative.

With a lightness characteristic of the New York poet Fanny (Frances) Osgood (1811–1850), Melintha, Harriet Gould's sister-in-law, aligns Harriet's "volume"—her "Album"—with Harriet's "Heart"[13] in her poem (page 11) (lines 1, 9, 15). The poems, "signets of love" (1), stand in for their writers as ways of inscribing themselves upon the heart of the receiver. Melintha's poem asks its reader, Harriet, to incorporate Melintha into herself. The relationship between the women was based on more than just the legal fiction created by a marriage. Despite Melintha's understanding of the fragility of friendship and its expressions, "Friendship must fail like the pledge of its tracing," she hopes that her own "gift" / "flower" / "friendship" (2–3) / will be "a signet divine" (14) and the "seal of that real affection / Warm as the life-blood enduringly true" (5–6).

Melintha's husband was Harriet's brother L. Curtis Lazell, and he, too, wrote in his sister's book a poem that self-consciously points to its own purpose. Curtis's poem accompanies his wife's on the facing page (page 12), and its title, "At Parting," suggests the particular occasion for their writing in the album. Like so many New Englanders who faced a life of hardscrabble farming and who suffered both the unusually bad winters of the mid-1830s and the unusually unstable financial markets of the same time, Melintha and Curtis seem to have taken the earliest opportunity to emigrate west to the newly opened Western Reserve across the Appalachians. Curtis's poem, like Melintha's, is an attempt to prevent the effacement of his memory despite what Emerson might have called the "disagreeable fact" of his separation from his sister.[14] Their poems resonate against each other, magnifying the effect of their joint promises to remember Harriet and their shared desire to be remembered by her.

The functional nature of the sentimental poetics determines more than the topoi of *Harriet Gould's Book*. It also determines the rhetoric and diction of the poetry, which were determined not by any desire to "make it new" but by the desire to make it continue — to make the sense of self constituted through relationships with others able to continue despite the death or physical absence of those others. The blank book given to Harriet Gould was filled through a process of literary bricolage in which the fragments of several traditions and the artifacts of several individuals have been appropriated to serve a personal need. Not unlike the patchwork quilts known as "memory quilts" in the nineteenth century, the overall shape of *Harriet Gould's Book* is driven by the need to address loss.[15] The individual pieces (squares) are themselves conglomerations of fragments from preexisting texts and precise references to local particularities turned toward an immediate need. Each poem, like a fractal equation, tessellates from a shared pattern, which though predictable generates an almost infinite number of variations. The principles guiding the choices of the individual writers and the actual owner/compiler of the book, "at whose gentle direction / Thou [the album] goest forth the fond pledge to renew," are pragmatic (Melintha Lazell 11.7–8). Does a particular original poem, a tag-line from a hymn, a fragment of borrowed verse, act as a "seal of that real affection" (Melintha Lazell 11.5)? Real affection, for the writers of *Harriet Gould's Book,* seems to be the mark and the vehicle of authentic communication.[16] Without this communication, I argue more fully in the next chapter, the individual risked collapsing into isolated egoism. The aesthetic pleasure that the album's readers are meant to experience is also dependent on whether or not the "kind mementos" of "dearest friends" perform their stated function. The fulfillment of the sentimental aesthetic and the sentimental purpose are promised by Lois Gould in her inscription: "When distance or the grave hides form and face / Into this volume sweet t'will be to look."

PART TWO

Sentimental Collaborations:
Mourning and the American Self

GRAVES OF ABIGAIL AND LORENZO HOWE'S CHILDREN.
EAST DOVER CEMETERY.

Irwin L.
Son of
L. L. & A. M. Howe
DIED
Apr. 2, 1854
Æ. 10 m's.
———
Shall the dark grave
confine / Our darling
neath the sod
Oh no; his body
moulders here /
But Irwin is with God.

Wayland
Son of
L. L. & A. M. Howe
DIED
Aug. 9, 1858
Æ. 11 d's.
———
Our babe is safe in /
Jesus fold.

Lucian P.
Son of
L. L. & A. M. Howe
DIED
June 23, 1865
Æ. 3 ys. 4 m's.
———
How we miss thee
Lucian, / Words can
never tell, / But Jesus
gave and he has
taken, / The child we
loved so well.

Infant
Son of
L. L. & A. M.
Howe
DIED
Sep. 6, 1867
Æ. 8 d's.

Among democratic peoples new families continually rise from nothing while others fall, and nobody's position is quite stable. The woof of time is ever being broken and the track of past generations lost. Those who have gone before are easily forgotten, and no one gives a thought to those who will follow. All a man's interests are limited to those near himself.

—Alexis de Tocqueville, *Democracy in America*

Evidence of threatening loss was everywhere in antebellum New England, and not least in the families whose members made up the community of readers and writers represented in Harriet Gould's album. As children of parents who had left their parents to move to the hill country of "New Connecticut" and as the siblings of men and women who would move further west as opportunity arose or away to the factory towns, the members of Harriet and John Gould's cohort knew that voluntary bonds of affections were necessary to cement the easily broken bonds of kinship.[1] As parents, themselves, of young children during the years when cholera attacked the Atlantic coast and stayed to pose a recurrent summer threat, and later, as parents and siblings of men at risk of death and privation in the Civil War, they knew better than perhaps Alexis de Tocqueville could credit how fragile was the "woof of time."[2] Their poetry testifies to a belief that neither the ties of blood nor the ties of place could be sustained without shared efforts of will.

The cultural practice I call "sentimental collaboration" works essentially as a gift economy, establishing symbolic ties among separate persons and providing for what Theodor Adorno calls "the reproduction" of "man in so far as he is not entirely under the sway of the utility principle" (86).[3] I argue in this part that the sentimentality that structures sentimental poetry is part of a system that insures the existence of "a circle of family and friends" by producing a network of obligations that link together separate people and groups of people. Such a circle, *Harriet Gould's Book* suggests, provides not only a place of refuge but the very terms of existence. For again and again what this poetry by everyday, ordinary, non-elite Americans shows is that the inalienable possession of self fundamental to liberalism is produced through a free circulation of gifts of the self.[4] This circulation of selves engages those who participate in a joint effort—a collaboration of sentiment—to convert something established under temporary conditions and through a voluntary action of will (the individual self in this case) into something permanent and eternal. The way to keep the self is to give it away.

In other words, "sentimental collaboration" describes the system of exchange in which evidence of one's affection is given in such a way as to elicit not only a return donation of affection but also a continued circulation of affection among an increasing circle of associations. As practiced in mid-nineteenth-century New England, sentimental collaboration occurred through a set of practices that became increasingly articulated into an elaborate and important custom that seemed to have always been in place and yet was, in fact, a recent cultural innovation.[5] In this tradition, material articles become specially imbued with the emotions of the people who come into contact with them through mere association or through the process of production and exchange.[6] Such tokens of affection are not something *like* what is lost, but are actual vehicles or vessels of some essential quality of a person. Or, to use literary terms, they are not metaphors but synecdoches. They signify not what is lost but what is not lost. As Emerson explains in his 1844 essay "Gifts," such gifts of "compliment and love" are the only perfect gifts: "The only gift is a portion of thyself" (94). Such a gift "is right and pleasing, for it restores societies in so far to its primary basis, when a man's biography is conveyed in a gift" (Emerson 94).[7] The circulation of these portions of selves is not only restorative, as claimed by Emerson, but constitutive, since it also provides a strategy for the creation of both a ground of common interest and the ties of association necessary for a community, large or small, to function. In other words, as a symbolic operation related directly to mourning ritual, "sentimental collaboration" is both conservative and generative.[8] It is conservative in that it aims at restoring something that has been lost, generative in that it must create something new in order to achieve this. What becomes clear when we look at the traces of this practice is that the logic of sentimental collaboration tends to hide its generative aspect beneath its conservative one. It engages the participants in a joint or shared effort to create something from nothing as it provides for reproduction and growth under the rubric of conserving the status quo.

The relationships formed and maintained in such an ostentatiously voluntaristic way (through the exchange of gifts) are triumphs of the imagination over the forces operating against the formation of such relationships under the conditions of democracy and in the situation of the New World. Strangely, these relationships are almost always described in terms of bondage: a bondage that has power because it is the product of a collaboration rather than the product, imaginative or otherwise, of appropriation.[9] No one individual can then be responsible for the results of such bonds; no one individual, in fact, exists independent of such bonds. To give the self, possible only through the mediation of a synechdochically related object such as a tear, a lock of hair, or a verse remembrance, not only declares one's possession of self but also declares the dependence of that self on its society.

As I described in chapter 1, Harriet Gould and her cohorts are typical of the Americans Tocqueville would have met in his research for *Democracy in America*. In fact, Harriet was given the blank pages of her *Book* the same year that Tocqueville's exhaustive description of America was published. Like Tocqueville, Harriet and her group seemed to fear the degeneration of the individual into an unstable and unsustainable unit of one. The promise of sentiment to enforce or coerce a joining of interests was one way of negotiating this threat. While many have argued that sentimentality is the typical expression of middle-class subjectivity, it would be more accurate to say that sentimentality is the constitutive instrument of the middle class. It is through sentimental collaboration that those who would become increasingly identified over the course of the nineteenth century as the authentic representatives of "We, the People" established the parameters by which they would be known and by which they would know themselves. Over and over the artifacts of sentimental culture trace the conversion from the isolated, dysfunctional "one" or "I" into a "we" able to act on and promote communal interests among the competing interests of other "we's." In other words, as the gift economy of sentiment gave each member of the "little societ[ies]" of family and friends formed and dispersed according to taste a first-person plural voice, sentimental collaboration among these many "individual" voices generated a larger, national, and authoritative "We." And it was through validation and reproduction of these memories in a system of circulation and exchange that this present "we" could be guaranteed a connection both to the past and to the future.

The grammar of sentiment describes the operation of a cultural discourse inclusive of, but beyond, literary or material representation. The literary vestiges of this collaboration remain in the form of family mourning poems and in the form of narrative representations of the exchange of affections. All of these point to the central role played by mourning in the construction of the American self. The discursive mode of sentimentality structured an interaction between the writer and the reader in which they could collaborate on the solutions to the problems of meaning that they faced individually in the form of grief. Loss through death, especially the death of a child, seemed to be a sanctioned moment for articulating one's skepticism about religious teachings or even the possibility of meaning itself. In the course of a symbolic process designed to allay these feelings and to rebind the mourner to the community, sentimental collaboration entailed the creation of images of both the mourner and the mourned through a joint effort.

And this is a new role for mourning to play, for it differs both from the classical models of mourning that preceded it and the Freudian models that follow. The consolation of philosophy, for example, as described by the sixth-century philosopher Boethius, was freedom from the wheel of fortune which binds us to the world, its people, and its things. This is not, for example, the consolation sought by the writers in *Harriet Gould's Book,* who, like many ordinary New Englanders of the antebellum era, participated in the formation of the culture of sentiment at the same time that they were creating what it would mean to *be* the ordinary, middle-class American. Rather, as post-Calvinist Protestants, the members of Harriet Gould's community of friends and family sought consolation for their losses by attempting to maintain and reinforce their bonds with one another. In contrast to the conventional wisdom concerning the nature of American individualism, it was within and through (rather than against) this web of affectionate bonds that the American sense of individualism was constituted.

Or, at least, so Tocqueville suggests in his 1837 *Democracy in America*. American democratic "individualism," Tocqueville explains,

is a calm and considered feeling which disposes each citizen to iso-
late himself from the mass of his fellows and withdraw into the
circle of family and friends; with this little society formed to his
taste, he gladly leaves the greater society to look after itself. (506)

The poems in *Harriet Gould's Book,* discussed in the preceding chapter as
a key to the formal parameters of American sentimentality, demonstrate
the role of sentimentality in constructing and maintaining this sense of
individualism.[10] Tocqueville, as many have noted, wondered about the
prospects for a society composed of such individuals, since "each man is
forever thrown back upon himself alone, and there is danger that he may
be shut up in the solitude of his own heart" (508). Danger, that is, to
society, for then, "all a man's interests are limited to those near himself"
(507).

But as the poems in *Harriet Gould's Book* testify, to be "shut up in the
solitude" of one's own heart, "himself alone" within a family, was not
something these writers would have feared. Such a state was not at odds
with the greater good, for the heart was itself both a product of and a
type for society; it was nothing less than a collaboration among the members of the "circle of family and friends." To have a heart to be shut up
in, then, was the perceivable sign of the successful continuation of the
"little society formed to his taste." Where Tocqueville worries about how
society can continue to exist under these conditions, antebellum Americans themselves worried more about the vulnerability of such little societies (such collaborated selves) to the threats of loss, change, and dissolution. The possessive, possessing individual at the base of liberal society
is not an autochthonous being but a deeply social, possessed, creature.
The celebrated mobility and freedom of Americans to form and reform
themselves and their associations was at the same time a source of anxiety,
an anxiety that was met by the power of memory.[11]

This group of geographically and culturally marginal New Englanders feared, like Tocqueville, the collapse of such corporate "individualism" into the singularity of egoism, the collapse of the social being into
anomie, alienation, and disaffection. Their poetry and the larger system
of meaning within which it operated mitigates this fear. If self, family,
home, nation are concentric, voluntary constructions, each subject to the
forces of entropy which constantly threatened to dissolve such complex

structures, then sentimental collaboration is the mechanism of active maintenance.[12]

In the following two chapters I offer some examples of how the circulation of sentiments enables the construction of a collaborative self. The first two examples are from *Harriet Gould's Book,* for these raw poems uniquely illustrate the basic elements of the sentimental project of self-creation. As a model, I offer, first, a brief reading of a poem written by Isaac Gould to his sister Harriet. I then turn to the more complex example offered by the set of child elegies associated with *Harriet Gould's Book* (see appendix 2 for transcripts of the full set). In these readings I am interested in two issues. First and foremost, I hope to interrogate just how the collaboration of sentiment works, what are its essential gestures, what is the sequence for these gestures, who can participate, when, and under what circumstances. But second, I would like to investigate the way that the mode of sentiment inflects the genre of the lyric. Conventionally, lyrics are understood to work against or to stop the movement of time by fully representing one experiential status. But, as I have suggested and as these readings show, the mode of sentiment works to establish connections across the distances of time. The mode of sentiment, then, infuses into lyric one of the definitive aspects of narrative (temporal movement) without converting the lyric into a story.

Having established an understanding of sentimental collaboration based on the traces left by actual, historical collaborators, I turn (in chapter 4) to examples of how representations of such collaborations functioned within two famous and widely read midcentury domestic novels, *Uncle Tom's Cabin* (1852) by Harriet Beecher Stowe and *The Gates Ajar* (1868) by Elizabeth Stuart Phelps. The plot of each of these novels depends on the circulation of tokens of the dead to achieve resolution. As in the examples from the poetry of *Harriet Gould's Book, The Gates Ajar* features the circulation of affections among a community of adults constituted by choice. In this book, the economy of sentiment allows for the reconstitution of the collaborated subjectivity of a sister whose sense of self has been jeopardized by the loss of her brother during the Civil War. *Uncle Tom's Cabin* features the presentation and re-presentation of dead children in an economy of sentiment that effects the constitution not just of the individuals concerned but of the nation. While these novels provide indirect evidence of the actual existence of something like "sentimental collaboration," they also show how the mode of sentiment inflects the narrative discourse of the novel. In contrast to its effect on the genre of lyric, sentiment temporarily impedes the forward movement of the story through time by establishing affective ties among the reader, writer, and the subject of representation and, thus, breaks open the fiction's temporal framework.

CHAPTER 3

"And Sister Sing the Song I Love": Circulation of the Self and Other within the Stasis of Lyric

> Then when our thoughts are raised above
> This world and all this world can give
> Oh Sister, sing the song I love
> And tears of gratitude receive.
> —Isaac M. Lazell, *Harriet Gould's Book*

Has there ever been a child like Eva? Yes, there have been; but their names are always on grave-stones, and their sweet smiles, their heavenly eyes, their singular words and ways, are among the buried treasures of yearning hearts. In how many families do you hear the legend that all the goodness and graces of the living are nothing to the peculiar charms of the one who *is not.*—Harriet Beecher Stowe, *Uncle Tom's Cabin*

> I've felt it all — as thou art feeling now;
> Like thee, with stricken heart and aching brow
> I've sat by dying beauty's bed,
> And burning tears of hopeless anguish shed.
> —poem V, *Harriet Gould's Book*

Mourning, it would seem, replaced conversion as the primary spiritual and social event of the American's life.[1] There are many examples from across the registers of nineteenth-century American literature, but the poems of *Harriet Gould's Book* offer rare evidence of just how true this was for the ordinary people who were struggling to define what it would mean to be an American in the course of their lives as farmers, mill hands, and shopkeepers. When Isaac Lazell asks his sister to "sing the song" he loves in exchange for "tears of gratitude" (page 14), he invokes an economy of sentiment whose traces remain throughout the manuscript of *Harriet Gould's Book*. The presence of Isaac Lazell's poem in Harriet's album marks it as already participating in a system of reciprocal gifts. Harriet might have merely given Isaac the opportunity to write in her book; or (since we can't know for certain what really happened) Harriet might have asked explicitly for the gift of a "token" of Isaac's affection that we now have available to us in her book. Whatever the case may have been in that spring of 1837, Isaac complied with Harriet's overt or covert request and in his gift of affection lays out what it is that he, in turn, expects from Harriet:

> When evening spreads her shades around
> And darkness fills the arch of heaven
> When not a murmer not a sound
> To fancy's sportive ear is given
>
> When the broad orb of heaven is bright
> And looks around with golden eye
> When nature softened by her light
> Seems calmly solemnly to lie
>
> Then when our thoughts are raised above
> This world and all this world can give
> Oh Sister, sing the song I love
> And tears of gratitude receive
>
> When sleeping in my grass grown bed
> Shouldst thou still linger here above
> Wilt thou not kneel beside my head
> And Sister sing the song I love.

In the time-present of Isaac's poem, the utopian communion between brother and sister occurs only under special circumstances. Not "a murmer not a sound" should interrupt or mediate the experience of nature so that, together, Harriet and Isaac can raise their thoughts "above / This world and all this world can give." These conditions establish the circumstances in which Harriet and Isaac might exchange the tokens of their communion (song and tears, the two privileged vehicles of authentic sentiment) through which their existence might be perpetuated into infinity. While neither Harriet's song nor Isaac's tears are extant, Isaac's poem suggests a belief in the theoretical possibility of their success. In the final quatrain of his poem, Isaac invokes this future moment:

> When sleeping in my grass grown bed
> Shouldst thou still linger here above
> Wilt thou not kneel beside my head
> And Sister sing the song I love.
>
> (13–16)

The unspoken hope is that the binding economy of sentiment will continue after death. The gift of Isaac's poem calls for a return; the gift returned (in the form of Harriet's song) elicits an even less symbolic or mediated proof of affection: tears. Isaac's poem promises to operate as an agent for his affections even in the eventuality of his death or absence. Acting for Isaac, this poem carries his affections and so enables him to remain a part of the "circle of family and friends" that defines both his own and his sister's sense of ongoing individuality.

Both the elegy and the sentimental lyric have a more direct connection with a social act, mourning, than with other literary modes such as comedy, tragedy, or romance, whose social connections are either historical or metaphorical. In this respect, Isaac's poem shares much with conventional elegy. Yet the sentimental poem commands, through the logic of the gift, that its reader take a particularly active and responsible role in maintaining the author's memory. In contrast to the classic elegy, which celebrates the power of the author's individual actions in the form of words to overcome the exigencies of life, the poems in *Harriet Gould's Book* insist on the insufficiency of any one writer. Instead they coerce a collaborative response to loss that depends as much on the reader's symbolic actions as on the writer's. These poems insist—in their topoi, their diction, and in their rhetoric—on the inability of the author to reconstitute him or her self in the face of loss without the aid of another.[2]

Before I go on to elaborate the formal distinction between the sentimental lyric and the elegy I want to point out that what the writers in *Harriet Gould's Book* meant by mourning differs as much from contemporary models of mourning as the sentimental lyric differs from the elegy. Freud's classic description of mourning, like the classic definitions of the literary elegy, privileges the autonomy of the individual subject performing the act of mourning or writing the elegy. In contrast, the sentimental mode, as it inflects either the cultural practices of mourning or literature, is not interested in autonomy or liberation but in the restoration of constitutive bonds, which make subjectivity possible. In Isaac Lazell's poem, for example, the speaker is not the mourner but the one who will be mourned. Writing in the present, Isaac uses his words to create a thread in the "woof of time" that will bind him to the future. His own presence in the memory of his sister will depend on and be signaled by an act of signification: song. Neither the literary projection of the mourner nor of the mourned, alone, is a guarantee of immortality. Only the mutually dependent individualities of each, melded together into a shared and transferable memory, will serve.

Freud's account of "Mourning and Melancholia" has underwritten most twentieth-century accounts of the relationship between elegy and mourning. He describes the importance of what he calls "successful mourning" to the ego or operative self of an individual in this way: "when the work of mourning is completed the ego becomes free and uninhibited again" (249). But as I discussed earlier, the free ego is exactly what Harriet Gould would have feared most, for the free, unbound (uninhibited) ego is the antithesis of the individual who exists only in an ongoing reciprocal relationship with others. Mourning, since Freud, has been understood as a process of compensation in which the lost object of desire is replaced with another different but equivalent object: "Each single one of the memories and expectations in which the libido is bound to the object is brought up and hypercathected, and detachment of the libido is accomplished in respect of it" so that "withdrawal of the libido from this object and a displacement of it on to a new one" occurs (Freud 245, 249). In other words, the work of mourning is accomplished once the mourner has found an adequate replacement for what is lost. This replacement performs two important functions: it becomes the receptacle for the feelings and desires that had once been elicited by the dead person and it signifies the finality of the loss.

The mourning that gives rise to the sentimental mode operates differently from that described by Freud. If the end point of mourning for Freud would be a freed ego, then a free ego—unbound and unbinding—would be the beginning point for sentimental mourning. Successful mourning, within the culture of sentiment, occurs not when a replacement has been found but when restoration has been achieved. The most successful restorations occur through the production and circulation of a remembrance or token of the lost person. Such a restoration does not displace the dead but conserves the living as it carries some essential aspect of the person being remembered, and something of the person remembering, imbued within it. Rather than marking the acceptance of an irredeemable gap made by the death of a particular person, the sentimental poem attempts to close that gap. It continues the constitutive relay of communication via ongoing exchanges of affection in which the individual may find meaning.

Isaac Lazell's poem imagines a future time when he would be separated from his sister either by death or by travel. Such a prospect occasions his testament of affection and his display of optimistic faith in the solace that will follow upon Harriet reading his poem and remembering him as he directs. Isaac recognizes a threat to both himself and Harriet, a threat he attempts to counter with the poem I've been discussing. The deaths of children, however, posed an even more serious challenge to the religious faith of the parents and to their sense of personal subjectivity than did the deaths of siblings or friends.[3] Such challenges were met by extraordinary responses whose traces remain in the posthumous mourning portraits, complicated mourning dresses, elaborate grave markers, mourning embroideries, hair pictures and mourning poetry that crowd local museums.[4] The last three of these were practices available to most people since they could be manufactured at home and from easily available materials.[5] And many who would not otherwise think of themselves as "artists" and who seem not to have left any other trace of creative expression did devote scarce resources of time and money into the project of commemorating their dead children.

The currency of dead children within a material and symbolic economy of sentiment can be accounted for in several ways. William Simonds, the influential author of an 1858 compilation of sermons, poems, and stories devoted to this subject, explains that, familiar as this form of bereavement is, the loss of a child in its early years is ordinarily one of the most sorrowful calamities that can overtake those whom God has permitted to enter into the parental relation. (Preface)

Simonds's *Our Little Ones in Heaven* is both an argument for why this should be so and a catalog of the "many peculiar sources of consolation opened to those who are weeping over empty cradles and tenantless little beds" (preface).[6] Unlike in the Christian medieval era, when to love one's spouse too much (uxoriousness) was to cheat God of what rightly belonged to him, in the nineteenth century one could not love one's children enough.[7] To love one's child so much as to refuse to acknowledge its death was a testament to and a condition of loving God. But the death of a child, to whom the mother at least has indisputable proofs of connection, posed a fundamental challenge to an idea of selfhood based on mutual nonverbal recognition and reciprocity of affection.[8] Each of the child elegies associated with *Harriet Gould's Book* expresses anger, fear, and dismay at what it feels like when such a defining relationship is severed. Each poem seeks to engage help in the project of restoring this relationship.

The strategies addressing this personal anxiety served the needs of society and were thus sanctioned on various levels. Simonds's book suggests that the cultural logic of sentimental mourning was underscored by an interpretation of several key biblical texts. One was undoubtedly the favorite line of children who were forced to memorize biblical verses, "Jesus wept" (John 11.35). Another, cited by Simonds, occurs first in the Old Testament and later in the New. Simonds's interpretation of this biblical passage causally links mourning to the generation of a new dispensation:

> Thus said the Lord, a voice was heard in Ramah, lamentation, and bitter weeping; Rachel weeping for her children, refused to be comforted for her children, because they were not. Thus saith the Lord, refrain thy voice from weeping, and thine ears from tears: for thy work shall be rewarded, saith the Lord; and they shall come again from the land of the enemy. And there is hope in thine end, saith the Lord, that thy children shall come again to their own border. (Jeremiah.15–17)

Simonds, summarizing and reiterating the arguments of at least two other contemporary ministers on the matter of infant salvation, takes this and its reiteration within Matthew's story of Herod's slaughter of the innocents to mean that "hence the word of comfort uttered to Rachel, may be laid hold of by all parents bereaved of infants, as applicable to themselves" (26). Rachel need not weep any longer, "for" God says, "thy work shall be rewarded." Whether the prophet is speaking here of Rachel's work of mourning or of some other work, the Lord promises that "they shall come again from the land of the enemy" and "thy children shall come again to their own border." Again, in contrast to Freud's theory wherein mourning is complete only with the recognition of loss, here mourning is complete only when the lost is restored. Simonds recalls these texts as part of a setting forth of the "general view of the grounds on which the Protestant Church has come to a common and united belief in the salvation of those who die in infancy" (9). Implicitly, Simonds links this interpretation to the more conventional exegetical tradition in which this text serves as part of the prophetic prefiguration of an Israel "Gathered and Restored" through the "everlasting love" of God (Jeremiah 31; Simonds's subtitle). Rachel's twin actions, her gift of lamentation and her gift of the cessation of lamentation, elicit from God the return of gifts in the forms of his promise and its fulfillment.

Harriet Gould's Book contains a set of closely related texts that demonstrate how the circulation of poems on the deaths of children facilitated a collaboration among the members of Harriet Gould's community on the sentimental subject. As I've described earlier, six mourning poems and two consolatory verse epistles had been kept in an envelope within the covers of the *Harriet Gould's Book* manuscript and had, apparently, been passed on with the album for as long as anyone could remember (see appendix 2 for full transcriptions).[9] These eight poems provide a chorus of phrases echoing Stowe's list of the "sweet smiles," "heavenly eyes," and "singular words and ways" describing the dead children. Several, on very high-quality paper and bearing addresses, were folded carefully into the discrete packages characteristic of letters of that era. Others seem to have been cut from the pages of other books, perhaps ledgers with lined pages like Harriet's *Book* itself, yet they are written in no less careful hands than the formal letters. The physical condition of each sheet shows significant evidence of much folding and refolding through the years.

"Lines on the Death of Warren S. Gould" (I), for example, appears to have been cut by a razor from a longer letter. It is written in ink on one side of a sheet of thick blue paper bearing an embossed mark of an eagle in the upper left-hand corner of the first page. Copied in the hand of Harriet Gould but bearing an internal attribution to her husband, John Gould, this poem contains the death date of 1843 within the title while internally placing the time of composition as one year after that date. Following the text is the date October 20, 1851, which signals its status as a reproduced, rather than original, object. For what reason did Harriet Gould copy or recopy this poem in the early 1850s, and why had Abigail Gould Howe kept it along with the remembrances of her own dead children? It, along with a consolatory verse epistle "written merely to beguile a lonely hour . . . as a token of respect" by a neighbor Sarah Sparks, commemorates the death of John Warren Gould, dead at the age of six and a half.[10] This, and the generally clean condition of the pages, suggests that these are not hastily produced drafts but carefully polished copies whose physical presentation and existence played an integral role in the cultural economy of at least some part of the small Vermont community. The remaining six examples are also "child elegies": three occasioned by the deaths of three of Abigail Gould Howe's children, two having no name attached but directly addressing a child's death, and one addressed to an unnamed "weeping mother" and signed by an also unnamed "mother."

Although they are physically distinct texts and although their survival together is a product of chance, these eight poems have a greater thematic coherence than do the rest of the poems in *Harriet Gould's Book*. All of the poems concern infant death and parental grief. All are occasional elegies dominated formally by the mode of sentimentality. Each poem features the topoi, rhetorical devices, and diction characteristic of sentimentality as I have described them in part I of this study. All of the poems acknowledge and anxiously try to suppress the experience and the expression of an angry skepticism toward a God who would disrupt the foundational parent-child dyad of the middle-class family.

Deploying sentimental collaboration in an operation that extends beyond the written word, this particular group of people created an interrelated set of poems, gravestones, and hair-remembrancers in an effort not only to preserve the memory of their lost children but also to create a world that would deny that loss. Part of this vision calls into being a reconstructed self of the mourner as well of the mourned through a process of descriptive apostrophe. These redundant selves, redundant because they are not replacements for (but vestiges of) the previous selves, are enjoined to work together to prevent the alienation that the separation of death might otherwise entail. The poems also refigure the dead child as a still living one. This remembered child helps to reconstitute the grieving parent as it continues, through the efficacy of the sentimental artifact, to share in the reciprocal communication of sentimental collaboration. Remembered and thus still living, the restored child continues to be able to remember, continues to be able to return the act of animating, gifting, giving.

Stone, paper, and hair could all be vehicles for the circulation of dead babies through the community of Dover. One of the women of this same community memorialized her family, and possibly the very children who are the subjects of these poems, by weaving their hair into an arrangement of flowers.[11] Surrounded by a deep-edged gilt frame, the intricate pattern of variously colored swirls and knots of hair is easily a physical manifestation of Abigail Gould Howe's vision of her dead children transformed into flowers: "Our lovely little flowers now bloom / In heaven where angels are" (VI.39–40). These poems also correlate with the gravestones of the children who occasioned them. Like their companion poems, the gravestones in the West and East Dover graveyards are also the vehicles of sentiment bearing either biblical or original verses. The picture of the four graves of Abigail Gould Howe's dead children shows them standing beneath the "fir tree bough" in her poem: "He sleeps beneath this fir tree bough / Our darling and our joy" (IV.1–2). Three of the graves carry verse inscriptions that relate to the written texts. The fourth grave, of the last of Abigail's children, has neither name nor extended inscription. This child, dead after only a few days, is merely "Infant / Son of L. L. & A. M. / Howe" (see illustration on p. 51). While the fact that no poem survives does not mean that none was written, it is also true that the "speechless gloom" which the writer of poem V declares (line 19) or the pessimism as to the efficacy of verbal expression carved onto the stone of their third dead child had become too much to overcome: "How we miss thee Lucien / Words can never tell."

Like the poems, these inscriptions directly address the reader of the stones and, often, even the dead child. Once the testaments are written on the stone or on the paper, the writer also becomes the reader, and so sentiment is not only an expression of grief and desire but also an instrument able to be turned on the self of the writer. The inscription on Irwin's grave begins with a question that poses the parents' skepticism and source of worry: "Shall the dark grave confine / Our darling neath the sod." The inscription insists on a commonality of affection between the readers and writers for the child whose monument is being looked at through the use of the first-person plural possessive "our." This conventional question yields the conventional answer that the reader (at least while reading) is forced to join in, "Oh no his body moulders here / But Irwin is with God."

None of the poems, grave inscriptions, or hair-wreaths associated with the midcentury losses of the Goulds and the Howes tells by itself the process by which the parents of Irwin were able to find or to accept the consolation they claim on his stone (or if they did). In fact, the declarations of salvation and faith seem more tenuous and speculative when the less cryptic, fuller, texts of the poems are examined. The poems written by and to the parents stress the dependency or interrelatedness of each individual artifact in a way that models the prevailing assumptions about the process of grief. In addition they provide traces of the way that personal subjectivity for these people was both structured by and dependent on social relationships. Successful mourning is the object of each poem, yet each is but one segment of a more extensive and symbolic gesture composed of reciprocal movements. Mourning is produced through a joint effort resulting in the reconstruction of a self whose collaborative nature had been challenged by the death of another.

The earliest poem of this group, "Lines on the Death of Warren S. Gould who died April 6th 1843" (I), is paradigmatic of the collaborative mourning facilitated through the circulation of the dead. It is not an isolated expression of grief and consolation but, like a gravestone, it is an object that performs significant work as a relic and as a remembrance of the dead child. The poem itself relates directly to both the gravestone of the child and one of the two extant, consolatory verse epistles. It also relates intertextually, as we shall see further on, to the poems written by Harriet's sister-in-law Abigail.[12] As in Abigail's own poems, this one exerts a great effort to speak not for a singular sense of self but for herself and her husband as a corporate being, the parent. For the authority of any particular sentimental expression was vested less in the status of author per se as in the "authenticity" of the emotions being expressed.[13]

The fifteen stanzas of rhyming quatrains that make up "Lines on the Death of Warren" begin with a question both addressed to the reader and meant to be voiced by the reader: "Oh can it be a year has fled / Its scenes of grief and joys" (I.1–2). This question establishes the problem that the poem as a whole seeks to solve: although a year has passed since the actual death, the speaker is still experiencing disruptive grief. Speaking sometimes in the singular and sometimes in the plural, the persona of the poem privileges his own and his wife's identities as parents. The poem as a whole traces a narrative trajectory from the past into the future and beyond into the immortal time of eternity, when

> I've trod life's journey o'er
> And at death's portal stand
> My Warren at the opening door
> May wave his little hand.
> (I.53–56)

This vision of the future, in which the dead child prepares the way for and welcomes the parent, replaces the hopes that the parent once held for the child:

> Ten thousand schemes of love and joy
> Which fathers always plan
> And dream about a smiling boy,
> When he shalt be a man.
> (I.13–16)

The time present of the poem is dominated by the force of "That fatal blow — that fatal blow, / That smote so fair a son" (I.25–26). More than half of the poem focuses on the "scenes of grief" so as to undercut the possibility of the deathbed as being simultaneously a scene of "joy" (I.2). The actual experience of tending the dying child is covered in four stanzas—two, three, six, and seven—as the locus of pathos, for this is evidence that, "almost with a broken heart," the "I" of the poem "watched each faint drawn breath" (I.5–6). While the child was still alive, the speaker "felt I could not with thee part / To meet the embrace of death" (I.7–8).

The scene of death and the memories of the formerly happy child continue to intrude on the present: "From drear oblivion's dreams awake / As fresh as e'er before," as if to challenge the tenuous consolation claimed rhetorically at the close of the tenth stanza:

> Alas my boy, though sundered far
> Beyond those orbs that shine,
> I look above those twinkling stars
> And claim thee still as mine.
> (I.35–40)

While the first nine stanzas describe vividly the experience of grief that is personal and localized, the final six stanzas describe the consolation or joy that the conventions of the "sentimental love religion" attempted to provide for its adherents.[14] In contrast to the earlier American elegy occasioned by the deaths of children, such as Anne Bradstreet's, the speaker of this poem does not recognize God's claim upon his and his wife's child as greater than their own.[15] For Bradstreet, the dead baby is figured as having been a loan from God that he has taken back to himself. Whatever happiness or sadness that accrued to the parent during the life of a child was meant to demonstrate God's power. The separation of death, figured by Warren's parents as a factor of distance ("sundered far"), violates or threatens the parents' right of possession in the child. To counter this threat, in an act whose importance is stressed by the direct address of the child, the speaker looks "above those twinkling stars / And claim thee still as mine."

The claim of continued connection with the now dead boy and of continued right of possession is the first step in countering the pain described in the first nine stanzas. The eleventh stanza rewrites the death scene that in earlier stanzas was marked by a violence of emotion and language. The language of violent dissolution ("fatal blow, / That smote so fair a son" [25–26], the "daggers" that the child's death "thrust" into the parent's heart [12], the "tie" of affection that is rent apart [9–10], and even the "almost . . . broken heart" [5]) are rewritten into the language of pacific resolution:

He's stepped within the peaceful tomb
As if he had gone to find
A quiet rest within his room
And left his friends behind.

(41–44)

The grave, from this point in the poem, is not the sign of his being "sundered far" but a peaceful tomb that is, in fact, the child's true "room." The ordinary activity of napping, with its connotations of brevity and restoration, becomes the type of the sleep of death.

Having turned the grave into the child's room, heaven itself becomes, not a mansion, but a home. The Gospel assurance that "In my Father's house are many mansions" seems to mean for nineteenth-century America that in my father's freestanding house are many rooms devoted to the specialized tasks of living a genteel, comfortable life. In the sixth stanza the perception of the child's "closing gasp" signified not only that "we were forced to part" but that the writer had not been fully aware of "how firm a grasp / He had upon my heart" (21–24). But having converted the grave and the afterlife into a domestic space, the writer is able to call into being an image of being welcomed home by a not really dead boy, Warren. In the climax of the poem's utopian vision of familial reconstitution, the writer reemphasizes his/her stake in "*My* Warren" who "at the opening door / May wave his little hand" (55–56; emphasis added). This conclusion suggests that the writer of the poem retains an identity as parent. But instead of being a parent to a dead boy, the writer is the parent of "an angel boy" (60).

This consolation is neither easily achieved nor easily sustained. In the twelfth and thirteenth stanzas, the writer interrupts the extended conceit linking the grave with the child's room and heaven with the child's home. Beginning with an interjected "Oh," and continuing with the subjunctive "shall," the writer suggests that this consolation is something that has been or must be deferred—"Oh it shall be a source of joy"—although perhaps it is not now, "That love can go and clasp my boy / And feel a welcome given" (45–48). Again, in the thirteenth stanza, the writer begins with an "Oh," but this time it is to get the attention of an apostrophized addressee: "Oh thow that smitest but to heal" (49). The writer then asks his God for the assistance without which he, himself, will be excluded from the heavenly home where his son will be able to advise and help his father: "And cry fear not the threshold crossed / You'll find no thrill but joy" (57–58).

While the writer invokes this hope as a means for consoling both himself and his wife, he is also describing the set of a priori assumptions authorizing a new way of conceptualizing the role and nature of individualism. These poems express the hope that the corporate subjectivity of each family member, an individualism impossible outside the context of the voluntary family, will be proved to be sustainable even after death. The collaborative nature of both the speaker and the child is maintained through this mechanism. What John Gould aspires to here is what Tocqueville called the "calm and considered feeling which disposes each citizen . . . to withdraw into the circle of family and friends" (506) without which he would not exist.

"Lines on the Death of Warren" deploys all the features of the sentimental mode in order to attract the collaboration of the reader in the operation of mourning. Participating in this shared exercise of mourning is a privileged means of establishing and conserving the voluntary association of the "circle of family and friends" that is necessary to support the subjectivity of the individual within a democracy. On the level of language, the poet uses the highly inflected, ornamented, "poetic diction" to infuse the vocabulary of everyday domestic discourse with a sense of urgency and importance. The home and family are introduced under the threat of loss in order to celebrate the triumph of this social formulation on the eternal plane. And the topoi of bonding is repeatedly invoked. Not only does the poem represent bonds directly, it also makes great use of apostrophe directed at various levels in an effort to meld all the various readers, including the poet and the copyist, into a corporate "We." The dead child, Warren, who is addressed directly by the poem, is also asked to join in the transformative mourning. He is asked to mourn with the parents for the loss they have sustained as a first step to joining them once more.

This poem is not the only "remembrance" of Warren Gould created by his family (see illustration on p. 11). As Harriet's sister-in-law would do for her own children, the Goulds engraved the tombstone they erected to Warren's memory in a manner that parallels the movement of this poem.[16] It, too, details particulars of the child; but in the language of stone this becomes, for the most part, abstracted to numbers. The date of death (contained also within the title of the poem) is followed by a precise reckoning of the boy's age: six years, seven months, and twenty-nine days. What was lost is indicated in the gap between the date of death and the days that he lived. Also, as in the poem, the parents declare the grounds for their hope of consolation in the inscription that covers the bottom half of the stone: "Jesus said suffer little children to come unto me and / forbid them not for of such is the kingdom of heaven." Heaven, this verse acknowledges, is the true and permanent home of children. But unlike in the poems written by Anne Bradstreet on the occasions of infant or child death, God and his heaven are not in conflict with the parents' claim to the child. John Gould's "angel boy" will still be John Gould's boy as long as the child reciprocates John Gould's remembrances.

Warren Gould was also memorialized in a verse epistle by his family's Dover neighbor and fellow Baptist, Sarah A. Sparks (see example II in appendix 2). The compact packet formed by the double sheet of thick, high-quality white paper on which this poem is written is addressed to Mrs. Gould. Despite the conventional apologia that "these lines were written merely to beguile a lonely hour, without a design of presenting them to the eyes of any," this is the most self-consciously "poetic" item in this set. It is a compendium of stereotypically sentimental devices ranging from the highly embellished lines of the writer's opening apostrophe to her harp ("Wake harp, assume again thy plaintive strains") to her closing second-person address to the lost child. Rejecting the celebration of the "touching theme" the writer, herself, has been indulging in, she concludes:

> We will not lament, for *our* loss is *thy* gain;
> We wish not thy return to this region of pain;
> For we feel, thou hast entered a permanent rest,
> In that happy Country — the land of the blest.
>
> (emphasis in original)

The strong use of the first-person plural "We" expresses a claim to a share in the process of mourning through which she, too, can reinforce her own stake in the collaboration of subjectivity. Yet, it could also be read as an appropriation of the grief of the actual parents of the child by a member of the non-kin community of friends and church members. Addressed initially to Harriet Gould, this "we" attempts to force her (the reader) to articulate, if not to join wholeheartedly in, what rings as a credo of consolation.

In overall design, Sparks's "Lines Written on the death of Warren" parallels John and Harriet's own "Lines on the Death of Warren," although the percentage of ornate metaphorical language to homely, ordinary language is inverted. Sparks's elaborate language points to an important gesture in the economy of sentiment, for "Tho' empty be thy seat, around thy father's board; / Yet faith beholds thee now around thy other Father's throne." Beginning a new verse paragraph, Sparks claims that "We view thy glorious change, and sinking out of self, / Adore that God, who cleansed thee by his own dear blood." "Sinking out of self," a self limited by the perception of absence, the speaker calls into being the collaborative self able to perceive and participate in the ongoing, constitutive bonds of subjectivity.

The occasion of Warren's death is, for Sparks, the opportunity to affirm a collectively held faith and also to counteract the danger to this community posed by the parents' experience of death as something that estranges them from community. The primary strategy of this affirmation is the restorative representation of the child as living. Sparks first refers to Warren in relatively plain language as "a lovely boy, a child of promise fair." She immediately replaces this with a conceit of the child as flower. Sparks's analogy allows two successive accounts: "A bud just bursting into bloom, when, nipped by / Frosts of dire disease," is at first described as "too fragile / To endure . . . Earth's hard soil, it fell." The insufficient consolation of this natural law explanation is immediately remedied by this qualification: "or rather by its heavenly Sire / Transplanted to more genial lands — to a far gentler clime —/ To its own native soil, forever there to bloom, a fadeless flower." The "glorious change" experienced by Warren is thus a restoration to his "native soil" where instead of being dead he can be an eternally "happy child" able "Forever to be with thy Savior, at home." Sparks's giving of this poem is an attempt to correct the parents' perception of the "vacant place amid the social band" so they may "See thee as thou *art,* all holy — heavenly — pure": still present. As a self-described "token of respect," Sparks's lugubrious effort is an attempt not only to maintain the ties among the parents and the child but to reinforce the ties between herself and the self of the parents, which depends on an ongoing relationship to the child.

The rest of the extant infant elegies in this set tessellate out of the basic pattern set by the interactions among these two poems and the gravestone occasioned by Warren Gould's death.[17] As part of a mourning process, the larger community of the mourners joins together to help create one or several redundant images of the dead child. These redundancies, remembrances, operate like holy relics within a Catholic or orthodox Christian sense. They are invested with the capacity to continue to act as part of the network of family and friends that defines the individual.

Harriet Gould's sister-in-law Abigail Gould Howe employs similar strategies in the 1850s and 1860s when she, too, is challenged by her own experiences of infant loss.[18] As in "Lines on the Death of Warren," the speaker's grief dominates more than half of "Lines on the death of Lucien P Howe who died June 19th 1865; by his mother" (poem VI). Her grief yields to the hope of a tenuous joy to be found at some much later date: "Our hearts are bowed with heavy grief / Our dwelling lone and sad" (lines 5–6). The source of the "deepest gloom" (37) being experienced by the speaker (and her husband, for whom she speaks) is described in concrete and homely details:

> There's not a place within our home
> Or scene to which we turn
> But speaks unto our bleeding hearts
> Lucien will not return.
> (9–12)

Lucien's death, the third experienced by the Howes, threatens to prove an irredeemable threat to their home and heart. Throughout the initial nine stanzas of the poem the speaker describes the quality of her and her husband's unresolved grief:

> We miss him through the weary day
> And when our work is done
> We still can see his vacant place
> Alas, Alas, he's gone.
> (25–28)

Elevated language describing the dead as the "idol of our home" and "our first sweet bud" mixes unevenly but characteristically with concrete imagery of this particular child:

> At dawn of day we miss the voice
> That once our hearts did cheer
> "Good morning father" mother too
> On earth no more we'll hear.
>
> (21–24)

The speaker asks "How can we cease to mourn," for she and her husband are experiencing the accumulated grief of having lost three children in succession (16). The loss of the first child was "a heavy blow to bear / But not a blow like this" (19–20). These deaths challenged the adequacy of love or kinship to bind the child to the parents, "We loved him Oh could love have saved / He had been ours to day" (35–36).

Again, as in the earlier poem by her sister-in-law, Abigail Howe looks for relief from her sorrows to "a light from far" that may illuminate the mistaken nature of her grief and enable her to envision a time when "we may meet / In Heaven's eternal day" (38, 47–48). Compared to either the poem by the parents of Warren Gould or the one by Sarah Sparks, however, Lucien's mother is less able to depict the sensation of relief from grief in positive terms. The poem copied by Harriet Gould figuratively represented Warren at home in heaven as an angel boy able to allay his parents' anxieties and fears as they, too, died. Abigail Howe's consolation is less palpable, as she seems to echo Sparks's letter: "Our lovely little flowers now bloom / In heaven where angels are" (VI.39–40). For Howe, the heavenly state consists of the absence of "sickness and pain earth's partings too" (43). Her feeling that "earth has lost its charm" drives her toward a hope that her sufferings will be redeemed in heaven by "Him who once had trod / Afflictions thorny way" (53–54). The God whom her brother and sister-in-law had represented as wielding a "chastening rod," is now "A man of sorrows used to grief / He'll not turn us away" (55–56).[19] Warren's parents had drawn comfort from the evidence in the Bible of infant salvation; Lucien's parents' hope of consolation is based on an assumption of sympathy from God.

No poem by Abigail has survived that records her experience of that first bereavement. In the introduction to this book I touched upon the skepticism betrayed in the poem she wrote on the death of her second son, Wayland, and her efforts to control this. As in her later poem on the death of a third son, Lucien, Abigail expresses a depth of grief that comes close to challenging the ability of her religion and society to provide solace. It seems that the belief in sentiment's promise of utopian consolation did not mean that one believed that this promise was fulfilled without effort. The verse epistles sent to "Mrs. Gould" by Sarah A. Sparks and to Abigail and Lorenzo Howe by Marian Gould Sherman (see appendix 2, poems II and VII) suggest that poetry and "poetic prose" were directed toward intervening and collaborating with the mourners in meeting this challenge. In these admonitive poems, the writers openly seek to influence the behavior of others. The authority for this intervention is dependent on an expression of an earnest and spontaneous experience of sympathy. Sarah Sparks avers that "these lines were written merely to beguile a lonely hour, without a design of presenting them to the eyes of any," as if they were written for herself alone. Gould's bereavement leaves her open to Sparks's elevated "plaintive strains" because Sparks's sympathy erases the distinction between her and them. The Goulds' grief is validated and converted into mourning as Sparks validates and converts her own grief. As in the paradigm of "Lines on the Death of Warren," consolation is signaled by the negation of grief. In other words, consolation occurs through the active intervention of various members of the community who persuade the grieving person that no loss has actually occurred.

In this case, as in the other gestures of sentimental collaboration, the single dead child is replaced by multiple redundant representations whose accumulated force restores the child to the parent and the parent to the child by rebinding and reinforcing the "ties of affection." Both Sparks and Marian Gould Sherman begin by setting forth the subject of their text. For Sparks, this is a "touching theme, of blighted youth, of hopes parental, / Blasted" (II). Sherman, as in a homily, quotes what within the American culture of mourning has become a self-evident, but still problematic, truth: "Death loves a shining mark" (VII). Both personify death, as if to raise up an adequate object on which to direct the parents' anger and grief as a means of introducing their narratives of the death scene. Sherman's text, which, overall, avoids the excesses of Sparks's, relies on more concrete imagery and focuses more clearly on her own experience of this death: "A few short days ago I saw a lovely babe, sleeping in death's cold arms" (VII). The surge of sympathy expressed in the openings and closing of these poems authorizes the application of the corrective dose of an "eye of faith," as Sherman puts it, which will show that the "same hand that afflicts can heal" (VII). Despite slight differences, these two texts are close variations on the same conventions. In fact, Sherman's affirmation that "there is a balm for every wound and that same hand that afflicts can heal," echoes almost verbatim the periphrasis John Gould used to address his God in the conclusion of his consolatory poem written almost twenty years before in the same community.

The consolatory texts supply a mirror reflecting the behaviors that are sanctioned by society and that fulfill the psychic demands of the grieving process. Both poems give the bereaved an object onto which any anger felt can be channeled in the apostrophized entity of "death." In addition, they fulfill the need of the bereaved to create an attractive picture of the deceased to supplant, through corrective supplementation, the painful image of the dying child. The possibly disturbing image from Sherman's poem of the "cold inanimate form of a dear child scarce a year old" is transformed in the next verse paragraph into "the remains of the lovely sleeper, beautiful even in death" (VII). By the end of the epistle, in the closing quatrain of the poem within a poem, the child is pictured with

> His little hands clasp on the throne
> Singing "Father, Mother come:
> And Stay with me in my bright home,
> Where sorrow cannot enter in.["]

Most important, the consolers offer a reflection of the mourners themselves as objects deserving of pity: "How my heart bled for that mother as she bent for the last time over the remains of the lovely sleeper" (VII). Properly composed and mannered, in a way belied by the parents' own initial descriptions of themselves as torn and severed by grief, "it well becomes thee to weep for the departed" (VII). Having established an image with which the mourners can identify, the consolatory texts then present a way to achieve resolution or closure on the process of grief that otherwise might have disruptive consequences within the self of the mourner and the mourner's larger community. This model encourages them to

"Adore that God" (II) whom they might be questioning or be angry with and to be assured that the one who is dead "is far beyond the pains of this world of sorrow and death in the bright abodes of Heaven" (VII). It stresses the difficulty of achieving this assurance without the aid of God, family, and friends.

Poem V of this group varies significantly from the others in that it carries traces of both its circulation in the economy of sentiment and of the writer's repudiation of the efficacy of sentimental collaboration. Of this group, this poem alone fully suggests the flip side — the negative consequences inherent in sentimental collaboration. For, as I've explained earlier, collaboration is one of those "funny" words whose connotation is clear only in context, for it can mean either "to participate in a joint intellectual effort," or "to cooperate treasonously, as with an enemy."

> V.
> Weeping Mother; what can feeble friendship say
> To sooth the anguish of this mournful day
> They, they alone, whose hearts like thine have bled
> Know how the living sorrow for the dead
> Each tutored voice that seeks such grief to cheer
> Strikes cold upon the weeping parent's ear
>
> I've felt it all alas too well I know
> How vain all earthly power to hush thy wo
> God cheer the childless Mother, tis not given
> For man to ward the blow that falls from heaven
>
> I've felt it all as thou art feeling now
> Like thee with stricken heart and aching brow
> I've sat and watch'd by dying beauty's bed
> and burning tears of hopeless, anguish shed
> I've gazed upon the sweet but pallid face
> And vainly tried some comfort there to trace
> I've listen'd to the short and struggling breaths
> I've seen the cherub's eye grow dim in death
> Alas I've veiled my head in speechless gloom
> And laid my little ones to rest in the cold and silent tomb.
> Mother

This untitled poem, in pencil on blue-lined paper, seems to have been written by Abigail Howe, for it is in her hand.[20] It begins with a direct address to the reader, who is described as a "Weeping Mother." The writer, or copyist, signs herself, in closing, "Mother." Between the salutation and the closing, the speaker denies her ability to console her friend despite their shared status as mothers: "what can feeble friendship say / To sooth the anguish of this mournful day" (lines 1–2). As if in answer to the breathy consolation offered by Sparks, the poem assiduously refuses to proffer any consolation except empathy. While "Each tutored voice that seeks such grief to cheer / Strikes cold upon the weeping parent's ear," the speaker of the poem has "felt it all alas too well I know / How vain all earthly power to hush thy wo" (5–6, 7–8). The second stanza ends with what can be read as either an exclamation of skepticism or an earnest apostrophe: "God cheer the childless Mother, tis not given / For man to ward the blow that falls from heaven" (9–10). Having claimed the authority of empathy, the speaker offers an image of herself under the duress of grief. Beginning "I've felt it all as thou art feeling now," the speaker does not present a beatified idealization of the bereaved:

> Like thee with stricken heart and aching brow
> I've sat and watch'd by dying beauty's bed
> And burning tears of hopeless, anguish shed.
>
> (11–14)

Nor is the dying child represented as experiencing a kind of domesticated Christ-like transfiguration (as is Eva's death in *Uncle Tom's Cabin*) but as a struggle for breath that ends only when the child's eye "grow[s] dim in death" (18). Unlike the writers of the other five poems written by parents, this speaker does not close with an affirmation of reconstructed bonds with her dead child, her community, her husband, or her god. Instead, for the surviving speaker, death leads not to a reinvigoration of her relationships through acceptance of Providence, but to a "speechless gloom" that is betrayed only by the existence of the poem itself (19).

As I mentioned earlier, the grave of the last of Abigail Howe's children to die young carries no inscription. This poem, from one who has "laid my little ones to rest in the cold and silent tomb," would seem to represent eloquently Abigail Gould's particular situation. But what is even more interesting is that this poem was actually written and published by a man, Charles Sprague. Although I had originally read it assuming it was written by a woman (in *Harriet Gould's Book,* it is signed "Mother"), I discovered my error when reading Karen Haltunnen's *Confidence Men and Painted Women,* which quotes part of this poem. In the published version, the poem bears a title, "God Shield Thee, Childless Mother," and is addressed not to a "Weeping Mother" but to a "Young Mother." Nor does Sprague sign himself Mother. It does not appear that the author was appropriating a feminine voice; he was not "cross-dressing," but speaking for himself as a father and a parent in a way that is consistent with John Gould's "Lines on the Death of Warren," and with the testimony in William Simonds's treatise on parental grief. It seems that Abigail Howe must have adopted this poem either from a book like Simonds's or, perhaps, from a newspaper reprint of the poem. Although the poem was apparently written by a man, she is able to make it serve her purpose with little changes.

The most significant difference between this poem and the others is its refusal to complete the gestures of sentimental collaboration as it refuses to envision either a temporal or an eternal future where grief has been replaced by mourning. It ends with the moment of grief, a grief continuing and unameliorated by a vision of reunited family. The speaker's children are laid in the "tomb," the speaker veiled in "gloom," there is no promise (as in "Lines on the Death of Warren") that any one of them will "cry fear not the threshold crossed / You'll find no thrill but joy" (I.57–58). In other words, through these differences this poem serves as a foil to one of the most important properties of the sentimental mode: the establishment of two different kinds of continuities. One is the continuity of association formed by linking people together in a common practice of mourning. The conversion of grief into mourning converts otherwise isolated "I"s and "you"s into a "we" through the mutual recognition of common loss. Reinforcing such personal connections in the time present facilitates a second continuity, a temporal continuity, which allows the self to travel into the future. That is, the remembrances or memories embodied in these works link the past self of the mourner (a self recognizable in relation to what is lost) with a present self and a future, eternal self. To be remembered seems to be the key to existing in the present and in the future. As several of the poems show, the dead, too, have the responsibility to maintain their own continued existence and in the continued existence of others.

Both of these continuities work against the common understanding of the Romantic lyric. For these poems are not concerned with expressing or constituting an isolated, freestanding ego but a situated, dependent individual. The singular, melodic voice of the lyric is replaced by the polyphony of the collaborated speaker. Further, they seem devoted to violating the formal quality of the lyric that disassociates the moment being described from the continuum of moments leading up to and succeeding it.[21] By serving as a medium through which past griefs may be connected to present and present to future, the sentimental mode injects the narrative element of diachronic movement into the lyric.

These mourning poems show the degree to which average, ordinary Americans participated in the solution to what both they and critics such as Tocqueville saw as a clear threat to the continued existence of a society under the conditions of democracy. But the conventional metaphor of society as a woven cloth (in which the "woof of time" accretes within a structure of kinship which is extraneous to those whose separate lives are shuttled back and forth in the creation of a predetermined pattern) does not, as Tocqueville discovered, pertain. In the new democratic model being patched together in America, the work done by the woof of time (the work of connecting the present to the past and the future) was being done by sentimental collaboration. The sentimental subject is determined by its functional relationship to others. It reproduces and thus conserves some aspect of what precedes it, yet in this reproduction generates increasingly complicated, different yet related patterns of signification which contain the inherent threat of dissolving into incoherent fragments.

CHAPTER 4

The Circulation of the Dead and the
Making of the Self in the Novel

If we could push ajar the gates of life,
And stand within, and all God's working see,
We could interpret all this doubt and strife,
And for each mystery find a key.
—"Some Time," poem VIII, *Harriet Gould's Book*

"Roy never forget me here!" I said, not meaning to sob.
"That is just it. He was not constituted so that he, remaining himself, Roy, could forget you. If he goes out into this other life forgetting, he becomes other than himself."
—Elizabeth Stuart Phelps, *The Gates Ajar*

"Mary, I don't know how you'd feel about it, but there's that draw full of things—of—of—poor little Henry's." So saying, he turned quickly on his heel, and shut the door after him.
—Harriet Beecher Stowe, *Uncle Tom's Cabin*

Stone, paper, hair. The material traces of what I call sentimental collaboration have been left in attics, graveyards, and archives for us to piece together. But these are not the only sources. Many of the most powerful novels of the mid–nineteenth century provide supporting evidence for the importance of such a practice. In fact, the circulation of memories of the dead through an exchange of gifts could be said to be one of the main plot devices of the domestic novel during its American heyday.[1] Over and over, these "women's fictions" show women and marginalized men coming together and empowering each other through the exchange of sentiments and sympathy. These exchanges generate a sentimental subject whose power derives from its collaborated nature. Although the impulse behind these collaborations is almost always conservative, aimed at preserving or restoring something that is figured as having been lost, they frequently result in the generation of new solutions that have the effect of challenging or displacing the former status quo with a new one. In *Uncle Tom's Cabin* by Harriet Beecher Stowe, for example, the fetishized memories of dead children circulate through the plot to effect great change in the lives of her characters even as Stowe tries to change the political affiliations of her readers. But perhaps the fullest example is provided by the extremely popular post–Civil War novel *The Gates Ajar,* by Elizabeth Stuart Phelps. In the aftermath of the war, Phelps's novel offered survivors the clearest articulation of the promise of sentimental collaboration. These two books also demonstrate the way that the mode of sentiment inflects the genre of the novel. Where it injects some of the qualities of narrative, such as polyvocality and diachronic movement, into the powerful genre of the lyric, it has the opposite effect when deployed in novels. Placing the power of secular narrative in the service of prayer, it breaks both the flow of fictional time and the fictional frame to allow for the construction of affective ties among reader, writer, and characters.

One of the most famous American novels, Harriet Beecher Stowe's *Uncle Tom's Cabin: or, Life among the Lowly,* underscores the role of a gift economy in which affections circulate in the operation of sentimental collaboration. On the level of story, the most important forms in which affections can be circulated are the memories of dead children: it is these memories that convert slaves, senators, and boys into "men."[2] It is these memories, again on the level of story, that allow the protagonists to gain the "Victory" of becoming themselves through a process of sentimental collaboration. In fact, the multiple plots of *Uncle Tom's Cabin* all turn on the circulation of child relics.

The beginning of chapter 18, "Miss Ophelia's Experiences and Opinions," finds most of the protagonists in between crises. Harry, Eliza, and little Harry have successfully made their "Freeman's Defence"; young George Shelby, Mrs. Shelby, and Tom's Chloe are working hard to redeem Tom; and Tom seems to have fallen on his feet in the household of Augustus St. Clare, where his main duties are to nurture the spirits of his new master and his new little mistress, Eva. Stowe makes it clear that

Eva, unlike her father and mother, has not yet been corrupted by slavery. She is not cruel, lazy, or selfish but only indulged and indulging. But by the end of chapter 18 the trajectory of Eva's story and those of the other protagonists have been changed utterly by the force of a remembered story. Eva, hearing from Tom of how the slave woman Prue was haunted by the dying cries of her child as it starved to death, "did not exclaim or wonder, or weep, as other children do. Her cheeks grew pale, and a deep, earnest shadow passed over her eyes. She laid both hands on her bosom, and sighed heavily" (189). This story—a story that depicts what happens when the sentimental economy of affection linking parent and child is broken—poses a crisis for Eva that is resolved only with her own death. As Stowe's novel unfolds, Eva realizes that only in dying can she convert herself into a more effective agent of change by converting herself into a token for circulation through the sentimental economy.

The story that so "sink[s] within" Eva's heart that she is irrevocably changed is first told to Tom and the reader by "the old rusk-woman," Prue, whose drunken, beaten down figure bears the cost of slavery that heretofore has been hidden to Eva beneath the relative comfort of St. Clare's slaves. In response to Tom's attempt to console and reform her by reminding her of Christ's mercy, Prue explains that she is beyond hope and that she drinks to erase the memory of her inability to respond to her last child's dying cries. Prue's story underscores that the slave economy, built on theft rather than gift, systematically works to destroy the subjectivity of the slaves as it systematically interrupts the constitutive economy of sentiment. All of her children, Prue explains in her rejection of Tom's consolation, had been taken from her by a previous owner who had "speculated" in the market of native-born blacks.[3] Prue had hoped to keep this one of her many children out of circulation in the slave market, because her present owner was not a "speculator" in slave children. But, since the requirements of Prue's mistress clashed fatally with the requirements of Prue's child, this last child was placed forever beyond the market's reach "in a little kind o' garret," where "it cried itself to death" (189).

Like a figure from an ancient fable who was not careful with what she asked for (of all her children, this one *does* escape a life of slavery), Prue's story is simple and horrible.[4] She does not share her story gratuitously—it is not a gift, but a refusal of a gift—and it provides no consolation either for herself or for her immediate listeners. Told to Tom, it is merely an explanation for her drinking and for her preference to "go to torment" (324). Prue's experience seems to contradict the claims of sentiment made by Stowe elsewhere in the novel. The real cries of her living child had done nothing to bind her and her mistress into a community of affection based on a shared subject-position of motherhood. Instead, the child's crying had been a sign and demonstration of the power of the slave-owner over the slave: "She wished it was dead, she said; it kept me awake, and made me good for nothing" (189). Although Prue's child had been kept from the market economy of slavery, Prue was unable to enter her child into the symbolic economy of affection that would have granted humanity to both herself and her child.

Tom can make no response to Prue but walks "sorrowfully back to the house" where Eva waits standing with "a crown of tuberoses on her head," for him to take her for a ride in the carriage (189). Tom's gift to Eva of the story of a dead baby is instrumental in revealing the cruelest nature of slavery to a beneficiary of that system.[5] When Tom shares the source of his sorrow with Eva, the dead child is transformed into a gift of revelation. It serves as a token of Tom's recognition of Eva's spiritual maturity through which Eva and Tom are increasingly bound together. The story binds Tom and Eva even closer together than they had been before in a new shared project of ameliorating the conditions of amorality that characterize the St. Clare household.

On receiving this gift, Eva is transformed from a good little girl to a better little girl, from a living little girl to a dying little girl. Neither Prue nor Eva can "keep [the baby's] crying out" of their ears. But Eva, unlike Prue, can return the child's appeal. She does so by placing the cry into circulation by re-presenting what had been given to her as a present and by amplifying it so that it can no longer be ignored. Seventy-five pages or so past the point at which Eva hears the story of the wasting of Prue's "likely and fat" child into "skin and bones," Eva tries to turn the persuasive power of that image against her father's moral entropy:

> Poor old Prue's child was all that she had,—and yet she had to hear it crying, and she couldn't help it! Papa, these poor creatures love their children as much as you do me. O! do something for them! (241)

St. Clare refuses to take Eva's recitation of the story of Prue's dead baby for what it is, a gift meant to transform the receiver: "There, there, darling . . . only don't distress yourself, don't talk of dying, and I will do anything you wish" (241–42). Not taking it, he cannot return an equivalent symbolic gesture, and therefore, he cannot console his dying daughter. Like Prue's final mistress, and like Prue herself he risks breaking the economy of sentiment. The punishment for St. Clare, as for Prue, is mortal. In order to save her father from this risk, Eva has no choice but to amplify the rhetorical force of the cries of Prue's dead child with her death. She transforms herself into a gift—a symbol, a rhetorical gesture—to convert her father to a Christianity that would preclude slave-owning: "When I am dead, papa, then you will think of me, and do it [free the slaves] for my sake" (241). And once Eva is dead, she does live on in the memories of her father and of Tom, both of whom owe their ability to reach heaven to the intervention of her remembered self.

Prue, it might be said, dies of a collapse of self when her final chance of claiming herself through a connection with another is destroyed. Her claim to selfhood is negated when her claim to motherhood is denied once and for all. It is Tom, who relates the story to Eva, and Eva, who relates the story to her father, who make use of the symbolic capital of Prue's dead child. Eva's death does not restore Prue's dead infant to life or return any of the other "speculated" babies to Prue. However, the entrance of the story of Eva's death into an economy of exchange and signification does depend on and is a response to the story of the death of Prue's child. On the level of the story, Stowe has Eva offer the self-constructed drama of her death not as a way to suppress the crying of the infant whose mother cannot come to it, but as a way to amplify it.

The dying and then the dead Eva are of greater use to Stowe's narrator than the live Eva. The dead Eva becomes available as a site around which Stowe grafts a community of those touched by her "remembrances":

> There isn't one of you that hasn't always been very kind to me; and I want to give you something that, when you look at, you shall always remember me, I'm going to give all of you a curl of my hair; and, when you look at it, think that I loved you and am gone to heaven, and that I want to see you all there. (251)

If the living Eva was unable to secure the freedom of her father's slaves, eventually one the tangible relics of Eva (the lock of hair carried by Uncle Tom) *does* facilitate the freedom of at least some slaves. Through the strong magic of this token, the family of one of the other protagonists of Stowe's novel (Eliza's family) is able to reconstitute itself. It is partially through the agency of this lock of hair, evoking Legree's mother and Eva, that Cassy and Emmeline escape Legree's control and are reunited with their family to live in freedom.[6]

The main armature of Stowe's plot is shaped by the power of memory circulating through an economy of sentiment to bind the characters together in a collaboration against legal and social mores. However, Stowe also depicts sentimental collaboration in various subplots of the novel. One paradigmatic instance occurs when Mrs. Bird, at her husband's suggestion, gives to Eliza the clothes of her dead child which they had been keeping as remembrances.[7] The relics of a dead white child (the "things—of—of—poor little Henry's") are put in the service of a living "black" child's life and family. Mrs. Bird does not cast off her relics because she has "displaced" her libidinous attachment to a new "object," as Freud might say, but because giving enhances her attachment to her own lost child. Giving, in this case, is one of the best ways of keeping, for this exchange does not cancel the force of the symbolic integer but multiplies it.

The process of exchange, as in the case of Mrs. Bird, Senator Bird, and Eliza, establishes a collaboration among three very differently situated people on a project at odds with the dominant mores and laws of the society in which they find themselves. This collaboration abolishes the differences among the three levels of society that shape the status quo of the world Stowe is representing: the private sphere of domesticity, the public sphere of government, and the underclass of servitude. This collaboration occurs under the rubric of mourning and hence is essentially a conservative, conserving gesture, and yet it generates two subversive possibilities. On the one hand, as the title of Stowe's chapter suggests, it transforms the senator from an instrument of the state to "but a man" who will act on emotional evidence rather than legal precedence. On the other, it makes possible the free black family, for it enables Eliza, young Harry, and George Harris to be reunited. As Stowe's George Harris has explained in chapter 17, "The Freeman's Defence," the possibility of possessive individualism, the foundation of liberal thought, has been denied to George Harris because he has been denied the right to "form to his taste" (as Tocqueville would say) a circle of family and friends within which to withdraw.[8] The collaboration that occurs among the senator, the senator's wife, and the slave's wife as parents give the remembrances of their child and the other parent receives them on behalf of her own living child, actively establishes the conditions for democratic individualism.

The mode of sentiment and sentimental collaboration are two different things. While sentimental collaboration is a cultural practice that can be depicted within stories, sentimentality is a discursive mode with its own extrageneric imperatives. One of these is to turn the impulse power of narrative against itself. *Uncle Tom's Cabin* provides a good opportunity for illustrating this distinction, for, while sentimental collaboration figures importantly in the story, the narrative discourse of Stowe's novel is also inflected by the mode of sentiment. In other words, Stowe's novel not only depicts sentimental collaboration but tries, discursively, to coerce the reader into collaborating with the author. For the sake of argument I am relying on the following reductive but useful suppositions about the genre of the novel. One is that novels aim to tell a story and that stories, following Aristotle, have beginnings, middles, and ends; that is, stories represent a movement through time. The other is that the novel, in contrast to lyric, following M. M. Bakhtin, is composed of competing, multiple voices held in tension. *Uncle Tom's Cabin* shows that sentiment operates in the novel to stop temporarily the ongoing movement of time and to subsume the particularity of the fictional moment into a universal experience. The dissolution of particularity, and hence the achievement of universal sympathy, is marked by the occasional melding of the many disparate voices of the novel into the unified voice of lyric. The degree to which sentimentality inflects a novel is measured by the degree to which it interrupts the diachronicity and polyvocality of the novel by enlarging or opening up a univocal and static moment.[9]

Each of the plots of *Uncle Tom's Cabin* provides examples of the generative conflict between the teleology of narrative and the teleology of sentiment. But perhaps the best example occurs in chapter 22, "The Grass Withereth—the Flower Fadeth" which begins the denouement of Eva's story. A world without time (or within sacred time) is opened here for the characters in just one of the many instances of sentimental collaboration in the book. But more important, the *story* of the death of the child and the *story* of the death of a slave is interrupted, even contradicted, by a collaborated experience of transcendence which is atemporal and utopian. This same mechanism of sentiment serves to disrupt the reader's sense of difference from the characters of the novel and to force them into a relationship of emotional affinity with the characters and with the author by conflating the boundaries between her own story and theirs.[10]

As chapter 22 opens, Stowe's narrator explains that Eva and Tom feel the same way about their favorite books of the Bible, the book of Revelation and the Old Testament books of prophecies. In previous chapters, also, Stowe has been detailing the mutual responsibilities these characters have for the spiritual improvement of each other. But nowhere is this demonstrated as strongly as here. Reading the Bible together, each experiences the awakening of their souls as of "a trembling stranger, between two dim eternities,—the eternal past, the eternal future" (226). As Eva reads "And I saw a sea of glass, mingled with fire" from the book of Revelation, the representation of a future dreamt of by the Evangelist blends with the reality of the characters' present situation:

> "Tom," said Eva, suddenly stopping, and pointing to the lake, "there 't is."
>
> "What, Miss Eva?"
>
> "Don't you see,—there?" said the child, pointing to the glassy water, which, as it rose and fell, reflected the golden glow of the sky. "There's a 'sea of glass, mingled with fire.'"
>
> "True enough, Miss Eva." (226)

"True enough," agrees Tom, for just as the view of the horizon over the lake collapses the distinction between water and sky so that the stars "looked down upon themselves," his and Eva's collaborative interpretation of these Bible verses has collapsed the distinction between the limited time of mortality and the infinite time of immortality.

Further on in this episode Eva announces to Tom that she will be going "*there*" to where the "spirits bright" call her. Here Stowe presents Tom with further evidence of the collapse of time and distance under the imperative of sentimentality when the "child rose, and pointed her little hand to the sky; the glow of evening lit her golden hair and flushed cheek with a kind of unearthly radiance, and her eyes were bent earnestly on the skies" (227). Eva, while remaining herself, is simultaneously a sign of grace. Although on one level Eva's announcement causes Tom to realize that she is in fact dying, the iconography of the scene denies the permanence of death by explicitly constructing Eva, not as a dying child, but as a living angel whose nature does not change over time. For Tom, the angelic interpretation of Eva is reinforced at the conclusion of his own story when she comes to him as she was in that moment "sitting on the mossy seat by Lake Pontchartrain" (303). After infusing him with "rays of warmth and comfort . . . she seemed to rise on shining wings, from which flakes and spangles of gold fell off like stars" (303). It is this vision that rescues Tom from what Stowe calls the "dark places" of despair so that he can achieve the "Victory" of self-sacrifice which is the final instance in Stowe's novel of the necessity to give the self in order to keep the self. Only in this way does Tom finally escape the subjugation of slavery.

As time has stopped for the characters, so it stops for the readers, for fundamentally *nothing* happens in this scene, no action, only the representation of a collaboration between the characters which results in a mutual revelation of an eternal moment. In addition to interrupting the narration of events and deferring the conclusion of Eva's story, Stowe attempts to force an analogous experience of lyric time on her readers. One way that she does this is by directly addressing the reader, which, as Robyn Warhol has so nicely pointed out, serves to engage the reader actively and intimately in the work of the novel. As a form of apostrophe, direct address serves, of itself, to turn the course of the novel away from the unraveling of events in the story. In this case the direct address of the actual reader, gestured to at the beginning of this episode and intensified at the close, turns the reader's attention away from the characters, Tom and Eva, and toward the self: "In how many families do you hear the legend that all the goodness and graces of the living are nothing to the peculiar charms of one who is *not*." (227). Of course, the reader's memories—if they are as Stowe suggests—should lend authority to the representation of what might seem like a fanciful scene. But this invocation of memory also forces an expansion of the reader's experience of the present to include, consciously, the past. Such memories provide the grounds for an analogy between the reader's own experiences and the characters. This analogy between the past of the reader (either personally experienced or learned vicariously through "legend") and the representation in the novel allows the prediction of a future event in the reader's experience: "When you see that deep spiritual light in the eye" (228). This analogy also allows Stowe to offer advice to the reader as to how to respond to such a situation in the future: "hope not to retain that child; for the seal of heaven is on it, and the light of immortality looks out from its eyes" (228). The present moment of reading a novel is infused with a remembered past moment and an imagined future and the differences between these temporalities are collapsed: each moment is marked as the same by being an experience of "immortality" that is beyond time.

But this scene also demonstrates sentimentality's ability to close down temporarily the polyvocality of the novel into something closer to the univocality of the lyric. I've been suggesting that the direct address of the reader, in this case, has been to force an enlargement of the reader's present moment. But this scene also features the more classic form of apostrophe by closing with the prayer-like address of Eva by the narrator: "Even so, beloved Eva! Fair star of thy dwelling! Thou are passing away; but they that love thee dearest know it not" (228). Having turned the reader's attention away from the story through directly appealing to the reader, Stowe now deploys classic apostrophe to turn the reader's attention once again back to the story, whose status as fictional representation has been challenged as its tropological truth has been affirmed. The reader reading the words "Even so, beloved Eva!" is asked to collaborate with the speaker, the narrator, on the interpellation, or the calling forth, of Eva that instantiates her as a subject with a different status of reality than the other characters. She can be spoken to ("Thou are passing away") and commiserated with ("they that love thee dearest know it not") from a position shared by the reader and the narrator and in a voice composed of both (228).

The voice of this formal apostrophe (and all the apostrophes of the book) is distinct from the narrator's usual voice (which is typified by the lines that initiate the continuation of the narrative: "The colloquy between Tom and Eva was interrupted by a hasty call from Miss Ophelia" [228]). It features the use of the archaic familiar second-person "thy," "thou," and "thee" as well as the rather heavy metaphoric paraphrases:

"fair star of thy dwelling!" (228). The diction is more similar to the language of prayer than to the language of storytelling, for it puts the reader into a relation to Eva that is similar to the one Stowe has previously ascribed to Tom: "He gazed on her as the Italian sailor gazes on his image of the child Jesus" (224). Eva is no longer merely a fictional character in a topical novel, but has been apotheosized into an avatar of Christ.

The collapse of polyvocality into univocality through the office of sentimentality is also represented or modeled within the scene itself. What Stowe calls the "colloquy between Tom and Eva" is really a demonstration of the necessity of collaboration to the "reconfiguration of common sense" which numerous critics such as Philip Fisher have deemed the defining effect of sentimentalism. As in *Romeo and Juliet* when the lovers, dancing together, together create a sonnet in the interchange of their conversation—the disparate voices of Tom and Eva meld to create one lyric voice. In a similar collaborative exchange, Eva and Tom reconfigure the "commonsense" interpretation of their reality (they are on the shores of a lake, the sun is setting in the sky and reflected in the lake) into another: they are on "Canaan's shore" approaching the "new Jerusalem" (226). In this collaboration the words of the Bible, the words of two different Methodist hymns, and the individual perspectives of each character are bound together and the differences of register, provenance, and authority collapse to make one utterance.

Previous to this Stowe has detailed the gift exchange that Tom and Eva have been participating in: Eva exchanges reading the Bible for Tom's renditions of hymns. It might be possible to say that it is this exchange that binds the disparate pieces together: Eva gives Tom the voiced words of the Evangelist; Eva gives Tom her revelation, which applies the words of Revelation to their present moment; Tom gives Eva his assent and confirms that he shares Eva's revelation by singing a verse from a Methodist hymn which is itself an interpretation of the book of Revelation. Each round of exchange repeats and slightly changes the terms of the first so that together Eva and Tom call into being a rich reinterpretation of their environment as sacred space. Neither Tom's intuitive spirituality and powerful ability to sing from memory, nor Eva's intuitive spirituality and ability to read aloud the Scriptures seems enough on its own to align the secular and the sacred worlds. Instead, the two voices need to be melded together (even if imperfectly); each needs to affirm the other through the reception of what each already has. Eva and Tom's individual voices join in a responsorial prayer that underscores their shared positions as figures of the Evangelist subsuming their differences into the sameness of the Christian prophetic voice.

Here, as earlier when Stowe addresses her reader as a mother of a dead child ("And Oh! mother that reads this, has there never been in your house a drawer, or a closet, the opening of which has been to you like the opening again of a little grave?" [75]), the author explicitly seeks to enjoin her reader into a collaboration with herself and the characters in the book. *Harriet Gould's Book* suggests that sentimental collaboration was a well-established practice by the time that Stowe incorporates it into the structure of her book. Her poetic blazon of the dead children whose "names are always on grave-stones" is offered in a direct address to the reader who is rhetorically asked to join the narrator in the catalogue of "peculiar charms" of the typical child *"who is not."* Through, and on account of, the dead infants and children that link Stowe with her readers, her readers and herself with her characters, her characters with each other, Stowe asks for participation in the project of overturning the mores of slave-holding America through the power of moral suasion.

The war that Stowe's novel anticipated is the immediate occasion for Elizabeth Stuart Phelps's *The Gates Ajar*.[11] Stowe had offered sentimental collaboration as a solution for the evils that might otherwise, she feared, drive the nation to war. Published in 1868, Phelps's novel deploys sentimental collaboration as a spiritual response to the losses caused by the war Stowe had feared. Where the circulation of dead children is at the center of Stowe's novel, the center of Phelps's is the circulation of dead men. One of these, Roy, was killed in the military sphere fighting to conserve the Union. The other, the Reverend Forceythe, was killed in the spiritual sphere, having exhausted himself on the southwestern frontier and in Lawrence, Kansas.[12] Both deaths leave a void that threatens the ability of those who survive to continue living. The single action of the plot is structured as a sentimental collaboration between the two main mourners. The fictional narrator of the novel, Roy's sister Mary Cabot, joins her widowed aunt Winifred Forceythe in a project that results in the realization that they, in fact, have no grounds for grief. The dead remember the living as the living remember the dead within an ongoing economy of affection and sentiment. The rhetorical devices of the novel also seek to extend the circle of collaboration from the fictional characters to the historical readers as it offers the promise of consolation through sentimental collaboration as a way of dealing with the consequences of the recent Civil War.

As in the child elegies of *Harriet Gould's Book,* Mary's initial rage, grief, and despair bespeak a self alienated both from her community and from a sense of herself as a whole. Early on, Mary writes that, though she has "been praying for a touch, a sign, only for something to break the silence into which he has gone," there has been "no answer, none" (21). Also, as in those poems, Mary's grief is assuaged through the circulation of affections. Her brother's death had disturbed the "circle of family and friends" that had determined her individuality, an individuality constructed relative to and dependent on only this other person. Through conversation with her widowed aunt Winifred, Mary is able to call into being and to sustain an image of her dead brother as "not any the less your own real Roy, who will love you and wait for you and be very glad to see you, as he used to love and wait and be glad when you came home from a journey on a cold winter night" (53). Just as relationships with living people are shown to depend on the reciprocal exchange of tokens of affection in an active display of love, so are the relationships with the dead.

Aunt Winifred engages Mary in a series of conversations during which the women collaboratively generate a concept of heaven that restores Roy to Mary and Mary to herself as it binds Winifred and Mary to each other.

The book opens with an explanation of the protagonist's social alienation and spiritual skepticism on learning that her brother has been killed. Offers of solace that account for Roy's death as either the will of God or the justified cost of war conflict with her own cynical account: "Why, it seems to me as if the world were spinning around in the light and wind and laughter, and God just stretched down His hand one morning and put it out" (2). While rejecting conventional justifications for death, Mary subscribes to the conventional accounts of her own behavior that castigate her as "rebellious" or self-pitying (15, 21). Writing in the form of a diary, Mary explains that she has transformed a "poor little book in which I used to keep memoranda of the weather, and my lovers, when I was a school-girl" into a testament of her despair and into an object for the indulgence of what she considers a morbid grief. Claiming to the unnamed reader of the diary that she has turned to literary self-examination only for want of "something to do," Phelps's fictional diarist enhances her claim to authenticity. As the narrative takes on the shape of a sentimental conversion narrative, this initial avowal of spontaneity displays the diarist's spiritual modesty as it establishes the conditions for a spiritual comedy.

Mary and Roy had been orphans who had formed a "soul's society" in the absence of their parents. Although Mary is twenty-four and her brother at least that old, they had enjoyed a relationship in which they were each all to each other: "we have lived together so long, we two alone, since father died, that he had grown to me, heart of my heart, and life of my life" (8).[13] Mary's romantic feelings for her brother are shared with the reader (who within the fiction of Phelps's novel would be Mary, herself, since the novel takes the form of a diary) in an extended appositive of the dead man: "Roy, all I had in the wide world, —Roy, with the flash in his eyes, with his smile that lighted the house all up; with his pretty, soft hair that I used to kiss and curl about my finger" (9). Learning that her brother has been killed, Mary describes her own state in an inverted credo of sensibility:

> The house feels like a prison. I walk up and down and wonder that I ever called it home. Something is the matter with the sunsets; they come and go, and I do not notice them. Something ails the voices of the children, snowballing down the street; all the music has gone out of them, and they hurt me like knives. The harmless, happy children! —and Roy loved the little children. (2)

Feeling that "I am nothing any more to Roy," Mary becomes afraid that she "should hate God" (51).

With the house a not-home, and without an ability to perceive beauty in such highly sanctioned sources as nature and children, Mary finds herself unable even to participate in expected social rituals. Without the complementarity provided by Roy, Mary's wonted constitution of herself as a subject is seriously threatened. Having defined herself within such narrow terms, only in relation to her brother, Mary's grieving self is so fractured that she cannot take part in the give and take that would have reintegrated her into her local society. For reasons that the narrator does not reveal, she had already foreclosed on the possibility of marriage.

Mary supposes that such a probability might make "the very incompleteness of life sweet, because of the symmetry which is waiting somewhere" (8).[14] The Freudian solution to grief, whereby a substitution is found to replace whatever object has been lost, is not open to Mary.

The Gates Ajar, like *Uncle Tom's Cabin,* shows the degree to which the conservative force of sentimental collaboration can generate sometimes threateningly new solutions. The conventional gifts of solace offered both by the male representatives of the church and by the female representatives of the local women irritate rather than soothe and are rudely refused by Phelps's narrator. Where Mary sees her grief as solely a personal matter, her neighbors perceive this as a crisis affecting the whole of the community and intervene out of a sympathy that Mary cannot accept because she cannot reciprocate it. Her behavior makes her an object of interest if not of gossip in the town. The town of "Homer," Mary explains, "has made up its mind that I shall become resigned in an arithmetical manner, and comforted upon the rule of three" (11, 12). When a schoolmate, Meta Tripp (who has also lost a brother in the war), comes to offer her condolences, Mary cannot help but see this as hypocritical and self-serving on Meta's part (7). Meta's observation "as she went out, that I shouldn't feel so sad by and by," is a sign of the distance between her own loss and Meta's. It is obvious to the narrator that Meta had not really loved her brother if she could feel so. The outward expression of Mary's anger and grief takes the form of refusing to take communion in church. This brings upon her the unwanted intervention of Deacon Quirk, an unregenerated Calvinist Yankee, of stern visage and few words. Quirk claims the right to interfere with Mary as a "Christian brother," but Mary rejects his pseudo-brotherhood as she had rejected communion: "God does not seem to me just now what He used to. He has dealt very bitterly with me" (14). Mary's rejection comes close, in her readings of unnamed Romantic German poets, to a sublime acceptance of alienation.[15] She will accept neither the teachings of the church nor of her neighbors.

Mary's state corresponds to the early movements of the child elegies of *Harriet Gould's Book.* Although more guarded and more cryptic, the parental subjects of these poems ask repeatedly, "How can I check the falling tear / How can I hush the sigh" even as they assert a belief that their dead child "though lost to me / has reached the blissful shore"

(III.17–18, 21–22). Although Mary knows that "Roy is an angel," she is unable to receive comfort from this because her definition of the state of salvation precludes the continuation of individual subjectivity. It is Mary's widowed aunt Winifred, her mother's youngest sister come to visit from the West, who disabuses Mary of this notion and leads her toward a new definition of salvation predicated on the continuation of the personal subjectivity of the possessive individual. The middle section of the book contains the dialogues between Mary and Winifred in which they develop and flesh out this new definition of a paradise that affirms worldly connections to both things and people. Together they come to reject the iconoclastic vision of heaven offered by the Congregational church and replace it with one patched together from various sources including Swedenborg, their own original readings of the Bible, and Augustine. Working together at the task of comforting each other, Winifred and Mary develop what they themselves recognize as "beautiful heresies" (141). "If Deacon Quirk *should* hear!" exclaims Mary after her aunt has concluded that

> Eternity cannot be — it cannot be the great blank ocean which most of us have somehow or other been brought up to feel that it is, which shall swallow up, in a pitiless, glorified way, all the little brooks of our delight. So I expect to have my beautiful home, my husband, and Faith, as I had them here; with many differences and great ones, but *mine* just the same. (141; emphasis in original)

This consoling dialogue eventually becomes a group discussion among a large number of people and is therefore the vehicle of the sentimental conversion of the Deacon Quirks and Meta Tripps of the town.

It is important to remember that Phelps's book functions as a mourning manual as well as a novel. In contrast to the tactless interventions of Meta Tripp and the Deacon Quirks, Winifred Forceythe entices her niece out of alienation. The others conspicuously had failed to establish the authority of empathy born by shared experience, thereby violating the sentimental assumption that "none but those who feel can tell / The sorrow which the bosom swells" (Abigail Lazell, *Harriet Gould's Book,* 10). Widowed three years earlier soon after the birth of her only child, this older woman is better able to assert the sentimental authority of empathy. She uses this authority to coerce her niece into joining with her, not submitting to her, in finding a solace that will enable Mary to continue to function in the world. Without having to be told, Winifred notices that it makes Mary uncomfortable to see someone else in the place at the table that used to be Roy's. As a token of her understanding, Winifred asks her hostess, the younger woman Mary, if she may sit somewhere else rather than seem to have assumed the "vacant place" (44). Although, as Mary says, "it was such a little thing," it serves as a sign of the older woman's "quick perception" and "unusual delicacy" (44). Winifred's perception elicits the beginning of Mary's interest in another human being: "I almost wish that she had stayed a little longer. I almost think that I could bear to have her speak to me about him" (44). But Winifred does not tell her niece about Roy. Instead, she asks Mary for the favor of hearing "all about it" (49). She affirms without judgment Mary's experience, which is summed up by Mary this way: "Why, you do not know,—it is just as if a great black gate had swung to and barred out the future, and barred out him, and left me all alone in any world that I can ever live in, forever and forever" (50). Winifred's response is to offer her own brief account of cynical despair and a narrative of her reversion from it. This exchange of memories, hopes, and fears for themselves and the people they have lost establishes the ground for the re-formation of the family ties that are the necessary prerequisites for a sense of possessive individualism. By page 100, Mary asks Winifred "to stay and help me bear my life," acknowledging that "*I* am not a 'family'" (100, 101; emphasis in original). This new family is related by kinship ties, but more by the ties of affection that have been actively created. The voluntary nature of this association reinforces the acknowledgedly weaker ties of blood.

Winifred teaches Mary through a process of engaging conversation. Mary feels "that, if I sat as a little child at her feet, she could teach me through the kinship of her pain" (51). Since Mary suffers most from having been "severed" from her relationship with her brother, much of the conversation concerns him. Winifred appeals to a "common sense" as the key interpreter of biblical teachings on the afterlife: "if there is such a thing as common sense, you will talk with Roy as you talked with him here" (81). The burden of Winifred and Mary's collaborative interpretation is that after death one retains one's particularity even while joining the utopian community of the saved. Winifred asserts early on that "wherever the Bible touches the subject, it premises our individuality as a matter of course" (80). This particularity is dependent upon the willed reciprocal relationships among both the living and the dead. The dead maintain their connections with the living by fostering their memories just as the living must foster their memories of the dead: "Heaven will not be less heaven, but more, for this pleasant remembering" (135). For the most part, it is Winifred that does the talking, while Mary appropriates her teachings to her own personal situation in the privacy of her journal. Having become convinced of Roy's continued individuality and ability to be a presence in her life, Mary begins to accept that she will be able to continue in this life. The women also together imagine the necessary heavenly environment for such a subject. As in midcentury America, one's self will be largely defined by one's possessions. If it is a piano that makes one most authentically oneself, then a piano will be there, if it is an orchard or a sofa, they, too, will be there. In this task, too, memory is seen to be crucial: Winifred believes that memories of this life will prepare her to appreciate the next. Hence, if mountain views from cozy domestic interiors embody one's happiest moment, this could be a prefiguration of how heaven will be experienced. The many mansions of Jesus' father's house become just so many independent domestic spaces structuring the families and friends chosen by the mutual exercise of taste among these individuals.

The success of sentimental collaboration as a means of reconstructing the foundations of society and the family, even in the face of profound loss, is signaled by the conclusion of the plot. Having aided Mary in recovering from her loss by exchanging with her both memories and hopes, Winifred then passes responsibility for her own child, Faith, on to the younger woman at the moment of her death. Where at the beginning of the novel Mary had been disconnected from both her immediate family and from a larger circle of society, at the end she is re-bound to both. Her new family does not erase the old one but supplements it, since she "cannot doubt that our absent dead are very present with us" (88).

Phelps's novel is a much more deeply conservative one than Stowe's. At the same time, it generates much more radical solutions to the problems it takes up. Standing in sharp contrast to the fractured, polysemous structure of Stowe's book that, like Melville's *Moby-Dick,* demands an allegorical reading, Phelps's novel (written in the form of diary entries) rehearses the conventions of eighteenth-century novels. The force of this semiautobiographical style is put in the service of a task usually undertaken in the compact lyric genre of elegy. On the level of discourse, it is a fictional prose elegy dominated by the strategies of sentimentalism, and on the level of story it contains one of the clearest representations of the operation of sentimental collaboration. The circulation of the memories of the dead men creates a situation in which the subsequent death of Aunt Winifred will cause no gap in the circle of the newly recomposed and extended family. By the conclusion of the novel, this collaboration has shifted Mary from being an orphan girl bereft of even her brother, to being the surrogate mother for a motherless child. Just as Faith's name had been given to her by her dying father as a sign and direction to her mother, Faith is given to Mary as a sign of her mother's faith in Mary and Mary's new-found faith in salvation.

The goal of sentimental collaboration is gestured to both in the title to Phelps's book and in at least one of the dead baby poems of *Harriet Gould's Book*. This goal was to "push ajar the gates of life" (VIII). This being done, "We could interpret all this doubt and strife and for each mystery find a key" (VIII). As the first step in a heuristic exercise, sentimental collaboration creates the interpretive subject, the "we," that will find and presumably use the key to resolve "this doubt and strife." Emerson had envisaged a poet who would perform an act of ongoing interpretation that would make the meaning of the hieroglyphics of nature transparent for the rest of Americans. Such a poet would be a truly "representative" person; representing to and representative of numerous less fully individuated and self-possessed beings. *Harriet Gould's Book* and the two novels I have briefly treated here suggest that the goal of such a poetics could only be achieved through a mutual collaborative action. It seems that the goal of the neighbors of Dover, Vermont, was not so removed from Emerson's, the main difference being that as active Christians they would have been more concerned with the mysteries of their God than with nature. Yet, in contrast to Emerson, their poetry displays a more open conception of who could become such a poet, of who would have access to the "key." In fact, without the active help of others, without the joining of interests, it would be impossible to establish either the grounds (representativeness) or the means (individualism) for such interpretation. Without the help of others, the power of grief threatened an isolation that would break the connections through which one recognized and was recognized as an individual. Through sentimental collaboration, the personal subjectivity of the mourner could be adjusted so as to experience a continuity of self, of family, and of time.

PART THREE

The Competition of Sentimental Nationalisms: Lydia Sigourney and Henry Wadsworth Longfellow

FLOWER ARRANGEMENT MADE OF HAIR.
Private collection of Ralph and Verne Howe, Wilmington, Vermont.
This arrangement came to the Howe's with the manuscript of Harriet Gould
from the collection of Florence Fox Howe.

Hail, brothers, hail,

Let nought on earth divide us.

—Sigourney, "The Thriving Family," 1848

Thou too, sail on, O Ship of State!

Sail on, O Union, strong and great!

—Longfellow, "The Building of the Ship," 1849

It is the powerful language of resistance . . . it is the dialect of common sense. —Whitman, preface to *Leaves of Grass,* 1855

The Americans of Harriet Gould's generation were faced with a problem. If neither blood, geography, nor established tradition was holding the composite parts together, what was? What could? They had inherited a grand, but almost uselessly, idealistic definition of America that, while inspiring, was too ephemeral. Now, as the number of states expanded, as immigration and emigration increased and as the problems of suffrage and slavery became more prominent, this vague and transcendent conception of America seemed unlikely to be able to hold the composite parts together, much less provide for the growth of the whole. Just as traditional ideas of selfhood had to be reworked to serve the new and still evolving conditions of democracy, so did the concept of nationhood. The nation itself, in other words, suffered from many of the same problems as Harriet and John Gould. Like the "circle of family and friends" that made up the American individual, the nation was the product of voluntary relationships and was subject to some of the same threats. Harriet and John Gould, like many other ordinary, non-elite farmers, shopkeepers, and mill workers, participated in the invented tradition of sentimental collaboration to address the problems of personal identity formation under the conditions of contingency and loss. Sentimental collaboration allowed them to instantiate imaginary bonds that would bridge the self-threatening differences of death, time, and distance. The work of two of the most popular poets of the antebellum period, Lydia Howard Huntley Sigourney (1791–1865) and Henry Wadsworth Longfellow (1807–1882), shows what happens when the same strategy is directed at the problem of national identity. When this problem is recast as one of emotional rather than rational logic, these poems show, the solution takes the form of a utopian promise of emotional cohesion which dissolves disruptive differences into amiable unity. It is this promise, which has been difficult for twentieth-century critics to see because we have been so sensitized to sentimentality's obvious threats, that accounts for the continued ideological force of sentimentality in America.

In the last chapter, I argued that the practice of what I call "sentimental collaboration" was quilted together during the early decades of the nineteenth century in response to personal and local experiences of loss. Engaging in a shared attempt to convert grief into mourning became instrumental for the construction and perpetuation of the possessive, because possessed, individual. Although this practice is represented in many mimetic genres of this time, including popular novels, lithographs, and dramas, the key to how it actually operated in the lives of historical Americans is found in the traces they have left in the form of mourning poetry, condolence letters, gravestones, and material "remembrancers" such as hair-wreaths, clothes, or embroideries. These "tokens," imbued with what was seen as the essence of personhood—the affections—of those who have touched them, circulated in a cultural economy of gift and presentation. This gift economy, as I have explained above, facilitated the collaborative reimagination of the contingent and vulnerable into the permanent. Mourning was achieved through collaborations structured by the exchange of sentiment which converted many into one, the devisible into the indivisible.

In this third part I turn away from the private realm of personal grief and mourning to the related but public domain of politics. I would like to suggest that sentimental collaboration also provided crucial strategies for defining what the adjective "American" could mean for those who inhabited the United States of America. In other words, if, as Benedict Anderson claims, communities "are to be distinguished, not by their falsity/genuineness, but by the style in which they are imagined" (6), then it is sentimentality that determined the style or manner in which the community of the United States of America would be imagined by those whose lived there. Earlier definitions of America, those formulated in the colonial era under the sway of the Enlightenment, were theoretical propositions derived through an earnest application of "reason" that merely needed to be substantiated by historical experience. Just one example would be the Declaration of Independence, which gave a composite title, the United States of America, to the incipient nation. The last word, "America," serves merely as a rubric conveniently locating the constituent states geographically and corraling them conceptually. But the name, as often is the case, preceded the thing to which it referred. The nation itself, the United States of America, had yet to be constituted through the violent, military contest of rebellion and through the verbal contests of the 1787 Constitutional Convention. In other words, "America" provided a theoretical framework, but not a methodology, for how the national project was to unfold.

Even after the Revolution and after the Constitution was ratified, and well into the following century, a consensus on what the national project was to be—and how it was to become that—had yet to be achieved. "America," as a concept, remained an unstable potentiality. The geographic shape of the country, like the political and economic relation of the parts to each other and to the whole, was undergoing a transformative crisis throughout the early nineteenth century which had not been—could not have been—anticipated by the framers of the Constitution. Their all-encompassing, but not concrete, conceptualization of the nation ceased to function in a positive or enabling way. What had been liberating became limiting as the vagueness of "America" as a defining term began to generate a cultural anxiety. This anxiety was met by the efforts of many, including Sigourney and Longfellow but also historians and politicians, to delimit and specify its nature. Later I discuss several of these poets' attempts, for they pose a marked contrast to the efforts during the Enlightenment to decree a national identity. These nineteenth-century poets discovered for themselves what political theorists such as Partha Chatterjee and Benedict Anderson have since described, that nationalist identities are seldom determined on a rational basis.[1] Those who, like Sigourney and Longfellow, were inventing what it would mean to be an American turned to sentiment, which enabled them to structure a project of imagining their country which would be ongoing, sustainable, and broad based because it depended on collaboration. And this collaboration begins to close down the proliferation of possible Americans by binding it, America, to a concept of identity dependent on voluntary relationships and demonstrated by shared, mutually felt emotional truths.

A useful contrast might be Crèvecoeur's use of the qualifier "American" in the title to his *Letters from an American Farmer* (1782). This typifies the abstraction and idealism of the term "America" as a geographic concept during the late colonial and early national era. "America," for Crèvecoeur, was that place where a certain way of being was possible: "*He* is an American, who leaving behind him all his ancient prejudices and manners, receives new ones from the mode of life he has embraced, the new government he obeys, and the new rank he holds" (70; emphasis in original). "The Americans," explains Crèvecoeur, "were once scattered all over Europe" (70). Crèvecoeur suggests that "American-ness" was an essential, though latent, quality inherent in individuals which a new political environment and geographic locale merely encouraged and revealed: "here they are incorporated into one of the finest systems of population which has ever appeared, and which will hereafter become distinct by the power of the different climates they inhabit" (70).[2] America, therefore, was a place not wholly defined by political or geographical demarcations. Instead, "America" existed on the cusp between the Old World of Europe and the New Worlds of the American continents. For example, late in *Letters,* when the press of Revolution threatens this liminal space of potentiality—when Crèvecoeur's letter writer is asked to choose between retaining allegiance to the British colonial government or pledging allegiance to the newly forming independent states of America and thus fixing a new center of government and authority for himself—he finds a solution in the removal of his family deeper into the frontier. Crèvecoeur's "Farmer," being the perfect example of the American, just moves his "America" with him to outside of what can no longer be considered "British America."[3] Like Thomas Paine, who declared that "where liberty is *not,* there is my country," the ostensible writer of Crèvecoeur's *Letters from an American Farmer* might be recognized as one of what Whitman would later call "the Americans of all nations at any time upon the earth" (preface, 1855 *Leaves of Grass*).[4] In contrast to those who in the nineteenth century would have described themselves as "native Americans" (white, Protestant, born of parents who had been born in New England), Paine and Crèvecoeur are not Americans by virtue of birth but by virtue of their voluntary attempts to fulfill the a priori potential of human nature. America, for these writers, is wherever it is possible to do this. America is the end point of a rational pursuit of the good life.

Another example of a revolutionary-era attempt to define America is the Connecticut Wit Joel Barlow (1754–1812). Born a British subject in colonial America, he found his true "Americanness" only (as standard biographies suggest) in the geographic space of Europe as the atmosphere of revolutionary France and the company of radicals such as Mary Wollstonecraft and the Marquis de Lafayette fostered a more enlightened and broader sense of republicanism than he had experienced even in revolutionary America.[5] Barlow, like Crèvecoeur, derived his definition of America according to a process of logical deduction governed by Enlightenment assumptions. But his attempt differs significantly from Crèvecoeur's in both form and purpose. Where Crèvecoeur wrote in the forward-looking and developing genre of the epistolary, speculative novel, Barlow, like many of his compatriots in the closing quarter of the eighteenth century, continued to believe in the efficacy of the traditional epic. For Crèvecoeur, the term "America" might as well have been "Erehwon," a utopia whose value lay precisely in its nonexistence. But Barlow would sing a democratic America into being as Virgil had sung imperial Rome.

Although the epic had little success in the eighteenth century, the enthusiasm of Dryden and Pope for this genre continued to inspire emulation in the former colonies of Britain. Only an epic could perform the necessary work of providing Americans with a way to recognize and make sense of themselves. What is more, America would be the salvation of poetry. Here in postrevolutionary America, Barlow thought, was the material and the necessity for what he envisioned as a republican epic.[6] "This is the moment in America," claimed Barlow in his preface to the *Columbiad,* "to give such a direction to poetry, painting and the other fine arts, that true and useful ideas of glory may be implanted in the minds of men" (389). Only the topic of America, Barlow thought, could adequately use epic's ability to provide the underpinnings to a political project.

In fact, Barlow repeatedly and without embarrassment emphasized that this ideological work was the "real object of the poem" (382). Both epics that he eventually wrote, the *Vision of Columbus* in 1787 and *The Columbiad* in 1807, were written with specific political goals in mind:

to inculcate the love of rational liberty, and to discountenance the deleterious passion for violence and war; to show that on the basis of republican principle all good morals, as well as good government and hopes of permanent peace, must be founded; and to convince the student of political science that the theoretical question of future advancement of human society, till states as well as individuals arrive at universal civilization, is held in dispute and still unsettled only because we have had too little experience of organized liberty in the government to have well considered its effects. (382)

The national project of America, according to Barlow, would be to provide data for an analysis of the "organized liberty in the government," and thus to provide proof of the attainability of "universal civilization." In a secularization of John Winthrop's claim in a "Model of Christian Charity" that the Massachusetts Bay colony is "as a city upon a hill" with the "eyes of all people upon Us," Barlow's America would provide the empirical proof of the rationalist theories of self-government driving the antimonarchical revolutions of the eighteenth century.

Conscious of living in a mythical time, Barlow strove to provide a narrative—to frame a political unconscious—which would guide future interpretations of the Constitution as well as the future growth and actions of the country.[7] In both poems, Barlow's epic seer presents Columbus as a victim and a creature of all the abuses of traditional and monarchical power. Over the course of the story, Columbus is spiritually and emotionally healed of these abuses only by the hope held out by the future, embodied in the history of the American colonies and the establishment of the United States of America, which comes to him in a dream vision. Barlow's epic (both versions) weaves Europe, Columbus, Native Americans, and North and South America into one unified story in which all participants work together to create and sustain a radically republican form of government. The story details the widespread achievement of a utopia founded on the free exercise of republican virtues. "Americans," in Barlow's epics, are the product of Columbus's mission to spread the values of the democratic Enlightenment.

Crèvecoeur's choice of the epistolary novel allowed him to engage in a speculative meditation—or rather in a staged speculative dialogue—on the nature of life's possibilities in the American colonies on behalf of his British and European audience. Like Voltaire in *Candide,* Crèvecoeur uses the setting of the New World (in this case British America) as the opportunity to philosophize on human nature and as a place for his speaker to enact a shift from naive optimism to cynical pessimism. Barlow's choice of the epic genre, on the other hand, rests on his unabashed desire to undergird the legal instrument of the U.S. Constitution with a logically derived explanatory myth addressed to those who knew themselves to be "American" but did not, exactly, understand what that entailed. Epic was, for Barlow, the best available way to define just who is meant by the "We, the people" who ordained and established the Constitution and to define just what exactly are "The United States of America."

Despite the differences in genre, Barlow shared Crèvecoeur's understanding of "America" as a transcendental signifier, an abstract formula from which a new conception of nation that would be independent of blood, force, and injustice could be derived. But this understanding didn't completely serve the needs of the nationalism that emerged in the early nineteenth century. Questions of geographical and political borders, questions of jurisdiction, and questions of money arose to complicate the theorem.[8] Unlike Crèvecoeur, Barlow never lost faith in the possibility of America because he had more faith, perhaps, in its reality. But for Barlow, and the others who agreed with him on the need for an American Academy of Arts and Letters, the ongoing reality of America depended upon the active intervention of those who knew best in the construction and imposition of what has been called a "national symbolic" as the necessary complement and completion of the work of the Revolution.[9] Barlow understood that the presently inchoate "American" political and geographic entity needed a myth, and he did not shy away from providing it. Sensitive to the power of genre, Barlow deployed the strong arm of epic to make it impossible for his readers to escape becoming the stuff of republican heroes.[10] But Barlow's myth, despite his best efforts, didn't take. His epics, even his revised version, didn't sell and certainly didn't enter the common storehouse of popular reference. For whatever reasons, in the nativist atmosphere of Jacksonian America, the constitutive "We" of the preamble to the Constitution demanded a more precise and limiting definition than it had in Barlow's day, or perhaps it just needed to be defined in a different way, in a different genre?

Did this American "we" include women, did it include blacks or Catholic immigrants? If anyone could be American then maybe no one, really, is American? Given this question, perhaps a good way to understand the problem of Harriet Gould's generation, which was after all the generation of Lincoln, would be this: how can we define America so that we can be both American by birth and by choice? How can we define America so that it can both grow and remain intact? Walt Whitman, Harriet Gould's contemporary, more famously struggled to answer these same questions. When he prefaced his first (1855) edition of *Leaves of Grass* with the claim that "Americans of all nations at any time upon the earth have probably the fullest poetical nature," he must already have been aware that such a universalizing use of the descriptor "American" was no longer wholly justified nor fully useful. It was losing value as it was being replaced by more concrete, more excluding, and yet more popular definitions such as those I discuss below. Even in this sentence the effort to subsume the categories of place and time into the broader term "America" is resisted by the words "all nations at any time upon the earth." Whitman, like Crèvecoeur, Paine, and Barlow, seems to be making "American" equivalent to the concept of man in his highest fulfillment no matter where he lived or what his heritage.[11] But, as in Paine's disavowal of any prior claims of national identity, Whitman's invocation of "all the nations" marks the increasing strength of a more narrowly conceived and material sense of nationalism. *Leaves of Grass*, in its various incarnations, sustains two opposing impulses: the impulse to claim a universal status for America and Americans and the need to articulate a particularized definitive vision of America. To do this, to "indicate the path between reality and their [the people's] souls," Whitman appropriated not only epic conventions and tried to turn them to a democratic purpose (as had Barlow) but also the power of a mode of discourse more often associated with poets such as Sigourney and Longfellow (10, 24).

Both Sigourney and Longfellow provide some of the best examples of what Whitman calls the "dialect of common sense" in their efforts to correct the proliferation of definitions of America which were springing up in the gap left by the breakdown of both the Federalist and Jeffersonian models of American development. The all-encompassing, idealized, and transcendent definitions of America generated by writers such as Crèvecoeur and Barlow did not provide, as I noted earlier, appropriately enabling limits to the term. For Crèvecoeur and Barlow, the set of individuals who were American did not have to be coterminous with that place called the United States of America.

Since the definition of the status "American" transcended geographic or political boundaries, the exact delineation of those boundaries wasn't necessary, nor was a perception of concrete organic wholeness, since the true America existed as an Ideal. Yet after the War of 1812, such a large and nonspecific definition of America became a source of anxiety. One example of the way this anxiety operated is offered by the treatment of the Cherokee Amerindians.[12] Treaties made during the early national period had recognized the sovereignty of certain native peoples whose domains were contiguous with or even within the borders of a particular American state. The state of Georgia, for example, encompassed the independently governed "state" of the Cherokees from the time of the Revolution until 1835. Increasingly, however, as the sense of what America was changed, the existence of native "nations" within the bounds of the United States of America came to be seen as disruptive.[13] In a series of wars ending only in the 1840s, these early treaties were successfully voided and the remnants of the Amerindians were violently displaced west, outside of the political bounds of the United States. For the "Indian-fighter" Andrew Jackson's generation, the Amerindians as individuals and as citizens of competing "nations" prevented the possibility of a sense of national identity based on geographic or racial cohesion.[14] Of course, paradoxically, it was through the establishment of this opposing category of alien states and the destruction of those who fit into it that Andrew Jackson, himself, was constituted as a representative American when he won the presidential election of 1828.

A second example of the cultural anxiety caused by the lack of an agreed-upon definition of America which could both prescribe and project the growth of the nation is the furor over the Mexican-American War, which caused poets (such as the established and socially prominent Sigourney, as well as the younger and obscure Thoreau) to protest the imperialist and militarist audacity of the American belligerents. The Mexican-American War raised the stakes on the question of how the United States could expand their geographical borders. Could American identity be forced upon another or must it be voluntarily assumed? Yet another concern raised during the same period was the question of what would be the nature of the reciprocal relations between the state and federal branches of the government: who would tax, who would spend, and for what? All of these questions had corollaries in the hotly contested questions of who was a citizen and what were the citizens' relations to the two levels of government, to each other, and to those who were noncitizens, such as women and slaves.

Sigourney and Longfellow (like Whitman) continued to share Barlow's belief in the need to define America in order both to prescribe what should and to proscribe what should not happen in the future. But Barlow's attempts to call into being a national identity through the vehicle of the epic and on the basis of rational deduction from logical premises had not attained widespread currency and did not provide a viable poetic model for poets such as Longfellow and Sigourney to follow. Instead, as their poetry shows, it was through the "humbler" genre of sentimental lyric and on the basis of an emotional logic that the imaginative work of national definition occurred. It is this mode that coerces the kind of shared emotional participation in an imaginative project that collapses the differences between disparate interests into one. I will argue that it is the "dialect of common sense," the discourse of sentiment, that succeeds, where the discourse of reason had failed, to define America. The competition to define America and its corollary the American subject occurred on the grounds delineated by the functional poetics of American sentimentality; this was also the ground on which the contest to define the "American Poet" occurred.[15]

CHAPTER 5

The Competition of
Sentimental Nationalisms

Only now did Karl understand how huge America was.
—Franz Kafka, *Amerika*

The critical commonplace that, while male poets "turned their attention to . . . the creation of that masculine nationalistic image, the American Adam," women poets "looked at themselves and their situations and found many other things to say," has made the competition of sentimental nationalisms difficult to see (Watts 64). For while Sigourney was a woman, she nevertheless did turn her attention to the problem of creating an image of America. And she was not alone in this effort. Despite being excluded from the privileges of full citizenship, many of the major women poets of Jacksonian America, such as Fanny Osgood and Elizabeth Oakes Smith, did aggressively engage in the creation of a non-Adamic, though "nationalistic image" able to engender and support a commonly shared understanding of what the project of America would be in the changing world of the first half of the nineteenth century. This project of creating a national identity, which could be held by women as well as men, is one of the dominant themes of Lydia Sigourney's long and influential career and was an important predicate for the subsequent development of nineteenth-century feminisms. And, while Longfellow was a man and while he also turned his attention to the problem of creating a national image, his creation was not exactly "Adamic" in the sense that has become familiar since R. W. B. Lewis's mid-twentieth-century description in *The American Adam* (1955). Unlike Whitman, who according to Lewis gives the fullest portrayal of the American Adam in *Leaves*

of Grass, Longfellow's American persona is not "liberated, innocent, solitary, forward-thrusting" (28). The biblical reference for the "American Adam" as celebrated by Whitman is the second version of the creation of humans in the book of Genesis. In this version, man is created first, alone, and woman is fashioned subsequently and subordinately from Adam's rib (Gen. 2.21–23). This is not to say that Longfellow didn't sometimes offer a masculine image of America, but that Longfellow's American is bound by memories of the past, by responsibilities to the future, by relationships with others. In Longfellow's narrative poems (for example, *The Song of Hiawatha* and *The Courtship of Miles Standish*), his male protagonists begin as fully integrated social beings who suffer from the loss or the threat of the loss of the societies that have given them meaning. In Longfellow's poems, his Americans are Adamic in the sense deriving from the first Chapter of Genesis: "God created man in his *own* image, in the image of God created he him; male and female created he them." In other words, Longfellow's personifications of America, like Sigourney's, are composite subjects dependent for their very identities on relationships with others. And, again like Sigourney's, this American Adam inhabits a post-, not a pre-, lapsarian world in which the goal is to invent a new way of being in a situation in which the common denominator of existence is loss.

Both Sigourney and Longfellow developed and exploited the "matter of the Indians" as one way to define America. Sigourney pursued this project in several forms, from the prose essay to the long narrative poems such as "Pocahantas" or "Oriska." These delineate the American landscape and the American character by putting the subject of the heroic Amerindian, and in particular the Amerindian woman, in the center of the narrative frame. In fact one of the first books that she published anonymously during the early years of her marriage was *Traits of the Aborigines of America* (1822). One of the first sustained critiques of U.S. imperialism, it protests the abrogation of treaties with the native nations which was intensifying during these years. But her most serious long treatment of the subject is "Pocahontas" (1841). The descriptions of landscapes in these poems contributes importantly to the replacement of the Puritan image of the American wilderness as a place of unregenerate evil.[1] Her America is figured as a knowing subject who participates in a constitutive economy of recognition with the human and animal characters. Longfellow in his *Hiawatha* also used the romance of Indian youth to celebrate the geography of America. In these Romantic narratives, Sigourney's falls of Niagara ("Oriska") and Longfellow's shores of Gitche Gumee (*The Song of Hiawatha*) become the settings for the actions, not of "noble savages," but of proto-Americans. In this respect, Sigourney and Longfellow were in concert with many of the American graphic artists of the period, with whom they may be seen as collaborators, for the contemporary illustrations accompanying these poems often underscore the sublime geography of the America of these poems.[2]

But these poets also deployed occasional lyrics in their project of defining America by directly addressing America in such a way as to make America come alive. Using the sentimental mode, Sigourney and Longfellow create a corporate entity, the family, as the persona of America. This America contrasts greatly with Barlow's solitary, suffering Columbus who dreams America into existence. Both poets privilege the fundamental topic of sentimentality—the lost family—as the template with which to shape the parameters of the Americas they address. But these poets also use the discourse of sentiment to engage their readers in joining with them in this process of national imagining. They meld everyday language with the elaborately embellished language of poetry into the characteristic diction of the sentimental mode to decrease the distance between the professional author's voice and the reader's vernacular. And they also use the characteristic rhetorical figures of sentimentality, direct address to the reader and apostrophe to an absent or abstracted presence, to link the writer, reader, and represented personae in an economy of reciprocal affections and sentiments.

Longfellow and Sigourney use these strategies to put into place a vision of America that reflects their own personal situations and political agendas. The multiple, various Americas that result allow us to explore the consequences for selfhood and nationhood of this effort and to see a set of common denominators that mark the sentimental armature of American nationalism. In the following pages I will deal first with Longfellow's elaborate sentimental allegory, "The Building of the Ship" (1849), which uses the family to sanction a vision of the nation devoted to and modeled on the expansionism of a market economy. I then turn to three poems Sigourney wrote between 1837 and 1850: "On the Occasion of the Admission of Michigan into the Union" (1837), "The Thriving Family," and "Our Country" (both 1848). This set of poems, including Longfellow's, indicates the range of sentimental nationalisms that were current during this important decade preceding the Fugitive Slave Law of 1850. "The Building of the Ship" explores and celebrates the inter-relationship between a capitalist economy and democratic imperialism which both serve to unite the differences of a large and heterogeneous community into a family having one set of interests. Sigourney's poems, in contrast, invoke the threats to national unity inherent in certain familial models of government in order to raise the stakes for the adoption of the sentimental resolution to political strife.

Longfellow's model of sentimental nationalism differs significantly from Sigourney's various models, not least in the degree of poetic closure, which is nothing if not overdetermined. "The Building of the Ship" follows the poem entitled "Dedication" to initiate the thematically unified volume of poems entitled *The Seaside to the Fireside* (1849). The "Dedication" to this volume declares the essential sentimentality of the book as a whole. The book itself is, according to Longfellow's speaker, a means "to join your seaside walk / Saddened and mostly silent, with emotion" while simultaneously joining "as no unwelcome guest, / At your warm fireside, when lamps are lighted" (lines 37–38, 41–42). Believing, with Sigourney, in the "language of the soul," Longfellow claims here that it is "the sympathies that ye have shown," and the "silent token[s]" that have taught the speaker that "when seeming most alone, / Friends are around us, though no word be spoken" (13–16). The cusp of the book, between the first half, subtitled "By the Seaside," and the second, subtitled "By the Fireside," describes the gap from which the sentimental ethos arises. In the last poem of "By the Seaside," Longfellow recounts a fireside conversation in which the participants eventually come to share, or attempt to share,

> . . . all that fills the hearts of friends,
> When first they feel, with secret pain,
> Their lives thenceforth have separate ends,
> And never can be one again.
> ("The Fire of Driftwood" 17–20)

The longing or loss of this existential alienation is made concrete in the following poem, "Resignation," which opens the second part of the book with the claim that: "There is no fireside, howsoe'er defended, / But has one vacant chair!" (3–4). In a world in which the "air is full of farewells to the dying, / And mournings for the dead" ("Resignation" 5–6), sentimentality operated to link the seemingly random events of the outside world, the "drift-wood fire without that burned" with the "thoughts that burned and glowed within" ("The Fire of Driftwood" 47–48). If, as studies of the sentimental novel have shown, the locus classicus of sentimentality is the family, sentimental poetry reveals that the specific originary site of sentimentality is the felt sense of loss within the individual as a member of that family.[3]

Like Sigourney, Longfellow grappled with the problem of envisioning America under the conditions of a widespread perception of loss and anxiety. Also like her, Longfellow turned to the family as the strongest and most appropriate model or template for rectifying the entropic potential of the contemporary political situation. Not only did the family serve as a common ground out of which a shared "commonsense" understanding of the American project could be forged, but more particularly, the absolute ground zero of the shared human experience was viewed by these poets as being marked by "the one vacant chair." Unlike Sigourney, who met the problem of loss and difference by deploying sentimentality as an agent of homogenization, Longfellow creates a model of heterogeneity controlled, guided, and limited by one dominant will. In Longfellow's most famous formulation of the national project, the United States of America are figured as "a goodly vessel, / That shall laugh at all disaster, / And with wave and whirlwind wrestle": the Ship of State in his still famous poem "On the Building of a Ship."

The entire process of building this ship occurs under the command of one driving force, the "One thought, one word" of the Master-builder who acts at the desire or prayer of a kind of prime-mover Merchant:

> Build me straight, O worthy Master!
> Staunch and strong, a goodly vessel,
> That shall laugh at all disaster,
> And with wave and whirlwind wrestle!
>
> (65, 1–4)

This prayer-like quatrain begins the poem and then serves as a refrain punctuating the several sections of the narrative. As the poem develops, the original Merchant speaker is successively replaced by the Master, by the extradiegetic speaker of the poem, and, finally, by the workmen of the shipyard.[4] In fulfilling the desires of the Merchant, all the individual workers take on this project as their own as they collaborate on it together. This first phrase, "build me straight," contains an syntactical ambiguity that is not resolved until the beginning of the next stanza. At this crucial point in the poem, Longfellow allows a characteristically sentimental slippage, in which these lines seem to speak the will of both the Merchant and of the ship. These lines force the reader and all those who reiterate it within the poem into a position coterminous with the ship; the Merchant, the ship, the Union, and the reader voice the same desire.

Longfellow's model of a nation held together by "oaken brace and copper band" endorses an imperialistic and market-driven idea of America where "every climate, every soil, / Must bring its tribute, great or small, / And help to build the wooden wall" (200, 67–69). Not only does the ship-building project begin with the voice of a Merchant, but also the ultimate rationale of the project as a whole is to provide for the ever-growing need for more markets and more sources of raw materials. "Cedar of Maine and Georgia pine / Here together shall combine" to form the fabric of the nation-ship under the force of the Master-builder's plan and imperious "gesture[s] of command" (101–2, 341). The products of the differing parts of the nation stand in, metonymically, for states and territories that exist in an hierarchical, not democratic, relationship to produce a "perfect symmetry" (179). Only in the service of the "merchant's word" (incarnated as the ship) are the raw "knarred and crooked cedar knees" and the "timber of chestnut, elm and oak" which lies "scattered here and there" across the shipyard fashioned into a productive form able, eventually, to carry the "hopes of future years" (5, 59, 57, 58, 380).

Longfellow's allegorical narrative tells two stories culminating in one: the story of the building of the ship and the story of the courtship of the Master-builder's daughter and the apprentice youth. The conjunction of these stories is made plain early in the poem, when, like a father in one of Shakespeare's dark romances, Longfellow's Master-builder proclaims that the ship will be

> A goodly frame, and a goodly fame,
> And the UNION be her name!
> For the day that gives her to the sea
> Shall give my daughter unto thee!
>
> (104–7)

Throughout the body of the poem, the daughter is the middle term linking the narrative of the building of the ship with the narrative of the young people's romance. Only once the "fiery youth" succeeds in building and launching what the "elder head had planned" would he become the heir to the Master's house and "his daughter's hand" (83–93). In response to the Merchant's desire, which the Master takes on as his own, he creates a "little model" which "should be to the larger plan / What the child is to the man," but in this case the child is not a male child but a woman child who will share her qualities of grace and docility with the ship (19–21).[5] The unnamed youth later seals this relationship by carving the ship's figurehead in the shape of the "Master's daughter" (215).

These two stories, in turn, become factors of a third and more important story by the imposition of the explicit interpretive frame presented at the close of the poem in which the "Ship of State," the "Union," and the union of the newly married couple are addressed with the same words. The apostrophe, declaring, "How beautiful she is! How fair / She lies within those arms, that press / Her form with many a soft caress / Of tenderness and watchful care!" is addressed equally to the bride, the ship, and the nation (360–3). Later, she becomes the link between the prospects of the ship (the "Union") and the prospects of the United States of America (367–70).[6] In advice directed to the "gentle, loving, trusting wife" (simultaneously ship and bride), the speaker advises that "gentleness and love and trust / Prevail o'er angry wave and gust" (368, 373). This advice marks the point in Longfellow's allegory at which he collapses the three levels into one in his famous coda beginning:

> Thou, too, sail on, O Ship of State!
> Sail on, O Union, strong and great!
> Humanity with all its fears,

> With all the hopes of future years,
> Is hanging breathless on thy fate!
>
> (377–81)

Longfellow here refashions the conventional image of the ship of state by grafting it onto a sentimental framework. This framework gives the ship of state a history and makes it at one with, not opposed to, the values of the family. In Sophocles' *Antigone,* in contradistinction, the ship of state that Creon claims to command proves antagonistic to the spiritual and emotional needs of the family. Within Longfellow's formulation, the needs of the individual as a family member cannot be violated by the needs of the state, nor the needs of the market, because they are inextricably woven into one.

Just over ten years before Longfellow wrote "The Building of the Ship," in the crisis year of 1837, Lydia Sigourney addressed the problem of national unity and identity in "On the Admission of Michigan into the Union" (*Illustrated Poems,* 1849). In Sigourney's hands, sentimentality is a subtle and powerful tool. In this poem, as in her later attempts to figure America in verse, Sigourney deploys a model of nationhood that is, like Longfellow's, fundamentally familial and sentimental. In contrast to Longfellow, however, who uses sentimentality solely for its very powerful ability to forge emotional analogies, Sigourney uses sentimentality here both to invoke the power of such emotional analogies and to critique the danger inherent in some uses of familial metaphors. In "On the Admission of Michigan into the Union," Sigourney literalizes the metaphor of sister-states so that Michigan becomes "Little Michy," who is welcomed by the speaker of the poem into the "best parlour" of the household of the United States of America (lines 40, 2). This is a household made up exclusively of sisters in which a "father" is invoked but not present, and a mother does not seem to exist at all. What would it mean, Sigourney seems to be asking, for the community of America to be "imagined," to use Benedict Anderson's terms, as a community of sisters? What kind of spin does the substitution of sorority for fraternity put on the cry inherited from the revolutionary days of "Liberty, Equality, Fraternity"? Despite the almost obnoxiously coy and playful tone in this poem, Sigourney begins to lay claim here to an authority to participate in the negotiation of the tensions inherent in the geopolitical expansion of the United States at that time. Sigourney, like Longfellow and innumerable thinkers of this period, was attempting to divine and control the destiny becoming manifest for America.[7] Taken as a whole, these three poems show Sigourney's awareness of the complications which class and gender posed to the democratic project of America. As the century progressed Sigourney laid aside both her self-protective flippancy and the model of a sororal America in favor of greater seriousness and a more conservative familial figuration of America. In her later poems "The Thriving Family" (1848) and "Our Country" (1848) she continued to advocate a nationalist vision of an America that would be guided by the kinship rules and mores of the family. In each effort Sigourney pushes the limits of a different familial metaphor of national identity.

In all three poems Sigourney grapples with the problem of reproduction and growth. This problem of growth is related, as Barlow had shown, to the problem of the reproduction of values; and the process by which the country could continue to grow while maintaining a harmonious relationship between the newer states and the old had become problematic almost as soon as the Constitution was ratified. In "On the Admission of Michigan to the Union," Sigourney brings to the foreground one of the historically determined exigencies of the growth of the United States of America during this time when, after having celebrated all that Michigan would bring to the Union, the speaker asks Michigan, "But where are your Indians—so feeble and few?" and admonishes her to "soothe their sad hearts ere they vanish afar, / Nor quench the faint beams of their westering stars" (19, 24–25). On the one hand, this stanza seems to display the ineffectuality of the sentimental critique of a political event, since it evades the issue of why the Indians of Michigan are "so fall'n from the heights" or who is responsible for their now being so "feeble and few" and asks merely that Michigan not add insult to injury by refusing to "soothe their sad hearts" before they disappear completely (20, 19). On the other hand, as part of an effort to construct a definition of America, this poem is one of the few instances where the cost of that project is even gestured to. Sigourney's uneasiness over the disappearance of the Amerindian, in this poem as in her larger treatments of the topic, has interesting affinities with Thoreau's complex evocation of the absent presence of the Massachusetts Indians in *Walden*. Like her contemporary Lydia Maria Child, Sigourney could not suppress the knowledge that the territories which were becoming encompassed by "America" were not empty.

Unlike her later nationalist poems where her tone is unambiguously earnest, in this early poem Sigourney disguises her bid for cultural authority behind a veil of seemingly conventional humor and irony. The poem opens by depicting the United States as a group of sisters cozily crowding their "father's best parlour" as if to humorously reduce the tensions among the competing states' interests to the differences among childish siblings. But in this poem Sigourney begins to recast the vocabulary of rights inherited from the days of the early republic into the discourse of sentimentality, so that the relations among states, the responsibilities of states to the federal government, and the relation of the individual to the state are modeled on a not-unproblematic familial schema. Although Michigan is figured here as a young child who has merely been held in the nursery until mature enough to join her sisters, the poem's treatment of the former inhabitants of the land and the wilderness of Michigan's terrain emphasizes that a more significant transformation has occurred. In other words, that which had formerly been "other" has become, through the force of the symbolic family, the same. One of the strengths of this poem, especially given the period in which it was written, is Sigourney's recognition that this transformation is violent and entails the death of difference.

The most serious issue addressed by Sigourney's poem is the question of how the country will grow and what the relationship will be among the various parts to the whole and to each other. Deriving a model of the ideal state from an ideal of the family is certainly no innovation. But Sigourney's model of a sororal America—a model of united sister-states—is a peculiar twist on this time-honored convention. As I mentioned earlier, the family Sigourney sets up here as an analogue to the country is notable for the absence of both father and mother. At first glance, therefore, it seems as if the sister-states all exist in a more or less equal relation to one another as they are bound to one another through ties of politeness and kinship but not through the force or law of the father. Indeed, it is the "thirteen old sisters" who wield authority in this parlor, being both the keepers of the cupboard and the transmitters of the constitutive symbolic law (27). The oldest sisters indoctrinate the younger into the mysteries of her new status by showing her "the writing

that gleamed in the sky / In the year seventy-six, on the fourth of July"
(33–34). Patriarchal rules of primogeniture are not in operation here;
rather, the youngest and twenty-sixth state has had a "portion" of "freedom" reserved for her (47). Like the workers in the Lord's vineyards who
will, according to Christ's parable, be paid the same despite the amount
of time they have spent there, the sister-states have all an equal share in
their "sire's" democratic patrimony (7).

And yet this seemingly egalitarian national sorority is insistently
undermined by Sigourney.[8] Her opening stanza refers to the difference
in status ascribed to an actual state versus a territory: Little Michy, the
speaker asserts, has "been kept long enough at the nurse's," and only now,
after the admission of twenty-five other sister-states, is the "best parlour"
opened to her (3). Territories, as Sigourney describes them, existed in
the mediating position between the geographic areas which were still
part of the "Americas" and the geographic area actually governed by the
United States of America. They are already and always America while
not yet being part of the United States. In addition, those same oldest
sisters, with whom the youngest state will now be sharing a full portion
of the inheritance of democracy, enforce their authority with violence.
The speaker hints that acts of insubordination will be met with "a frown,
or box on the ear" (41). If the improved status of the youngest state is
marked by its admittance into the domesticated space of the nation, the
genteel accoutrements of the best parlor (the sofa) mark the distinctions
that operate even within a supposed democracy: "the stateliest dames of
our family" (original thirteen states) are ensconced "on the sofa so high"
(25–26). Sofas and best rooms are both markers of the attainment of a
certain amount of surplus capital, which can either "fill a nice cupboard,
or spread a broad board" (14, 7). But this surplus capital is dependent on
the "present[s]" and "dowr[ies]" brought into the common larder by the
incoming sisters (13). The present wealth and comfort of the oldest states,
within this schema, rests on the products of the younger. Despite the
glum economic situation of the 1830s, the America of this poem does
seem to be passively growing in size and comfort: cupboards are full and
parlors are furnished by an ever-increasing household of sister-states.

Yet, Sigourney's ostensible celebration of the "Admission of Michigan
into the Union" becomes an occasion for excavating the uneasy map-
ping of capitalism and domesticity during the Jacksonian period. The

sororal equality among the states is presented as unstable since it depends on force or coercion. The speaker implies that the economically vigorous younger state might well choose to "scorn" the more established states and implies that the greater deference due the older states derives from having "bore the burden and heat of the day" as a means of paying the "price of [our] freedom" (43–45). For Sigourney, the capital contributed by the original thirteen states is of the cultural, not the economic, variety.[9] Ultimately, the poem suggests that a harmonious and lasting relationship among the states relies on the reciprocal rules of manners and on the mutual recognition of the value of the two forms of capital brought to the Union by the different states: the younger Michigan, while deserving the full rights of one of the United States, must show polite deference (with a curtsy) to the older sisters, who, because of Michigan's "plentiful store" of incipient cities and raw products, must show her due respect in return (30, 15). Like genteel women of antebellum America who circulated cultural currency within a noncommercial gift economy, the younger states, in Sigourney's model, exchange their raw products for the "many stories" through which culture can be transmitted (29).[10]

At this time of the geographic expansion of the nation through the process of violent and commercial annexation, Sigourney seems to be suggesting that the country should instead grow the way that a family of sisters grows. I stress the word "seems," here as elsewhere when discussing Sigourney's sentimental strategy, because she does not hide the troubling aspects of this sororal model of growth. In Sigourney's poem, what Jacques Lacan would call the Law of the Father is clearly in the keeping of the older sisters, who "can teach you the names of the great ones to spell" (31).[11] In addition, images of incest, blood, and sterility dominate this poem as Sigourney's model literalizes the problems that might arise from the effort to create one homogeneous whole out of formerly disparate units by extending the boundaries of the normal to absorb and neutralize the alien much in the way that a family absorbs and neutralizes a daughter-in-law. For where are the grooms? The "dowry" that Michigan has "very cunningly stored" seems to be a present for the absent sire—will the young girl-state ever have a chance to bring that dowry to a lover as a means to set up a new household? When did the marriage occur that produced this generation of incipient and mature sister-states? Although, as in T. S. Eliot's "Journey of the Magi," "there was Birth, certainly" from which these national children sprang, sterility seems to be the fate of the sisters who join the best parlor of nationhood.

In the latter half of the poem Sigourney focuses disturbingly on the older sisters, who are not only "the stateliest dames of our family" but who were "notable spinsters before you [Michigan] were born" (26–28). In the genteel world of Sigourney's national parlor, the term spinster does not connote one who contributes to the household economy through productive work (there is no spinning wheel in the crowded parlor) but one who is unable to marry and who can only consume, not contribute to, the household's resources. They do not spin, but merely "sit on the sofa so high." Do the sisters with their dowries become incestuous "brides" of the father? Do the sisters give up their potential fecundity as the price of, or necessary result of, admission to the governance of the United States? In the concluding stanza, Sigourney presents a rationale for the higher status, the paradoxical greater equality, ascribed to the original thirteen states because "the price of our [the nation's] freedom they better have known, / Since they paid for it out of their purses alone" (45–46). Sigourney deploys the sexual puns of "purses" and "known" in such a way as to suggest that the sterility of these sisters might have resulted from the almost sexual violence of the revolutionary moment when they "bore the burden and heat of the day" (43). Experiencing the national parturition when "the flash of the Bunker-Hill flame was red, / And the blood gush'd forth from the breast of the dead," Sigourney suggests, precluded these sisters from a future fecundity (43, 35–36).

In "On the Admission of Michigan into the Union," Sigourney's ironic treatment of her topic allowed her to interrogate the disturbing slippage between the models of national identity based on the family and the simultaneously operating model of the capitalist market. It is important to note that although the mode of sentimentality is often considered incapable of critique, here, as elsewhere in her work, Sigourney uses sentimentality not only as a means of questioning the basis of a political system, but also as a means of questioning the basis of sentimentality's own deficiencies.[12] More than ten years later, around the same time that Longfellow was writing his sentimental vision of America which would be published as "The Building of the Ship," Sigourney returned to the problem of adequately defining America in two separate poems. In one, she once again takes up the problems of a homosocial familial model of the nation in her poem "The Thriving Family: A Song," which was written shortly after the admission of Wisconsin to the United States. This time, more conventionally, "thirty well grown sons" stand for the individual states of the Union (5). The problem of reproduction is finessed here, rather than interrogated, in order for Sigourney to pay more attention to modeling a means by which the North/South divisions could be healed. As in the biblical account of the children of Adam and Eve, the sons have become a "numerous race indeed, / Married and settled all" although the source of the wives remains mysterious (6–7). Part of the surface lightness of "Admission" comes from Sigourney's use of swift-moving iambic pentameter to construct the eight balanced stanzas composed of rhymed couplets. In contrast, "The Thriving Family" signals its more serious tone from the first line. The national family, the poem suggests, cannot be thriving so very well since the paterfamilias suffers a "world of cares" (1–2). In addition, "The Thriving Family" is composed of two complicated stanzas; one long, thirty-six-line stanza which itself falls into two balanced sections, and one concluding eighteen-line stanza. The rhyme scheme intricately weaves each eighteen-line portion together, and Sigourney marks the transition between each movement with the apostrophic refrain "Hail, Brothers, hail, / Let nought on earth divide us."

The hortatory tone of the poem remains consistent throughout the poem as the first-person speaker, again one of the children-states, addresses his brother-states, urging them "to draw the cords of union fast, / Whatever may betide us" (49–50). The anxiety that pervades this poem is introduced from the very first line, when the place of the absent father in "Admission" is filled by "Our father," who "lives in Washington, / And has a world of cares" (1–2). The claim of the title, "The Thriving Family," is immediately problematized by this admission that the father's world can no longer be figured (albeit disturbingly) as a cozy parlor but as a "world of cares." The national patriarch's troubles result from the divisiveness among the brother-states, each of whom is figured as possessing independent "farm[s]" which together make up the national "household": "Every quarrel cuts a thread / That healthful Love has spun" (3, 39, 47–48). Despite the fact that "Nature made us one," the full strength of the "cords of union" is being stressed by the differences between those brother-states who "dare the sharp north-east," those who "clover fields are mowing," and the others who "tend the cotton plants / That keep the looms a-going" or "build and steer the white-wing'd ships" (46, 49, 19–26).

In the face of such potential division Sigourney draws on the full repertoire of sentimental strategies. All of these rhetorical devices are designed to mold the nation into the shape of a family through the sentimental reliance upon the paradigm of the family as the interpretive frame of knowledge. Sigourney uses the first-person singular and plural to construct the reader as a brother of the speaker of the poem. Directly addressing all the brother-states, the speaker admonishes them to remain true to the neo-Jeffersonian faith that the wealth of the nation will take care of itself "if we wisely till our lands" (9) The closely connected rhetorical figure of apostrophe is deployed to reify the corporate nature of the United States: "Hail, brothers, hail." In her use of direct address, Sigourney moves the reader to literalize the metaphor of the nation as family; the use of apostrophe grants agency to an abstract, corporate noun; "the United States *are*" becomes "the United States *is*" in the moment between the turning from the ostensible to the real subject of the poem.[13] In the full refrain of the poem, Sigourney simultaneously insists on the integral corporate nature of this entity while raising the possibility of its destruction. "Hail, brothers, hail" is followed by the plea that we, the United States, "Let naught on earth divide us." Having acknowledged the disparity between the interests of the different sections of the country, Sigourney attempts to account for and to defuse the tensions between the states by the reminder that "other households have the same" (39). In fact, the poem insists, the "foible[s]," "fume[s] and frown[s]," and "hard names" are not only a "waste of time" but also wrongheaded, since, as brothers, the states should "closer cling through every blast" as they have before when "many a storm has tried us" (38–42, 48, 51).

Sigourney's anthem "Our Country," written in the same period as "The Thriving Family: A Song," replaces the metaphor of the nation as family with the metaphor of the nation as mother. As in her other nationalist poems, Sigourney uses the mode of sentimentality to push the limits of what might otherwise be an unexamined cliché. "Our Country" is one long apostrophe to the nation, who is addressed throughout by the speaker using the second-person archaic familiar pronouns — "thy" and "thine." The first movement of the poem is a blazon anatomizing "how glorious thou art" as a land "of broad rivers and ocean-lakes, / Sky-kissing cliffs and prairies prank'd with flowers" (8, 1–2). In Sigourney's hands, the alma mater of America becomes a parthenogenic progenitrix whose body is composed ("bound in one living whole") of the different political and geographic parts of the country whose "great, beating heart" is located in "the young, giant West" and whose head, the "East / Wrinkled with thought, doth nurse a nation's mind" (77, 34–36).[14] The second movement presumes on this to give advice and warnings. Like a paragon of the "cult of true womanhood" who has nevertheless not relinquished her role as the "republican mother," Sigourney's mother-land is figured dressed with the "robes of Liberty around thy breast," in order to "as a matron watch thy little ones" (56–57).[15] "America," as mother, does not shirk from active protection of her young but "spread'st thine eagle-pinion" over her many children (20). Unlike the other two poems we have looked at, this poem does not use the term children to denote individual states; instead children are the citizens who "share / One home, one destiny" on the lap of the national mother who is like "some fair hearth which hovering angels guard" (42–43, 49). In contrast to the nativist propaganda of this period, Sigourney's figuration of the nation has ample room for the "exiled, and the crush'd from every clime" on the maternal lap (21). The national mother gives equal attention to molding her own mysteriously generated children and the children of strangers into Americans.

The function of this national mother is to "gather thine offspring round thee, and make bright / Their hallow'd chain of love" (50–51). The object of the speaker's "ardent prayer" is "that God would hold thee safe, / And firmly knit thy children's hearts, to share / One home, one destiny" (40–43). In Sigourney's other attempts to use the family as a model for the nation, she was unable to ignore the weakness of the sororal or fraternal bonds; sisters will fight as will brothers. Where the children-states of the first two poems held the possibility of discord within themselves, in this poem, children are always figured as "salvation" and the source of danger to the nation is extrinsic: "May no vulture / Transpierce thee for thine hospitality" (22–25). This poem is an acknowledgment that neither the voluntary politeness of the parlor nor the voluntary drawing of "the cords of union fast" can be relied on. Neither can the abstracted power of the father, whether the completely unrealized "sire" of "Admission" or the worried "father" who "lives in Washington" solve the problems inherent in such familial models of the nation.

Instead, the best "hope" and "strength" of the country is modeled on the interaction between mothers and children: "thy strength" lies in "thy young children, and in those who lead / Their souls to righteousness" (63, 71–72, 63–65).

In the conclusion of "Our Country," Sigourney shifts her frame of reference slightly to close with an invocation of the national mother which seems to recall Longfellow's allegory of the ship of state. The "glorious," "fair," "free" land is refigured as a "lonely ark, that rid'st / A tossing deluge, dark with history's wrecks" (7–8, 73–74). Like Longfellow's, Sigourney's project of envisioning the nation is a strategy for keeping the nation "perfect in thy many parts, / Bound in one living whole" (76–77). Although both use sentimentality, the actual parameters of their utopian constructions vary tellingly. Sigourney's "ark" is a feminine image, a container and sanctuary, which carries, in its allusions to the biblical flood, the future within it. The growth and prosperity of the national future relies not, as in "The Building of the Ship," on market-driven expansionism, but on a shared, essentially conserving and benevolent collaboration between the ideals of the nation and the needs of the citizens: the "mother's prayer" with the prayer of "her sweet lisper" are "thy strength, my land!" (65–66, 71).

This last attempt of Sigourney to call into being a sentimental America displays the radical, even subversive, potential of the conservatively structured mode of sentiment. Against Longfellow's father-centered, authoritarian model of the nation, Sigourney's poem places an equally sentimental image of a family. But this family acts, not through subserving the wills of all to one, but by melding different voices into a harmony. It is this polyvocal harmony that, Sigourney hopes, will provide the flexibility and compassion needed to overcome the stresses on the national Union. Neither of these sentimental nationalisms wins the contest to define America that had begun even before the births of these poets. But the contest of one sentimental vision against another forever changed the rules by which the contest of national definition would continue to be

played. The struggle for national definition would have to be collaborative, it would have to invoke the threat of lost or broken families, lost or
broken selves, it would be expressed in a language that would be simultaneously "high falutin'" and authentically vernacular, for it would be
voicing a felt, emotional experience that is both universal and local.

CHAPTER 6

The Other American Poets

The sign and credentials of the poet are,
that he announces that which no man foretold.
—Emerson, "The Poet," 1844

I would like to suggest that Sigourney and Longfellow were just two typical participants in the contest to define America and that this participation warrants a revision of our understanding of what it meant to attempt to become *the* American poet.[1] It is hard, these days, to see beyond Walt Whitman to imagine any other way of fulfilling Emerson's description of *the* American poet. But since Emerson himself, even after he had had a chance to read *Leaves of Grass,* continued to "look in vain for the poet" he had described, it seems fair to consider some other possibilities.[2] Lydia Sigourney—the "Sweet Singer of Hartford," the "American Hemans," and the "Female Milton"—is known best as the paragon of the "damn mob of scribbling women" that so dismayed Hawthorne. And Longfellow, "dean of Frogpondia," has come to function almost as the antitype (the not-Poe and not-Whitman) of the American poet. Yet both, despite the fact that their poetry and their poetics has been seriously underanalyzed in recent discussions of American literary history, pursued a shared agenda for becoming the American poet.

The nationalistic poems I discussed earlier are good examples of their attempts to author the poetry that would "lead in the new age" (Emerson, "The American Scholar," 1837). But Sigourney and Longfellow also contributed in important and distinctive ways to the formation of the mass market for literature, shaping both the expectations of the literary consumers and the infrastructure of the distribution side of the literary market. More important, each shared with Emerson the belief that it was within the ability of poetry to correct the "dis-location and detachment from the life of God" ("The Poet," 1844). If setting the nationalistic efforts of these two poets against each other reveals some of the ways that American sentimentality operated in and on the public and political world, a close look at the poetics they articulated in their lives and in their non-nationalistic poetry might also begin to disclose the complex gender and class valences carried by American sentimentality.

Although both poets began life from almost diametrically opposed positions in society, they each came to hold considerable cultural authority in America of the mid–nineteenth century. The kind of cultural authority that Longfellow and Sigourney wielded was a new kind—they became secular mentors of ethics, manners, and mores. This was neither the conventionally masculine authority of the law or the clergy (two options Longfellow, though not Sigourney, had the luxury of rejecting), nor the conventionally feminine authority of motherhood (an authority that Sigourney did not repudiate).[3] Both owed this authority to the strategic deployment of the mode of sentimentality as expressed in various genres—lyric, narrative verse, and the essay. Like many of their generation they took seriously the biblical injunction from Romans 12.15: "Rejoice with them that do rejoice, and weep with them that weep" and made it a part their cultural poetics.[4] Each wrote poems arising from a feeling of loss—loss through death, loss by absence, loss due to change. Both also used this feeling of loss as a major theme in their poetry, representing it as the antithesis to and catalyst for a more authentic relation able to transcend physical separation. This "more perfect union" of self to others, self to God, state to nation is modeled by the fleeting sense of unity imagined to have been felt between a mother and her child. The most elemental terms of the family—the mother-child dyad—become the basic relation of the homology that binds the otherwise disunited and entropic forces of society into a comprehensible order established on the basis of feeling rather than logic.[5] In other words, the work of both poets not only participated in the culture of sentiment but helped to put in place the constituent structures of that culture.

Sigourney and Longfellow have been written out of most conventional accounts of American literary history.[6] Unlike the virtually anonymous writers of keepsake albums such as *Harriet Gould's Book*, these two writers most definitely considered themselves to be "authors."[7] Furthermore, each very consciously accepted the role and responsibility of being one of Shelley's "legislators of the world." Like Barlow they were unembarrassed about the ideological work of poetry—but unlike Barlow, they both chose to do this work in the genre of the sentimental lyric. Thus their works provide an unequaled opportunity to examine what happened when sentimentality was deployed by individuals fully conscious of its power and willing to use this power not only in the seemingly private domain of personal subjectivity but also in the public domain of the political landscape. The similarities between the two poets are startling given the tenacious image of women writers as somehow concerned only with the private sphere of domesticity and the corresponding image of male writers as avatars of the American Adam.[8]

Sigourney, who was already an established popular poet by the time Longfellow began his nonacademic literary career, played an important role in the transmission of British Romanticism to America.[9] While the publication in 1817 of William Cullen Bryant's poem "Thanatopsis" is often cited as the moment when European and British Romantic poetry is appropriated within the American context, Lydia Sigourney, as Emily Stipes Watts has noted, had published *Moral Pieces in Prose and Verse* two years earlier (in 1815). This collection sold well and brought the themes of death, nature, and the individual together in a celebration of an American landscape that can only be called Romanticized.[10] Perhaps more important, Sigourney was responsible for the American publication of the complete works of Felicia Hemans (1793–1835). Given the prevalence of Hemans's works in newspapers, giftbooks, and other venues of popular literacy, it might be said that her evocation of the Romantic aesthetic was as important to the development of American Romanticism as was Coleridge. Sigourney's tastes, not surprisingly given her affiliation with Hemans, stressed the aspects of Romantic poetry represented by Wordsworth's contributions to *Lyrical Ballads*. Wordsworth's call for the embrace of everyday language and the perceptions of the "simple" people sanctioned Sigourney's exploration of the domestic and the familiar as a source for poetic inspiration and topoi. Sigourney took Wordsworth's project at least one step further. Where Wordsworth celebrates the ability to appreciate, from a distance, the insights of the child who avers that "we are seven" though one lies in the grave, Sigourney attempts to recover this naive conflation of the differences between life and death.

Sigourney's several cognomens (the "American Hemans," the "Female Milton," and the "Sweet Singer of Hartford") were more than vestiges of the neoclassical penchant for allusive pen names. On the one hand, they signal her precarious condition as a woman writer whose femininity was protected by the partial elision of her name under the veil of another's. On the other hand, since these names were given to Sigourney by her reviewers, they also give some indication of the degree to which she was linked in her own time to the British Romantic movement. As one of these cognomens indicates and as I've mentioned above, Sigourney was highly influenced by the work of the British poet Felicia Hemans, who attempted to articulate an ideal of the feminine sublime in her many narrative poems celebrating the lives and heroism of women.[11] Hemans's construction of her public persona influenced Sigourney almost as much as her poetry, for Hemans carefully presented herself as unimpeachably, even superlatively, feminine despite irregularities in her domestic life and the fact that she was a serious poet associated with the Wordsworth circle.[12] It seems a stretch to connect the "Sweet Singer of Hartford" with the author of *Paradise Lost,* but like her British contemporaries Sigourney was fascinated with Milton's work. Those who called her the "Female Milton" recognized that much of her work seeks to justify the ways of God to man within the new contingencies of the American nineteenth century. Following Milton, Sigourney's strategy for this was to interpolate and so call into being biblical stories that would claim for women a more active and positive role within sacred history.

Like Sigourney, Longfellow was also an importer of the European and British traditions of literature into American culture. Not only did he bring the contemporary movements of British Romantic and Victorian aesthetics to a broad audience in America, but he also made the antecedents of European Romanticism available to Americans through his translation of European vernacular classics such as Dante's *Divina Commedia* and the Norse sagas into American English. More important, he attempted to co-opt the power of his Continental and British exemplars to the task of celebrating and constituting America and its culture. From *Tales of the Wayside Inn,* which follows a Chaucerian model, to *The Song of Hiawatha,* which uses the rhyme schema of the Norse sagas, Longfellow sought to create a poetic idiom that was both uniquely American and still connected to and benefiting from the heritage of European culture. In this way, as is the case with Sigourney, Longfellow's literary project was at one with the sentimental project of creating an individual American subject who would not be at odds with the bonds of family and community; an American subject willing to participate, not flee from, society.

The similarities between the two poets are even more remarkable given the contrast of their respective positions in society. Sigourney, born Lydia Huntley just three years after the ratification of the Constitution, was a self-made woman who rose from poverty to wealth, obscurity to fame. Her mother died when she was young, and she was brought up by her father, who worked as gardener and handyman to the wealthy Lathrop family of Hartford, Connecticut. The wife of her father's employer took Sigourney on as a protégée, giving her not money but an education. Sigourney, in common with several of the remarkable women of her generation—Margaret Fuller, Emma Willard, and Elizabeth Oakes Smith—partially owed her later success to her early and unconventional education. This education allowed her, as a very young woman, to support herself by operating a school for young ladies.[13] It was during this time that she began to publish poems as well as essays and short stories which arose directly from her experience as an educator. Her incipient careers as author and as educator were willingly aborted by her marriage with the Hartford banker Charles Sigourney. Or, at least, that is what Charles thought, for during this period Sigourney continued to publish anonymously without her husband's full blessing. As is so very common in the lives of literary women from this era—such as Susan Warren, Louisa May Alcott, and Elizabeth Oakes Smith—Sigourney began to support the family. Even then, she was only able to win this concession from her husband with difficulty.[14]

Increasingly Lydia Sigourney's contributions to magazines, gazettes, and newspapers under her own name commanded the highest prices in the business (Haight). If she was looked down on by other would-be "professional" authors such as Poe, Hawthorne, and Melville, they welcomed the increasing standard of wages for which she was partially responsible (Charvat). But she and her poetry were, in fact, respected by much of the publishing establishment. Despite her increasing prominence as a successful and envied lady poetess, Sigourney never fully escaped being a "lady poetess," with all the connotations of Johnson's walking dog that term carries.

In later years her claim to have been one of the leading poets of her generation was denied for the most part on the basis that her taste in dress was "florid" and that she was an overbearing, pushy woman who neglected the needs of her sons and husband while commodifying herself as the model of domestic decorum (Haight). Her last biographer, Gordon Haight, writing in 1930, paradoxically attacked her authenticity as a poet on the grounds that she was both too commercial and not professional enough. She was too commercial in that she drove a hard bargain for her verse and in that she took control of what might today be called "packaging." In the early 1840s, Haight explains, she sold the rights to her name and her face to *Godey's Ladies Book,* which used them as an endorsement of their genteel probity.[15] She also aggressively reprinted her poetry in ever new editions that sold well despite the fact that they sometimes contained little new verse. Yet, even in her lifetime, Sigourney was sometimes not considered "professional" enough. As Rufus Griswold complains in his headnote to entries about her in his 1852 *Female Poets of America,* she resisted the process of revision, writing "impulsively from an atmosphere of affectionate, pious, and elevated sentiment, rather than from the consciousness of subjective ability" (93). Of course, this seems to be Griswold's attempt to inoculate Sigourney against any taint of bluestockingism and is fully consistent with Sigourney's own representation of herself as driven by pure, feminine intuition and inspiration. Sigourney was famous, and famously criticized, for responding to requests from her "fans" by quickly composing and giving away poems to those who asked for them on behalf of spouses or children who were sick.[16] Such criticisms indicate that Sigourney's poetry operated in two separate, though related, economies—the commercial economy in which she was a path-breaker for women's rights, and the kind of noncommercial gift economy which, as I've described earlier, enabled community through the establishment of reciprocal bonds of affection and responsibility among individuals otherwise only tenuously associated.[17]

In contrast to Sigourney's career, which has been almost totally forgotten, Longfellow's career as poet and professor is still somewhat familiar to Americans despite his demotion from the canon of American literature.[18] But few are now familiar with much of his work save the coda to the "The Building of the Ship" ("Sail on, Oh Ship of State / Sail on, O Union, strong and great") or the beginning of "A Psalm of Life" ("Tell me not in mournful numbers"). Rightly associated with the feminized poetry of the nineteenth century by modernists such as Eliot and Pound, Longfellow's contributions to the formation of an "American" tradition of poetry has been all but elided from serious critical attention even if his name has continued to be remembered. Ironically, it was probably never imagined by Pound and Eliot that their project of instantiating a counter-aesthetic would be so successful as to make the opposite category almost invisible.

The best contrast of Longfellow with Sigourney is illustrated by the different ways they invented what it would mean to be a professional poet. In the earliest years of the nation, and through the first quarter of the nineteenth century, the profession of author hardly existed, but by the Civil War this situation was changed. Such publishing of original "American" writing as did go on in the early republic was in the belles-lettres tradition of coterie writing, where not profit but fame was the object. Increasingly newspapers began to pay for contributions from freelance writers when they were unable to steal what they wanted or needed.[19] Sigourney and Longfellow both initially published under this dispensation. But by the time Longfellow graduated from Bowdoin, and certainly by the time he took up his second academic position as professor at Harvard, Sigourney had been a publishing poet and essayist for years, and she was finding it possible to support her family by the fees she could command.[20] However, as I discussed earlier, Sigourney's relation to the role of author was always contingent on the permission of another. First, she withdrew from her earliest inchoate ambitions to be a professional educator and author on her husband's wishes. Later, also in response to her husband's situation and with his permission, she re-embraced these earlier ambitions.

In contrast, Longfellow's status as author was never contested, although the ramifications of that status and the dimensions of that role changed over the course of his long career. As a college student, during the days when literature was still a gentlemanly and amateur endeavor, Longfellow did publish frequently. These efforts, according to Samuel

Longfellow, Henry's brother and biographer, were sanctioned by their father, who often took it upon himself to correct Longfellow's verse.[21] During these days, the market for poetry and prose picked up (partially due to Sigourney's efforts) and Longfellow began to make occasional money (*Life* 46). But until well into his second teaching position, Longfellow's efforts at poetry were an adjunct and a polish to his scholarship. Longfellow's father, a lawyer, had early on admonished Longfellow to keep his priorities straight, since "there is not wealth enough in this country to afford encouragement and patronage to merely literary men" (*Life* 56). And Longfellow did not leave the security of the academy (he resigned from Harvard in 1854) until he had accumulated enough "encouragement and patronage" to reassure even someone as cautious as his father. By this time, the financial success of *Voices of the Night* (1839) and the publication of various occasional pieces had demonstrated the economic viability of the new literary marketplace. This marketplace had only been recently opened up by those like Sigourney and others who lacked the economic cushion and outlet for creativity provided by the pulpit or the academy. But even so, far from becoming an author out of necessity, Longfellow's inheritance from his wife together with the savings from his professorship had by this time made remunerative work redundant.

Despite the differences in their origins and in the ways that they came to be professional authors, Sigourney and Longfellow met on a common ground that both participated in creating. This was the common ground of sentimentality. In this field both authors became figures larger than themselves with the authority to influence the construction of mores in the double-sphered world of nineteenth-century America as they modeled what the middle-class American would feel like, wear, and think. Longfellow, like Sigourney, was the author of numerous poems that were completely governed by the mode of sentimentality.[22] The poet of "Suspira" ("Take them, O Death! and bear away / Whatever thou call thine own!") and "The Children's Hour" participated in the redefinition of gender roles during the antebellum years. In poems such as these, Longfellow actively sought to appropriate the moral power of the domestic and private sphere as a means to reinvigorate masculinity. If the head of the democratic family was still, for Longfellow, the father, the father was of a caring, nurturing cast who was bound to his children as much by reciprocal ties of affection as by force and duty. Sigourney, on the other hand, sought to expand the power of the domestic sphere to subsume the public, political and commercial sphere. Although known today, if at all, as the writer of sentimental mortuary verse, Sigourney more often treated political subjects such as Napoleon, the expulsion of the Amerindians, and the United States' policies on immigration.[23] Sigourney, like Stowe, co-opted the public domain of politics by making it an extension of, not the opponent of, the home.[24]

In an early, long poem, "Unspoken Language," Sigourney provides an excellent articulation of the theory of sentimental discourse which also might serve as an apt description of the course of Longfellow's career from scholar to poet of spontaneous inspiration. "Language," she begins, "is slow, the mastery of wants / Doth teach it to the infant, drop by drop" (lines 1–2). "Years of studious toil / Unfold its classic labyrinths to the boy" and "He who would acquire / The Speech of many lands, must make the lamp / His friend at midnight" (4–5, 10–12). Sigourney then proposes that this course is incomplete if it does not recognize the prior claims of the "unspoken language" of love, which is "Simple and sure, that asks no discipline / Of weary years" (16–17). This love, "the language of the soul," is not learned in books or from any rational practice (17). Instead it is "told through the eye" in an instantaneous moment of mutual identification between beholder and beheld (18). Sigourney establishes the mother and child as the perfect epitome of this superior form of communication, for "The mother speaks it well / To the unfolding spirit of her babe" (19–20). The supremacy of this nonverbal and extrarational communication is that it cannot be faked since it bears "the signet ring of truth" (38).[25] More and more after leaving the academy this was Longfellow's goal as he sought to express the "language of the soul," "the dialect of common sense," "the discourse of sentiment" as a medium to translate the cultural heritage of Europe for his American audience.

For both Sigourney and Longfellow, the "language of the soul" has a grammar and lexicon that can be reproduced, approximately, through words. In this way, as Longfellow says in his long poem "Dedication," "kind messages" can "pass from land to land" (line 17). What I call the mode of sentimentality, Longfellow articulates as "the heart's deep history" which allows the transmission of (which may actually "betray") "the pressure of a hand" across distances of time and space (18, 19). Longfellow's "Dedication" suggests that he understood that the exchange of sentiments offered a way to bridge alienation, to collaborate with another in "endeavor[s] for the selfsame ends / With the same hopes, and fears and aspirations" (35–36).

And Longfellow had had direct experience of sentimental collaborations in his life. Earlier in his career, Longfellow had published a book, *Poems on Slavery,* containing the traces of just such a sentimental collaboration. Although not an active abolitionist, Longfellow was inspired by the antislavery writings of the elder William Ellery Channing (1780–1842), which Longfellow read while returning from England in the summer of 1842. These so impressed Longfellow that he wrote a small set of verses evolving out of examples offered by Channing in his "Letter to Henry Clay on the Annexation of Texas" (1837). In the headnote to these verses, Longfellow establishes the context for these poems with a narrative account of how they came to be written while he was on board a homecoming ship. Longfellow did not know that Channing was already dead when he responded to the "Letter" by recasting some of its incidents into poetry. In the absence of Channing himself, but in the presence of his words, Longfellow wrote a dedicatory poem addressing Channing directly: "The pages of thy book I read, / My heart, responding, ever said, / 'Servant of God! Well done!'" (1–2). Upon learning of the author's death, Longfellow decided to retain this poem despite the fact that it spoke to Channing as if he were still alive. The rest of the poems in the book compress the potent and persuasive images from Channing's antislavery exposé out of narrative and into short, evocative lyrics. Thus, the dead Channing and the live Longfellow shared, in this instance, in the "joint intellectual project" of warning white America that "There is a poor, blind Samson in this land" ("The Warning"). This cumulative process of sentimental collaboration continues when Harriet Beecher Stowe takes up the imagery of one of these poems, "The Slave in the Dismal Swamp," as the epigraph and governing trope of her sequel to *Uncle Tom's Cabin* entitled *Dred, or the Tale of the Dismal Swamp* (1856). But it is important to remember, as I warned in the introduction above, that collaboration is an uncanny word, meaning both "to work together, especially in a joint intellectual effort" and "to cooperate treasonably as with an enemy occupying one's country." It is the simultaneous currency of both meanings that accounts for the complex force of sentimentality in American culture as both a utopian or liberating vehicle that generates a feeling of universal community and integration and as an oppressively ideological mechanism that enforces the exploitative differentiation of classes. Sigourney and Longfellow are two different American poets. Different, certainly, from the ideal of the American poet as the "solitary singer," an "American Adam," whose exploration and naming of a paradisical world is simultaneously a discovery of the self. Instead, both of these poets participated in the collaborative definition of an America that has a past, that is made up of differentiated parts whose meaning inheres only in relation to the other parts, and that, with luck, will have a future. And Sigourney and Longfellow are different from one another. They began as differently from each other as was possible in terms of inherited wealth and privilege, but they ended up as merely the feminine and masculine sides of the same kind of person: the middle-class American. The Americas they each sing even construct these differences, yet these differences hide the more important commonality. It is sentiment that structures not only the subject of America, but also the American subject.

PART FOUR

Mourning Sentimentality
in Reconstruction-Era America:
Mark Twain's Nostalgic Realism

GRAVE OF CHILD, 1977, DOVER COMMON CEMETERY.
"Charmaine L. / Cantrell / 1967–1977 / She brought love and joy."

I am loth to close. We are not enemies, but friends. We must not be enemies. Though passion may have strained, it must not break *the bonds of our affection.* The mystic chords of memory, stretching from every battle-field, and patriot grave, to every living heart and hearth-stone, all over this brave land, will yet swell the chorus of the Union, when again touched, as surely they will be, by the better angels of our nature.

—Abraham Lincoln, First Inaugural Address, 1861

Warning: Replications are copies. Only Hallmark carries authentic Keepsake Editions™ of the StarTrek Keepsake Ornament.

—September 1993 television commercial, Hallmark Greeting Card Inc.

There is nothing makes me prouder than to be regarded by intelligent people as "authentic."

—Mark Twain, *Autobiography*

While Samuel Clemens was relying on the conventional power of sentimentality to reconstruct himself as a suitable member of the American cultural elite, author Mark Twain insisted on publishing his sense of having been betrayed by the code of sentimentality. In the two chapters that make up this part, I examine the complex homage and critique of sentimentality played out in two of Twain's novels about boyhood: *The Adventures of Tom Sawyer* and *The Adventures of Huckleberry Finn.* These novels provide the opportunity to excavate Twain's complex attitude toward sentimentality as a case study of the changed function of sentimental discourse in the years following the war.[1] While losing to a great degree some of its cultural mandate, sentimentality itself helped to generate its own replacement by the poetics of realism. Both books enact a kind of mourning for the world that preceded the "eight years in America from 1860 to 1868" that had

uprooted institutions that were centuries old, changed the politics of a people, and wrought so profoundly upon the entire national character that the influence cannot be measured short of two or three generations. (*Gilded Age* 1.177)

The pre–Civil War world that Twain presents in *Tom Sawyer* and then re-presents in *Huck Finn* is a world structured by modes of thought and expression that are essentially sentimental. Sentimentality, Twain's early novels show, had given this world both its best promises and its most fatal limitations. Mourning the loss of these promises as he mourns the results of these limitations, Twain participates in the generation of the poetics of realism.

In earlier chapters I have shown the ways that sentimentality functioned as a means of creating and maintaining a sense of personal and societal cohesion in Jacksonian America. The large set of literary and nonliterary practices covered by the term "sentimental" are too vaguely explained as an appeal to the emotions over reason; sentimentality amounted to a poetics—a formal set of rules and strategies governing what could be said, by whom, to whom, and in what way. This poetics, I have argued, was especially dominant (if not hegemonic) in America throughout the first half of the nineteenth century for two reasons: one has to do with the way that the formal characteristics of American sentimentality took shape as part of a widely shared attempt to find solutions to the problems of grief and loss; the other has to do with the way these formal aspects contributed to the creation of the parameters of the American middle class. In particular, sentimentality allowed for the collaborative production of a concept of self and of nation that was both particular and corporate.

Through the ostensibly private and personal processes of converting grief into mourning—the experience of anomie into an experience of socialization and of spiritual skepticism into certainty—many individuals whose gender and economic status otherwise limited their claim to "Americanness" were able to define collaboratively the ground of "American" subjectivity. This is seen in the amateur literary productions of rural, frontier America, where it circulated through gift economies in which exchange not only marked but created boundaries of inclusion and exclusion.[2] It is also seen in the work of professional poets and novelists and in the intersection between the commercial and gift economies of the prewar period. By the midcentury such various poets as

Whitman, Longfellow, and Sigourney would agree that the empty chair beside the fireplace was the common denominator of the American experience; the feeling elicited by the empty chair was the nexus through which apparently disparate individuals could be joined together with a sense of communal identity and shared interests. The collaborative poetics of American sentimentality functioned positively to enable its users to reposition themselves from the margins to the center of cultural authority. In this way, sentimentality had been instrumental in solving (or seeming to solve) the conundrum—E Pluribus Unum—inscribed on the one-dollar bill as it helped to establish the outlines and content of the American middle class.

Sentimentality, I wish to stress, is a collaborative poetics not only in the sense that it facilitates joint intellectual efforts (definition 1) but also because it coerces a kind of "treasonous cooperation with an enemy occupying one's country" (definition 2); in the years following the Civil War, what might be called the ideological (or class-enforcing) functions of sentimentality became more perceptible to those who had been in part created through its instrumentality. What I mean by this is that those who identified themselves with the interests and values of the white middle classes of the northeastern United States and who, in fact, owed much of their cultural strength to the power of sentimentality became both disdainful and suspicious of sentimentality.

This dual stance toward sentimentality is epitomized in the work of Mark Twain. His early novels, in particular, document the debt owed by those members of the firmly dominant class of Americans to the culture of sentiment.[3] But, as Twain's early works also make clear, this was not a grateful acknowledgment. Twain's cynical disillusionment is driven, as cynicism often is, by a sense of betrayed trust. The economy of sentiment was not a closed system available only to those whose claim to participation was patent to those already in the system. It could be joined by anyone able to master and deploy its strategies despite their race or ethnic background.[4] Thus, the utopian potential inherent in sentimentality came to threaten the parameters of the class identity on which white, Protestant, New England–derived "Americans" had come to depend.[5]

Twain's project in these two books has most often been described as realist and as in opposition to the project of sentimentality. It is true that in dramatizing his anxiety over the limits and potentials of sentimentality in *The Adventures of Tom Sawyer* and *The Adventures of Huckleberry Finn* Twain suggests that there is something inherently dangerous in sentimentality's promise of expanding yet eternal continuity. The following reading of these books, however, suggests that Twain's project is reformist and conservative as it tries to save and fulfill the promises of sentimentality. Mark Twain's works show a canny appreciation of the way that sentimentality functioned to structure his own society. Having no urge to dismantle his world or challenge his own place in it, Twain's works display an uneven set of negotiations and adjustments to the mode of sentiment that end up being considered important movements toward the articulation of American realist poetics. Twain's critique of the culture of sentiment is deeper than a mere dismissal of "feminine" or "feminized culture"; he understood the degree to which the gilding of his age was the product of the same processes that had made an earlier period seem golden.[6]

Thematically, Twain's stories demonstrate his understanding that the America that he and many of his post–Civil War era generation figured as the Golden Age was a mourning America. This mourning was, of course, essentially a conservative practice. But the strategies it used to conserve and preserve relationships that had been severed by death or travel proved to be generative. Sentimentality, I have argued, took a situation characterized by lack and experienced as grief to produce a culture characterized by excess. The dead were not dead but present and re-presentable in an infinite number of forms from literary representations to fetishistic tokens made of hair or paper.[7] The dead were available, in this way, for circulation within an economy devoted to the exchange and accumulation of cultural capital.[8]

But, more important, the living mourners used the strategies of sentimentality to construct a form of personal subjectivity for themselves that was able to dominate, rather than be subjected to, the capital of culture.[9] Sentimentality empowered the creation of certain sense of self (a collaborative self) which was oriented toward community and toward cohesiveness and at odds with the definition of self as essentially isolated and alienated from others. Sentimentality had seemed, in addition, to provide a medium through which the hieroglyphics of nature could be made transparent and the "dis-location from the life of God," as Emerson put it, healed.[10] The associative power of sentimentality established ana-logical (synchronic) relationships that allowed nature, God, the cosmos, and other selves to be decoded through reliance on a template inscribed within the emotions of each individual by the action of loss.[11] The uto-pian promise of sentimentality offered not only the possibility of com-munity but also the possibility of community based on the inherent, not extrinsic, quality of each individual.

A thematic reading of Twain's early novels, however, also demon-strates his understanding of the threat posed by the reproductive power of sentimentality that functioned to suppress difference and disassocia-tion. *Huck Finn,* in particular, treats the crisis that ensues in a culture based on exchange and circulation from a system that demands both an ever-increasing inflation of the value of the dead *and* an unchecked re-production of the dead in the form of literary and nonliterary represen-tations. If the strategies of sentimentality can produce one self, they can produce others, and this multiplication of selves, which proceeds almost mechanistically, eventually came to overburden the ability of the system to continue circulation. Twain's extraordinary twin selves, which have been so commented on, are only one paradoxical product of the logic of sentimentality as it operated in the years after the Civil War. Trying to be "regarded by intelligent people as 'authentic,'" which Twain averred to be one of his most cherished personal and artistic goals, is itself an attempt to fulfill the demands of the cultural poetics of sentimentality. Such a goal, as Karen Halttunen claims, was the defining goal of genteel Americans.[12] The danger inherent in this approach is laid out Twain's early novels, beginning with the *The Gilded Age: A Tale of Today,* and con-tinuing in greater detail in *The Adventures of Tom Sawyer* and *The Adven-tures of Huckleberry Finn,* which posit violence and insincerity as the nec-essary result of a system that relied on the circulation of reproductions of the "authentic self" as a means of coherence. Both Twain's continued reliance on sentimentality and his development of what have come to seem as the counter-strategies of realism are part of a lifelong effort to solve the problems of a sentimental culture.

Twain's work provides just one example of the way that the promises of sentimentality generated their own replacement in the wake of the Civil War during the crisis of Reconstruction. I wish to frame my dis-cussion of Twain and sentimentality by touching on two instances from different cultural registers, art and politics, that resonate with Twain. Stresses on the culture of sentimentality began to register most strongly during the Civil War even as its deployment in the arenas of art, politics, and religion would have seemed to have signaled its status as a hegemonic discourse.[13] One example of this dissonance has been suggested by students of the photograph.[14] The reality of the battlefield was graphically represented for the first time through the techniques of photography, and these images defied the adhesive powers of the poetics of sentimentality. As an aesthetic, or description of what one experiences when viewing a work of art, sentimentality seems to give way to an aesthetic of realism.[15]

The new media of photoreproduction had seemed to promise the fullfillment of the sentimental aesthetic. "Every conceivable object of Nature and Art will soon scale off its surface for us," predicted Oliver Wendell Holmes in an 1859 essay on photography.[16] Photography had seemed to offer a technological access into an unmediated relation with nature that Emerson had advocated in 1837. The Transcendentalist goal articulated by Emerson was shared, as I have argued in part I, by many ordinary Americans, whose expressions of this goal were contained within the more conventional practice of Christianity and which have come to carry the label of "sentimental." Photography promised to bridge the distance of time, or the grave, in a manner similar and superior to graveyard poetry, pictures, or locks of hair. When it first entered the American market in the 1830s and diffused throughout America, early photographs supplemented these other practices in what I have argued was the social ritual of sentimentality. The "exigencies of life, in most cases," explained photographer Marcus Aurelius Root in 1864, "necessitate the dispersion of relatives, born and reared under the same roof, towards various points of the compass, and often to remote distances."[17] For Root, a portrait taker, the camera offered the chance to return "our loved ones, dead or distant." The images created by the various methods of photoreproduction might serve even better than verse as "remembrances" meant to keep fresh the bonds between people separated by circumstances.[18] Ironically, the greatest opportunity to prove the camera's potential to capture the authentic essence of a person in order to preserve this essence for memory, the Civil War, proved the insufficiency of the sentimental poetic.[19] Despite efforts by photographers and reviewers to account for the images in sentimental terms—terms privileging the qualities of nobility, pathos, honor, and beauty—the photographed reality of the battlefield called for some other language. Even when photographers altered the positions of their dead subjects or the negative in order to conform with the sentimental aesthetic, many of the photographs heightened rather than diminished the sense of loss: the dead brother was not nobly dead but butchered. As a remembrance, these pictures kept fresh the sense of grief rather than facilitating the process of mourning.[20] The aesthetic of realism that arises from the effort to contain and account for many of the war pictures is a continuation, not a repudiation of, sentimental representation. It is no less formal in its attempts to generate images that will transparently reveal the nature of their object.

Another example came from the world of politics as the war came to its end. National figures such as Abraham Lincoln or Elizabeth Cady Stanton invoked in their speeches the power of sentimental mourning rituals to achieve the rhetorical aim of reconstituting American society after the Civil War. This invocation contributed to, rather than derailed, the production of an America that was a substitution for, but not a reconstruction of, the America that was irrevocably lost. Like Twain in *The Adventures of Tom Sawyer,* Lincoln's use of sentimentalism appeals to and attempts to conserve the a priori assumptions that structured his world: authenticity, nationality, personality. Even as he spoke, however, these assumptions, the trueness of these assumptions, were being challenged by the very war that these assumptions had helped to produce. By the time Twain took up the story of Huck Finn, a boy without a home, a boy at the mercy of felt but inarticulable losses, the reconstruction of the national home for the benefit of the wounded soldier and his orphan had become a reconstruction of the very structures that had threatened to destroy that metaphorical home. The "passion," which Lincoln worries will "break the bonds of our affection," is the result, Twain's early novels suggest, of the nature of those bonds. The powerful utopian potential of sentiment to bind people together into families, communities, and countries contains within it the threat of dystopic self-annihilation.

At the close of his First Inaugural Address in March of 1861, Lincoln urged that "though passion may have strained, it must not break the bonds of our affection." Even though the armies of the Republic and of the Confederacy were poised to meet one another in the first battle of the war, Lincoln still hoped that it would be possible for the "mystic chords of memory" to be touched "by the better angels of our nature."[21] Lincoln's appeal to heart, memory, angels, and the "bonds of affection" sounds remarkably like language that would be dismissed today as hopelessly sentimental if the author under discussion were a woman—say, Lydia Sigourney or Elizabeth Cady Stanton. In his own day this shift in emotional key, contrasting with the body of the speech, which depends on measured rational analysis of the current situation, would be seen as a strong rhetorical move to diffuse the secessionist impulse. First, Lincoln had attempted to assure the slave-holding states that both his own and the legislators' oaths to "support the whole Constitution" will temper any threats to the sovereignty of any of the individual states. A second historical argument explains why Lincoln considered "that in view of the Constitution and the laws, the Union is unbroken" (582). Confederate Acts of Secession abrogate the main objective of the Constitution, Lincoln argued, which was "to form a more perfect Union." At the most critical moment in his speech, Lincoln replaces these appeals to the Constitution with an appeal to the bonds of affection. Perhaps the "bonds of affection" are the seat of the "universal law," which justifies Lincoln's faith that "the Union of these States is perpetual": "I hold, that in contemplation of universal law, and of the Constitution, the Union of theses States is perpetual" (582). Even within fifteen years, less than a generation, language such as Lincoln used to close this address would become the hallmark of institutionalized corruption that shielded (less and less efficiently) the self-serving actions of individuals under the cover of altruism. The language of Lincoln became the language of Dilworthy, the "Golden-Tongued Statesman" of *The Gilded Age* whose appeals on behalf of the "poor negroes" and the "ruined South" are designed to perpetrate an enormous financial scam on the U.S. government.[22]

As early as 1858, when Lincoln opened his famous debates with Stephen Douglas by reiterating the biblical injunction that a "house divided against itself cannot stand," the tropes and figures of sentimentality had already framed both the war and its foreseeable resolutions.[23] On both sides, the war was being fought to preserve community, and as such it was a large-scale enactment of the anxieties against which sentimentality was framed. The First Inaugural Address suggested the sentimental resolution to the conflict between the states: "the mystic chords of memory" (that is, the memory of a shared communal identity through the shared losses incurred during the Revolutionary War) would be touched "by the better angels of our nature" and thus heal the fraying "bonds of our affection." These affectionate bonds are posited by Lincoln here as the basis for the indissoluble union between individuals that parallels the function of the Constitution as the bond among the states. The bonds of affection had to be strong since neither the bonds of kin nor geography held together or defined the American people as they did in the more conventional states of Europe.[24] This relationship was clearly figured as the relationship among the members of a family bound by mutual consent with reciprocal ties of sentiment that link the parents to each other and to their children and link the children to their parents.[25] Lincoln, in this First Inaugural Address, hopes that the memory of a shared cultural childhood will restore the erring states to the national family.

The potential for the betrayal of this hope was figured in Harriet Beecher Stowe's paradigmatically sentimental novel, *Uncle Tom's Cabin*. Stowe's treatment of one of the pivotal characters of the novel, Simon Legree, illustrates the way that the power of sentiment can be difficult to contain once it is released, how it can generate passionate violence as well as ameliorative affection. Simon Legree is a lapsed Yankee. He has fallen from the New England way of virtue and self-reliance in which he had been raised. Profit, and the corrupting influence of a slave society, have overcome the passive moral influence of his mother. Legree's moral trajectory is emblematic of the way that many New Englanders viewed their southern neighbors. At its final climax, Stowe's plot depends on the intervention of a seemingly magical token of Legree's mother. This token of hair, which is not his mother's but Eva's, performs the sentimental action of playing the "mystic chords of memory" as it revives memories of Legree's mother's love. But though the "better angel" of Legree's nature is invoked, her "touch" does not restore him to her values. Rather, it precipitates Legree's final descent into a madness that is instrumental to the escape of the women characters and to his mortally sadistic beating of Uncle Tom.

The production, here, of an item that stands in for and does the same sentimental work as an actual piece of Legree's mother's hair widens the gap between Legree and all social mores. The sentiments raised by the simulacra of Legree's mother (the curl of hair, the visual and aural apparitions) do not tighten the bonds of affection but sever them. Stowe's sentimental text shows that the redundancy inherent to effective sentimentality *can* fracture, and in the process of fracturing, produce a violent wedge of skepticism. In like manner, Lincoln's appeal to sentiment fuels rather than impedes secession. Within secessionist discourse, the pull of the mystic chords of patriotic memory drives them violently to establish and protect an alternative to the United States of America: the Confederate States of America.

Although the military victory of the federal forces resolved the two factions into one nation, the "mystic chords of memory" were no closer to being in harmony with each other. As the war came to an end and Lincoln proposed what he called the "Reconstruction" of the nation, his thinking continued to be shaped by the discourse of sentimentality.[26] In his Second Inaugural Address, Lincoln called for a shared effort "to bind up the nation's wounds, to care for him who shall have borne the battle and for his widow and for his orphan." Lincoln refers throughout this speech to the nation as a whole, not just the secessionist states, as the object of this reconstruction. Here, Lincoln metaphorically imbues the nation with an organic sensibility that can suffer and be healed. The abstract nation is called into being as a particular kind of subject: it becomes a sentimental subject more worthy of respect and allegiance because it suffered; it also becomes stronger as a corporate individual because it sustained the threat of losing its integrity. In another strategy consistent with sentimentality, Lincoln directs his listeners to blend the subjectivity of the wounded nation with the subjectivity of the human victims of the war. The wounded nation becomes a composite of veteran, widow, and orphan meant to reposition his listeners as not merely citizens but as actual constituent parts or elements of the nation. He appeals to their sense of self-pity while suggesting an equivalence between acts of compassion and acts of self-interestedness. The sentiments of his listeners are appealed to directly as Lincoln establishes an analogy that blurs the distinctions between those of the unionists and those of the secessionists.

In this public call for Reconstruction, Lincoln deploys all the rhetorical moves associated with the mode of American sentimentality. On the level of trope or metaphor, the nation is the home that has been partially destroyed and must now be restored. Simultaneously, it is a wounded member of that household. Lincoln's words have the effect of apostrophe, calling into being a national subject who both authorizes the pity of its

citizens and is the object of pity.[27] As part of a speech directly addressed
to his listeners, Lincoln's words have a similar effect on his listeners, posi-
tioning them as both the object of pity and the givers of pity. After Lincoln's death, although Reconstruction took on an explicitly punitive cast,
the rhetoric used by the congressional proponents of what was considered Radical Reconstruction continued to operate under this sentimental
rubric.[28] Despite the distinct shift in their objective away from Lincoln's,
this rubric enabled the drafters of Reconstruction to maintain on at least
one level that what they were doing was not creating a new social and
political order to replace the previous one, but merely restoring a broken
part of the national home. The sentimental rhetoric of the Reconstruc-
tionists stressed the conservative rather than the radical nature of their
work just as the sentimental rhetoric of the secessionists had stressed the
conservative rather than the radical nature of their act.

The existence of the new Confederate Constitution with its new
presidency and its newly legitimated armies called into question not
only Lincoln's words, but the whole system underwriting his rhetoric
of sentimentality. The so-called bonds of affection holding these United
States together had rebounded—fractured—into bonds of mortal hatred
and antipathy. There was not one heir to the American Revolution but
two; each of them was vindicated by the "better angels" and the "mystic chords" of national memory. Lincoln's rhetorical strategy aimed at
dissolving these differences, but at the same time he knew that only military force could create the United States out of these differences. If the
rhetoric of sentimentality could not force reality into alignment with his
ideal, Lincoln was prepared to reconstruct reality to conform with his
ideal.

On the political stage Lincoln was deploying an operation fully ap-
proved and demonstrably effective within the personal sphere. In the
face of imminent or actual loss, sentimentality aimed at negating that
loss by instituting (or revealing) a structure that maintained connections. Through the making and sharing of an idealized image of both the
mourner and the mourned, say in a poem, middle-class parents could
force their grief into acceptable bounds. Through the preservation and
circulation of fetishes, such as locks of hair or miniature portraits, contact with what was considered the essence of the individual who was
lost could be preserved. This preservation took the form of a duplica-

tion or a representation of the person who had died. The act of conservation entailed, in this way, a successful act of creation or generation that denied the event of death. For Mrs. Lincoln, as Gary Wills points out, this strategy was successful to such an extent that she believed herself to be visited by the spirit form of her boy, Willie, who died while they were living in the White House.[29] For President Lincoln, the strategies of sentimentality worked less well on the political front. At best, his attempts to "strike the mystic chords of memory" failed; at worst they served to emphasize and reinforce the differences between the two sectional factions.

One way to see Reconstruction, at least in Lincoln's formulation, is as an attempt to accomplish the work of mourning for all the very real losses that individuals and states had experienced. Mourning practices, which had given rise to the various expressions of the mode of sentimentality during the antebellum years, seemed to offer a viable method for imposing an order on events following the war. More than that, sentimentality promised a way to reestablish connections that death and dislocation had apparently disrupted. As I detail in chapter 4, Elizabeth Stuart Phelps's postwar novel *The Gates Ajar* is the best and fullest example of the revolutionary potential of this application of sentimental collaboration. But Reconstruction as formulated after Lincoln's death betrayed the sentimental promise of mourning; the rituals of mourning failed to effect a utopian reunification of the national family. Instead, they brought about an increasing sense of nostalgia for a time when it was possible to imagine the nation as a family bound together on the mutual project of forming "a more perfect Union." This nostalgia informs and structures Twain's comedy in *The Adventures of Tom Sawyer,* while the profound cultural disappointment that followed the war informs *The Adventures of Huckleberry Finn.*[30]

CHAPTER 7

Invoking the Bonds of Affection:
Tom Sawyer and America's Morning

I'll stick to the widder till I rot, Tom; and if I git to be a reglar rip-
per of a robber, and everybody talking 'bout it, I reckon she'l be
proud she snaked me in out of the wet.

    —Huck Finn, in Twain's *The Adventures of Tom Sawyer*

The mourning culture prevalent throughout the states and territories before the Civil War aestheticized all the aspects of death: the death, the
dead, the mourners. This was done not merely because "When distance
or the grave hides form or face / Into this volume sweet t'will be to look,"
but also because it would give pleasure (Gould 2). The pleasure or "sweetness" it would bring was of a functional nature:

> Each fond remembrance oft will speak to you
> In language which may never be forgot
> Of those who ever constant were and true
> And gently whisper O forget me not.
>
>   (Gould 2)

The "language" of sentimentalism encoded the aesthetic "remembrances"
so that those who were gone could continue to speak to those who remained. Sentimentalism's language operated beyond the verbal level: remembrances could be locks of hair woven into rings, pictures of graves,
or poems. It shaped both the sender and the receiver, demanding that
after the experience of loss one engage in a compensatory and spiritually therapeutic process of personal reconstruction. As I have argued
earlier, these mourning rituals had served to create the parameters necessary for a cultural identity that assumes the rubric of "American." The

utopian potential of sentimentality, the potential of forming communities in which difference was suppressed and fulfillment was defined as a sense of boundless belonging, had driven its ideological success. But during the postwar period the nature and cost of this success comes under increasing suspicion even as it becomes the object of nostalgic longing. The promiscuity of the dead and the prevalence of mourning in the aftermath of the Civil War violence began to threaten to explode the class boundaries that sentimentality had earlier helped to establish. On the other hand, the gap between what sentimentality promised—the conversion of grief into mourning, absence into presence, other into self—and what it achieved was perceived as widening. The sentimental faith that a "sound heart" of the nation could conquer and reshape the self-approving but deformed conscience of an intrinsically corrupt and self-serving society had been repeatedly disappointed.

Coming into his own as a writer during the decade of the war, Twain in his fiction suggests that the very processes inherent in the mode of sentimentality were threatening to collapse upon themselves. Twain, of course, is of a different generation from Lincoln, Sigourney, or Long-fellow; his uneasy and suspicious understanding of sentimental culture is not theirs. Twain's oscillations between a reckless optimism based on material progress and a cautious pessimism arising out of spiritual despair have often been cited as characteristic of that postwar era. For the most part, it is Twain's suspicion or cynicism regarding the sentimental and his role in articulating the realist project (a project framed by most critics as in opposition to the sentimental one) that has attracted the most critical attention. This position came to be shared and reformulated in important ways by early-twentieth-century writers who had, perhaps, even more reasons to be suspicious of what was seen as the evasive idealization of painful truths. The valence of sentimentalism shifted so that rather than being understood as a way of coming to grips with reality—a reality defined by pain and loss—it became a way to avoid harsh realities and to practice deceptive manipulations.[1] As many students of college composition courses learn, George Orwell in his famous essay "The Politics of the English Language" warns against using or being impressed by figurative language that no longer refers to reality. Such "dead metaphors" are not merely useless; they can be actively pernicious. Orwell's fear of the dead metaphor (a kind of empty, beguiling language) is similar to the embarrassment caused by "abstract words such as glory, honor, courage, or hallow" to Hemingway's Frederick Henry. Henry's embarrassment arises partly from disappointment, from having "seen nothing sacred, and the things that were glorious had no glory and the sacrifices were like the stockyards at Chicago if nothing was done with the meat except to bury it" (*Farewell to Arms* 185). Frederick Henry suffers from having been betrayed by a set of cultural expectations which, at the very least, did not describe the experience he was undergoing. Henry's personal investment in these expectations—of glory, honor, courage—drives his cynicism. Orwell, Hemingway, and especially James Baldwin in his perceptive excoriation of the danger of sentimentality in "Everybody's Protest Novel" were registering the shift in the valence of sentimentality that occurs during the years Twain is writing. The emotional, analogical power of sentimentality was put in the service of Jim Crow, and later in the service of the American red-baiting of the 1920s and the European rise of fascism. Revealingly, Hemingway traced his literary genealogy back to Twain's *Huckleberry Finn* and what he perceived as its antagonism to false genteel culture and, more important, back to what Hemingway describes as Twain's uncompromising realism. But if *Huck Finn* can be seen as a modernist forebear, Twain himself was sometimes seen by this same generation as a cultural apostate—as a man who had, as Orwell points out in another essay, sold out both his artistic and social conscience in the service of hypocritical capitalists.[2] The discourse of sentimentality had proffered the opportunity for a cohesive, unified, and hegemonic "ideology" but the cost, as Twain clearly saw, could be fatal. The dissolution of many into one could just as easily result in a dangerous and violent mutual annihilation as in the empathetic merging of selves into a community that was promised by sentimentality.

The Adventures of Tom Sawyer has been read as, and in fact was considered by Twain to be, a lyrical evocation of Twain's and Twain's America's Golden Age of pastoral innocence and beauty. It is Twain's nostalgic depiction of time past. Coming on the heels of *The Gilded Age: A Tale of Today* (1873), it is a foil to the rottenness of the American society satirized in the earlier book.[3] The missing term between these putative "Ages"— between the Gilded and the Golden Age—is the period of the war. Twain resists the depiction of the war. Instead, he obliquely explains the declension from the past to the present by re-presenting Tom Sawyer's world from the perspective of one of the most marginalized characters of that world, Huckleberry Finn. In *The Adventures of Huckleberry Finn,* the violence, the meanness, and the loss in American antebellum society express Twain's recognition that the golden hue that had permeated his hymn to his own and America's prewar youth was itself a form of gilding, a gilding not so dissimilar in function to the gilt described by *The Gilded Age.*

Huck begins his book with the modest admission that the reader won't "know about me, without you have read a book by the name of "The Adventures of Tom Sawyer'" (9). The community celebrated in *Tom Sawyer* and repudiated in *Huck Finn* is a community in which it is necessary to deal with loss by imagining replacements, replacements for that which has been lost—say one's family or home—or for that which one has never had or been. The bonds constituting these communities on the frontier of America, Twain suggests, are forged through a process of sentimental mourning.

Both *Tom Sawyer* and *Huck Finn* are about the bonds of friendship: Tom and Huck's, Huck and Jim's. Although Twain's Huck qualifies his claim that "You don't know about me, without you have read a book by the name of 'The Adventures of Tom Sawyer,'" by politely saying "that ain't no matter," it does matter. *Tom Sawyer* makes clear Huck's position vis-à-vis normative sentimental culture. In the earlier book, Huck plays the conventional comedic sidekick to the protagonist. He is not even Tom's primary friend, but an alternate who is turned to when Joe Harper is not available. Like Jim's in *Huck Finn,* Huck's earnestness and essential social marginality allow him to play the necessary straight man upon which much of the humor of the book relies. In additional contrast to Tom, who has a family and a place in society even though he is technically an orphan, Huck has no family except for his Pap—which is to say he has no family at all.[4] Huck begins the novel as an unsentimentalized boy who lives in a hogshead barrel and who often depends on the adult ne'er-do-wells to provide for him. Although not legally an orphan during the time frame of *Tom Sawyer,* Huck could not be more of a social orphan.[5] Tom, also an orphan, offers a demonstration of the ability of the society as a whole to function despite the loss of certain individuals. Tom's birth parents may be dead but his extended family, in the form of Aunt Polly in St. Petersburg and Aunt Sally further downriver, is able to perform the roles stipulated for the middle-class family. They care for him as they see to the reproduction of their own values through his education. Huck, on the other hand, is a boy who is not linked to society in any of the conventional ways and for whom no one, initially, is willing to assume responsibility. The sentimental mechanics of *Tom Sawyer* work firmly to integrate both of these orphans into the whole of society.[6] And they seemingly succeed, since at the conclusion of *Tom Sawyer* Tom's new wealth and his love for Becky Thatcher bind Tom even more firmly into the community while Huck's new wealth and his transformation from village pariah to object of sentimental attention should both serve to shift fundamentally Huck's status within the community of St. Petersburg.[7] *Tom Sawyer* ends as an American comedy of the rise from poverty to wealth, from a state of lostness to a state of foundness. It is *Huck Finn* that calls the nature of this comedy into question.

In his recollections of his own childhood Twain admits that from a child's perspective all

> the negroes were friends of ours, and with those of our own age we were in effect comrades. We were comrades, and yet not comrades; color and condition interposed a subtle line which both parties were conscious of and which rendered complete fusion impossible. (*Autobiography* 1.100)

As in Twain's childhood relationship to the slave boy Sandy, who was Twain's closest buddy during that time, Huck and Tom share a common ground of childhood that is nevertheless marked by class divisions, which they perceive but cannot quite articulate. In *Tom Sawyer*, Huck and Tom are separated not by a barrier as impenetrable as color but by a more "subtle line" based on a condition that exists nevertheless between them. The subtle line of class is exactly what the sentimental elements of *Tom Sawyer*'s plot are designed to ameliorate.[8]

In one way, the plot of *Tom Sawyer* resolves Tom's relationship to his family and to the small society of St. Petersburg. More important, it allows for the amelioration of the differences in condition which kept Tom and Huck from being more than "in effect comrades." The highly romantic plot devices—including the adventure in the caves with Becky and Injun Joe and the recovery of the gold—have two results, which at the close of *Tom Sawyer* seemed to have the potential to change Huck's condition.[9] The most important one, as Twain has Huck make clear at the beginning of *Huck Finn,* is that Huck is now a person of property with a seemingly unlimited income for life.

The second result is that the funeral for Huck, Tom, and Joe in *Tom Sawyer* begins the important symbolic transposition of Huck from outsider to insider. This transposition is the ultimate function of sentimentalism in America.[10] Temporarily, at least, this is completed at the conclusion of the novel, as signaled by Huck's adoption by the paragon of genteel culture, the Widow Douglas. This final apotheosis has been foreshadowed by the conclusion of the first movement of the novel:

> Aunt Polly, Mary and the Harpers threw themselves upon their restored ones, smothered them with kisses and poured out thanksgivings, while poor Huck stood abashed and uncomfortable, not knowing exactly what to do or where to hide from so many unwelcoming eyes. He waved, and started to slink away, but Tom seized him and said:
> "Aunt Polly, it ain't fair. Somebody's got to be glad to see Huck."
> "And so they shall. *I'm* glad to see him, poor motherless thing!" And the loving attentions Aunt Polly lavished upon him were the one thing capable of making him more uncomfortable than he was before. (*Tom Sawyer* 115)

For the first time, Huck, "the juvenile pariah of the village," is redefined as a "poor motherless thing." Aunt Polly's reclassification of Huck occurs in the midst of the funeral service that was being held for the lost boys and is marked by sanction of the entire congregation in the form of the Protestant doxology, or as Twain conventionally calls it, the "Old Hundred" or the Hymn of Thanksgiving. The "loving attentions" of Tom's Aunt Polly and the discomfort they cause Huck are multiplied when the conclusion of the novel provides him with the two additional prerequisites for inclusion in the community of St. Petersburg: family in the form of the Widow Douglas and her sister, and money in the form of the robbers' hoard.[11] The ritual mourning of the lost boys that occurs in the first half of the novel restores Tom to his family and establishes the ground for integrating Huck into the community. The conclusion of the novel places Huck in a reciprocal relationship with the Widow Douglas that is based on loss and on the potential of a substitute to fill that gap:

Huck is to act as child to the Widow, the Widow is to act as parent to Huck.

Late in life, Twain described *Tom Sawyer* as "simply a hymn, put into prose form to give it a worldly air." To call *Tom Sawyer* a hymn suggests that the book, like the lyrical passages in Twain's autobiography, would convey a sustained, unified, and compact emotional tone or charge. Calling it a hymn, moreover, devalues the narrative content, suggesting that as time went on Twain became even more certain, at least in his mind, that the book was not about a person or persons — Tom and Huck — but an elegiac celebration of a way of life that was now an unapproachable ideal. More than that, as a hymn or prayer, *Tom Sawyer* can be read as an extended apostrophe, calling into being as it addresses the a priori conditions still underwriting Twain's own world. Twain's revision of this world in *Huck Finn* does not change its status as an ideal type, but does change his evaluation of it. The time of Tom and Becky may have been a Golden Age, a time when the gods still walked the earth; but the gods were wanton boys and rules were just as cruel and arbitrary.

CHAPTER 8

Mourning America's Morning:
The Adventures of Huckleberry Finn

> Poor Emmeline made poetry about all the dead people when she
> was alive, and it didn't seem right that there warn't nobody to make
> some about her, now she was gone; so I tried to sweat out a verse
> or two myself, but I couldn't seem to make it go some how.
> —Huck, in Twain's *The Adventures of Huckleberry Finn*

While Twain came to consider his *Adventures of Tom Sawyer* as a hymn, he
came to view *The Adventures of Huckleberry Finn* as an allegory: *Huckleberry
Finn* is "a book of mine where a sound heart and deformed conscience
come into collision and conscience suffers defeat" (qtd. in Kaplan 198).
The ground or field of this providential battle between "sound heart" and
"deformed conscience" is sentimental America. The immediate opening
of *Huck Finn* shows the inadequacy of sentimental mechanisms. Just as
the Emancipation Proclamation itself was not able nor ever expected to
erase the subtle line of color that had separated Sam Clemens from full
friendship with his playmate cum slave Sandy, neither the money, nor the
sanction of the community, nor the new family can erase the line separating Tom from Huck. By the end of *Huck Finn,* Twain has reinscribed this
difference as difference based not on wealth or social status but as difference in moral sense, the only difference, sentimentalists maintained,
that was essential. In *Huck Finn,* Twain uses the conventions of sentimentality to reverse the apparent distinctions between Tom and Huck.
In *Tom Sawyer,* Tom had been privileged over Huck because of his greater
cultural knowledge. By the end of *Huck Finn,* Tom is the one who seems
morally naive and ignorant. Like Twain as child or Twain's own mother,

"he has never had the chance to learn that slavery was an evil" (*Autobiography* 1.100), Tom is open to Twain's criticism because, unlike Huck, he has never learned to overcome his fatally deformed conscience.

In *The Adventures of Huckleberry Finn,* Twain exposes the ways in which the very fabric of prewar America was held together by strategies of mourning. Twain is not original in noticing this. Years earlier, at the very moment when the dream of the Mount Auburn Cemetery, where the living and the dead could better maintain their relationships in a carefully sculptured environment of nature and beauty, was becoming reality, Emerson had warned Americans not to build "sepulchres of the fathers" ("Nature"). Emerson, of course, was not arguing in "*Nature*" with the cemetery movement that swept New England during the 1820s and 1830s. In fact, his argument for "an original relation to the Universe," in which God and nature may be perceived "face to face," has much in common with the cemetery movement's goal to create a space for the proper and continued relation to the dead. In "*Nature,*" Emerson uses the set of terms that had arisen as a way of describing the pervasive anxiety over the proper way to mourn as a means of warning his listeners against a too moribund relationship to the intellectual inheritance of England and Europe. The correct relationship to the dead was one that propelled an individual into the future, not one that returned an individual to the past.

Opening "Nature" in this way is typical of the way that the discourse of mourning was beginning to provide the key elements for understanding the self in America. The culture of sentiment did more than merely provide Emerson with a set of rhetorical figures, it provided him with strategies for structuring some of his most important experiences. Emerson was pleased to be able to move the grave of his boy Waldo once the "Sleepy Hollow" cemetery in Concord was completed. He had responded to the death of his son in conventional ways, writing a long mourning poem, "Threnody," and later demanding to view the long-buried body of his son when the first grave was opened. Among other things, the essay "Experience" marks the disappointment Emerson feels when the promises of this mourning culture fail him: "There are moods in which we court suffering, in the hope that here at least we shall find reality, sharp peaks and edges of truth" (256). But Emerson had found that mourning neither restored the possibility of a transparent connection between the hieroglyphics of nature and their meaning, nor compensated for all that he lost when his son died. The seemingly affirmative resolution of "Threnody," taught by the "deep Heart," that the "House and tenant go to ground, / Lost in God, in Godhead found," is countered by Emerson's claim in "Experience" that "I grieve that grief can teach me nothing, nor carry me one step into real nature" (256).

Though a frontier town, the fictional St. Petersburg is part of that same American culture of the Mt. Auburn Cemetery and Emerson's Concord. St. Petersburg, like its prototype Hannibal, is connected not only by river commerce but by the print media, which brings not only the books of Dickens and Scott to boys like Tom and the latest fashions to girls like Becky, but the literary fashions of poetry and essays to the local paper. The provinciality of St. Petersburg, which is the object of so much of Twain's humor (especially in *Tom Sawyer*), is the provinciality of the nation as a whole. In the year 1876, when he published *Tom Sawyer* and began *Huck Finn,* Twain expressed his hatred of what he considered

> sham sentimentality—the kind a school-girl puts into her gradu-
> ating composition; the sort that makes up the Original Poetry col-
> umn of a country newspaper; the rot that deals in the "happy days
> of yore", the "sweet yet melancholy past," with its "blighted hopes,"
> and its "vanished dreams"—and all that sort of drivels. (Qtd. in
> Paine), *Mark Twain's Letters* 1.250

But though he claimed that this was the "one thing which I can't stand and won't stand, from many people," Twain's *Huck Finn* details the degree to which he understood how the various practices of sentimentality, whether "sham" or "authentic," worked to hold the culture of his youth in a tenuous cohesion.

Early on in *Huck Finn,* Twain repeats the climactic scene from *Tom Sawyer,* in which the townspeople fire cannon over the water to raise the bodies of the assumed dead boys. In *Tom Sawyer,* as in *Huck Finn,* this pseudo-scientific ritual fails in its explicit object of dislodging a corpse from an inaccessible and inappropriate resting place. In both instances, it doesn't actually work because, among other things, the boys aren't dead. In *Tom Sawyer,* however, it does work on a symbolic level. It initiates a ceremony of communal identification—the funeral—which has the boys as both its objects and its witnesses. Through the efficacy of this funeral, the lost are literally found and—in *Tom Sawyer*—rebound even more tightly into the community.

In *Huck Finn,* the ritual fails both symbolically and actually. Though the community is reinforced by its participation in this mourning ritual, Huck's alienation from that community is likewise reinforced rather than ameliorated. Hoping to raise the literal object of their loss, individuals as disparate as "Pap, and Judge Thatcher, and Becky Thatcher, and Joe Harper, and Tom Sawyer, and his Aunt Polly, and Sid and Mary and plenty more" are joined in a community based on their common loss of Huck (35). The basis for the association of individuals "booming" for Huck's body is a shared practice of mourning, and these named individuals stand in for the whole of the citizens of the town of St. Petersburg, representing as they do the entire social spectrum from the town drunk to the minister and lawyer. In fact, in this gathering the town drunk, Huck's father, has the prominent or central position as chief mourner despite his lack of financial or social status. In *Tom Sawyer,* Twain has the presumed dead boys participate emotionally—as mourners touched by the words of the service—in their own funerals. In *Huck Finn,* Twain stages the confrontation between the mourners and the mourned on two irreconcilable planes. This time there is no hymn of Thanksgiving sung as Huck is embraced by a surrogate mother and by a newly loving community of friends. Rather, Huck, alone on the shore of his island refuge, stares at the mass of townspeople as they float by on their riverboat: "They all crowded up and leaned over the rails, nearly in my face, and kept still, watching with all their might. I could see them first rate, but they couldn't see me" (35). In contrast to the effect of witnessing his own funeral in *Tom Sawyer,* this time, when Huck witnesses his own funeral the gap between these people who claim him as their own and himself resists all interventions. As with all the communities Huck visits as he travels down the river away from his one murderous blood relation, he ultimately rejects the community united on the riverboat to mourn for him.

This is not to say that Huck's rejection is a calculated rejection of the values of St. Petersburg; it is an emotional, a sentimental, rejection. In fact, despite Huck's claim that he "don't take no stock in dead people," he shares his culture's concern for the dead and an interest in the ways they are treated by the living (8). The long list of "homes" that present themselves to Huck only to be rejected are characterized for Huck by the way that mourning occurs within them. The "good Place" of Miss Watson, which would exclude Tom Sawyer; the shack, where "Pap struggles with the death angel"; the island, where Jim's death-like pose gives Huck the "fantods"; the wreck of the "Walter Scot" as well as the home of Mary Jane Wilks, are all examples of the prominent role played by the trope of the dead person in Twain's description of the various inadequate homes offered to Huck.

Above all other examples, the two-chapter interlude Huck spends in the Grangerford household marks the degree to which mourning is both constitutive and generative of the American middle class. As critics have noted, it is here that Twain indulges in his fullest description of this culture; but this is also where Twain offers his clearest statement of regret that the utopian aspirations of the culture have so degenerated into self-destructive violence. When Huck comes upon the Grangerford household, he has just endured two crises—one a crisis of faith, the other a physical crisis in which he comes as close as he ever does in either book to death. This is important to note in order to register Huck's sense of relief at being taken in by a "mighty nice family, and a mighty nice house, too" (82). The first crisis, the climactic moment in the allegorical battle between a sound heart and a deformed conscience, occurs as Huck approaches the confluence of the Ohio and the Mississippi rivers, where Jim had hoped to begin his life in the free states. In the course of Huck's internalized battle, which Twain stages as a dialogue between two selves, Huck tells how he "got to feeling so mean and so miserable I most wished I was dead" (73). As in the several other places where Twain has Huck express despair, this initiates an action on Huck's part that he had not anticipated. Exacerbated by Jim's vexed hopes to free his children, Huck's conscience "got to stirring me up hotter than ever, until at last I says to it, 'let up on me—it ain't too late yet—I'll paddle ashore at the first light and tell'" (74). Having made peace with his conscience, Huck feels the opposite of his more characteristic feelings of melancholy and loneliness, "I felt easy and happy and light as a feather right off. All my troubles was gone" (74). Temporarily, the teaching of "poor Miss Watson," who had "tried to learn" Huck "his book" and "his manners," was paying off for Huck.

But having temporarily reconciled his actions to conventional social ideals of right and wrong, Huck finds himself the victim of sentiment. He is forced by the gift of Jim's affection and trust to collaborate on the transformation of a piece of property into a man.[1] On his way to "do the right" thing and turn Jim in, Huck is assailed by Jim's reiteration of what he owes to Huck:

> I's a free man, an I couldn't ever ben free efit hadn ben for Huck; Huck done it. Jim won't ever forget you, Huck; you's de bes' fren' Jim's ever had; in you's de *only* fren' ole Jim's got now. (74)

Having already followed his heart into antisocial complicity with Jim, Huck finds himself a collaborator against the prevailing social system that had tried to claim his own heart.

Twice in his *Autobiography,* Twain describes the extent to which it was impossible in his youth to conceptualize slavery as morally or politically unjustifiable, for no one "heard it assailed in any pulpit" or otherwise subjected to criticism (1.123). His own mother, who was for Twain the epitome of a naturally and sincerely "kindhearted and compassionate" person, "was not conscious that slavery was a bald, grotesque, and unwarrantable usurpation" (*Autobiography* 1.123). Instead, like everyone else in the town, she did not question when she heard it

> defended and sanctified in a thousand [pulpits]; her ears were familiar with Bible texts that approved it, but if there were any that disapproved it they had not been quoted by her pastors; as far as her experience went, the wise and the good and the holy were unanimous in the conviction that slavery was righteous, sacred, the peculiar pet of the Deity, and a condition which the slave himself ought to be thankful for. (1.123)

Twain uses very similar language in his *Autobiography* when explaining his own early attitude toward slavery.[2] Of course, Huck was not a frequent visitor of churches, but nevertheless the claims of conventional morality are strong within him. When he lapses from his newfound conviction to do the right thing and turn Jim in to the bounty hunters, he is following no theory but the claims of sentiment.[3] Although early on in the novel

Huck disavows conventional heaven in favor of his allegiance to Tom, it at this place that Huck knows he has finally rescinded all possible claims to grace.

The Bre'r Rabbit–type tale Huck tells to ward off the slave catchers who threaten Jim's freedom successfully invokes the sentimental economy of affections. Huck has told his tale of woe and contagion to ward them away from the raft and Jim. The men feel sorry for the boy with the supposedly mortally sick family, floating homeless down the river. As a token of their concern and as a substitution for their own personal intervention, they each give Huck (once again a poor motherless boy) twenty-dollar gold pieces. If the facts of Huck's story had been true, this substitution would have actually served the stricken family as well or better than the presences of these particular men. Although the facts of Huck's story were not true, the cash comes as a bonus gift supplementing what would have been the satisfactory and crucial achievement of driving the men away. By gratuitously responding to sentiment, the men have joined and collaborated with Huck, in an act subversive to their own interests as individuals and as members of the slave-owning society. The unexpected bounty of the bounty hunters offers Huck and Jim the prospect of booking passage by steamboat into the free states.

The emotional crisis of this threatened double betrayal is immediately paralleled by a physical crisis that deprives Huck of his "only fren" and makes moot the debates that had anguished Huck. After having missed Cairo, Jim and Huck enter a nightmare scenario when "the night got gray and rather thick, which is the next meanest thing to fog" (78). Having just recently damned himself by betraying his race as well as his new class, Huck seems to be meeting hell when a steamboat bears down on them out of the dark: "all of a sudden she bulged out, big and scary, with a long row of wide-open furnace doors shining like red hot teeth, and her monstrous bows and guards hanging right over us" (78). "Jim," recounts Huck, "went overboard on one side and I on the other" as the boat came "smashing straight through the raft" (78). The dynamo of nineteenth-century America seems here to have successfully negated the "bonds of affection" that had joined the white boy to the black man. This physical disaster, however, eases the effect of the previous emotional one, since it separates Huck from Jim and interrupts their journey together into the free states. Accident does what Huck's conscience could not and offers Huck the opportunity, through the interlude at the Grangerfords', of becoming an accepted member of legitimate society.

In the two chapters that follow, Twain offers Huck a substitution for his lost friend and his lost life on the raft. Critics have often read these chapters as Twain's unmitigated critique of American middle-class culture, especially as expressed in its most provincial terms on the geographic frontiers, with its adaptations of imported and inappropriate cultural artifacts and practices.[4] They cite parallels between Twain's characterization of the Grangerford household and the frontier households depicted in *Life on the Mississippi*. In *Life on the Mississippi*, Twain's excoriations of the shabby incongruous gentility is much more pointed and reflects the educated taste of one of Hartford, Connecticut's esteemed residents.[5] They lack the mediation of Huck's naively appreciative eye. But while the Grangerford household is, undoubtedly, built from recollections of the "poor white" households Twain met in his early travels and as a riverman, it is also built from his memories of his uncle John's farm. The farm, "a heavenly place for a boy," was "a double log [house], with a spacious floor (roofed in) connecting it with the kitchen" (*Autobiography* 1.97). The Grangerford house, too, "was a double house, and the big open place betwixt them was roofed and floored, and sometimes the table was set there in the middle of the day, and it was a cool, comfortable place" (*Huck* 86). For Huck, as for Sam Clemens, "Nothing couldn't be better," especially since the cooking was good and there were "just bushels of it too!" (*Huck* 86). In his autobiography, Twain's memory of the food served on his uncle John's farm takes the form of an epic list. "Fried chicken, roastpig; wild and tame turkeys, ducks and geese," not only makes the older reminiscent Twain "cry to think of them," but also forms the basis for one of the few non-ironized statements of belief or credos indulged in by Twain (1.97).[6] What Twain unambiguously "knows" are things learned empirically through his own perceptions as a boy—the taste of watermelons, for example, whether legitimately or illegitimately procured. Uncle John's farm, as many have noticed, also seems to be behind Twain's depiction of Aunt Sally's farm. As a repetition, with a difference, of the Grangerford farm, Twain encourages the reader to see that Uncle John's farm and Tom's Aunt Sally's farm are really one and the same: they are both genteel, homely refuges of civilization on the frontier offering Huck a home, and both are rejected, like the Widow Douglas's home.

At the Grangerfords', with a parlor decorated with crayon sketches of weeping willows, artificial fruit, and a copy of *Friendship's Offering,* Twain satirizes the reliance on what he had come to view as inappropriate and inadequate substitutions for the real thing—for real art, for cultivated fruit, and for literature. But in Huck's response to the Grangerfords, Twain discloses his understanding of the urge behind these practices. Though the novel was written from the epicenter of American genteel culture (and Twain would be sensitive later on to the possibility that all American aspirations to the claim of artists were ridiculous and provincial to Europeans), Twain shows an understanding of their worth as cultural capital even while exposing their dangerous cost.

Even in areas where "Yankee" or "frontier" thrift dominated, the conversion of grief into mourning justified an expense of time, effort, and cash not devoted to other occasions. A contemporary of Twain's, James Jarvis, who was a prime mover in the establishment of American art museums, understood that Americans "are a composite people. Our knowledge is eclectic. . . . We beg, borrow, adopt and adapt" what is needed. In the "genteel adornments" of the Grangerfords' homestead or the graduation exercises of *Tom Sawyer,* Twain shows the products of this process of cultural bricolage. Twain's treatment shows their role in the process of creating and maintaining community under adverse conditions. But Twain also shows the danger inherent in this very same process, a danger that results in the mutual annilation of community members. Of all the homes opened to Huck over the course of the novel, this one attracts him most with its "bushels of food," and its "fine and handsome men," and its companion boy (Buck). It offers him access to a kind of American utopia where a sense of easiness and happiness displaces his more usual sense of alienation and melancholy. Only when this mournful utopia betrays itself as a self-annihilating dystopia does Huck return to the river, his raft, and his one friend, the "nigger" Jim.

At the center of this genteel frontier family is the memory of the dead daughter Emmeline. Her empty room is maintained as a shrine tended by the mother of the household with her own hands. It is in this sanctuary and under its auspices that Huck makes his most sincere effort to conform himself to imposed cultural conventions. Humor, as well as pathos, arises from his sincerity. The appeal of this family is so strong, ("I liked all that family, dead ones and all") that he "warn't going to let anything come between us" (86). Huck's attempts to conform to the usages of the Grangerford family contrast markedly with his rejection of Miss Watson's and later Aunt Sally's attempts to "sivilize" him. The sentimental artifacts generated by this now dead daughter have almost a totemlike power over the Grangerford family and over Huck as well. The last "crayon" or picture that Emmeline had been working on when she died has been established within a tabernacle placed in the innermost sanctum of the Grangerford home (her former bedroom).[7] Under a curtain that hides the picture for most of the year except on the Emmeline's birthday, when they expose it and adorn it with flowers, is a picture of an incongruously Shiva-like figure:

> It was a picture of a young woman in a long white gown, standing on a rail of a bridge all ready to jump off, with her hair all down her back, and looking up to the moon, with tears running down her face, and she had two arms folded across her breasts, and two arms stretched out in front, and two more reaching up towards the moon—and the idea was, to see which pair would look best and then scratch out all the other arms; but, as I was saying, she died before she got her mind made up, and now they kept this picture over the head of the bed in her room, and every time her birthday come they hung flowers on it. Other times it was hid with a little curtain. (84)

If these artifacts of Emmeline continue to exert a felt power over the family and Huck, it is nothing, so Huck tells us, to the power they exerted when she was alive. In the interpolated story of Emmeline's life and death, Twain has Huck describe the operation of the gift economy of mourning gestures that breached the isolation of the individualistic families (like the Grangerfords) so as to create and enable community. Like but unlike the professionals of death, the doctor and the undertaker, Emmeline intervenes in the death room: "Every time a man died, or a woman died, or a child died, she would be on hand with her 'tribute' before he was cold" (143). Before the undertaker could perform his ritual cleansing and preparation of the body for burial, Emmeline transforms, through her "tributes," the dead body into an aesthetic object, into a symbol, through the medium of poetry. In Huck's account of Emmeline, her death is itself caused by her inability to perform this function,

> the undertaker never got in ahead of Emmeline but once, and then she hung fire on a rhyme for a dead person's name, which was Whistler. She warn't ever the same after that; she never complained, but she kinder pined away after and did not live long. (85)

The inability to mourn in the proper way, to complete an aesthetically unified symbolic replacement for the dead person, seems, here, to be the cause of death. Huck tells the reader that he feels sorry for "Poor Emmeline," who "made poetry for all the dead people when she was alive, and it didn't seem right that there warn't nobody to make some about her now she was gone" (85). As if attempting to reverse the interruption to the symbolic economy of mourning posed by this death, or perhaps to himself enter in the symbolic economy that links this family together, Huck "tried to sweat out a verse or two myself," but admits defeat: "I couldn't make it go some how" (144).

As the second chapter of the Grangerford episode unfolds, Twain suggests that Emmeline played an important, though inadequate, role for the entire community.[8] Here, as elsewhere in the text, Twain's attitude toward sentimentality is both cynical and nostalgic. He has a deep understanding and appreciation of the limits of sentimentality's ability to perform its main function: the creation, the maintenance, and (if necessary) the extension of the bonds of the family so as to enable the construction of a more broadly based sense of community. Emmeline's mortal failure to mourn seems to lead not only to her death, but also to the death of the extended family and its counterpart family, the Shepardsons. Huck's account of the time before Emmeline died describes an economy in which the literal dead were re-presented by a symbol which can then produce beneficial cultural capital through its circulation. His account of the time-present describes an economy in which literally dead people are exchanged, cancelling each other out rather than adding to the sum population of the community. This equation is one of violent subtraction. Eventually even the youngest members are killed, leaving Huck with no way to mourn, to "get shut of them—lots of times I dream about them" (94). Huck accepts that "there warn't no home like a raft, after all" (96).

At the Grangerfords', Huck had begun to feel that he had found a home, since he had found a place, a community, that had seemed to supply him with a systematic way of dealing with the omnipresent but inarticulate feelings of loss and the susceptibility to the dead that characterizes his personality. The regularity of the Grangerfords' mourning practice seems a superlative extension of the more catch-as-catch-can system of prophylactics—charms, curses, dreams—Huck has had to deploy against bad luck, ghosts, spirits, and presentiments. Throughout the book, Twain's Huck is a paragon of sentimental sensibility; he is so at the mercy of his sensitivity that at the close of the first chapter he feels

> so lonesome I most wished I was dead. The stars were shining, and the leaves rustled in the woods ever so mournful; and I heard an owl, away off, who-whooing about somebody that was dead, and a whippowill and a dog crying about somebody that was going to die; and the wind was trying to whisper something to me, and I couldn't make out what it was, and so it made the cold shivers run over me. (9)[9]

Repeatedly, Huck's affections and his unconscious tendency to create analogies between himself and another in which difference—of color, of gender, of status—derails the action of either conventional mores or enlightened self-interest. Huck is so sentimental, in fact, that the sight of Emmeline Grangerford's "crayons"—with titles such as "Shall I never see thee more alas"—give him the "fantods," as had the uncanny sight of Jim lying as if dead (84). The "fantods," which affect Huck several times throughout the narrative, mark the intervention of the autonervous system into the rational or conscious control of the body with fainting, shortness of breath, or other bodily symptoms displaying the body's unconscious reaction to stimuli. They are the sign announcing the process through which, as Twain was to describe years later, "a sound heart and a deformed conscience come[s] into collision and conscience suffers defeat" (qtd. in Kaplan 198).

The Adventures of Huckleberry Finn describes the way that sentimental mourning in antebellum America, or at least in Twain's representations of antebellum America, played a constitutive role in that culture. One of the key ways that Twain's characters attempt to make sense of their situations is to participate in certain mourning practices. The written traces of these mourning practices are labeled sentimental because they favor emotion over reason as they aspire to create, maintain, and extend the bonds with which one individual is linked to another. Sentimental literature or art deals with the pain of loss by symbolically re-presenting it rather than eliding, covering over, or omitting it. The symbolic re-presentation of the loss provides the ground for the continued establishment of community. When this sign system breaks down, as in *Huck Finn,* the possibility of shared community and even of family becomes doubtful and even, scenes such as the Grangerford/Shepardson episode suggest, becomes the source of violence. Twain shows repeatedly how this way of making sense through these particular ways of mourning no longer works: Huck is given up for dead when he isn't, Pap is feared as alive when he is dead, the Duke and the King come perilously close to supplanting the heirs to the Wilks fortune. Twain links the failure of these mourning practices to a demonstration of the inadequacy of the alternative homes Huck passes through. As a paragon of authentic (versus sham) sentimentality, Huck is a touchstone indicating the worth of this culture for those who would like to live the sentimentalist dream of being able to reconcile one's heart with one's conscience and one's actions. Twain does not reject these homes and the practices that constitute them because they are silly, but because they are dangerous. Twain's frequent return to this topic, in *The Mysterious Stranger, Letters from Earth,* and other dark meditations can themselves be seen as mournful reenactments of his own sense of loss arising from this realization.

In *Huckleberry Finn,* the house of America, built through mourning, is revealed to have always been a "House of Death." In the dialogue preceding the famous conclusion to the novel (in which Huck declares that he has "got to light out for the territory ahead of the rest"), Jim resolves the novel's plot: he reveals the secret of Huck's father's death which he has carried since the ninth chapter, entitled "The House of Death Floats By." Jim's revelation is a brief interpolation in which the ending of the novel as a whole pauses for him to ask, "Doan' you 'member de house dat was float'n down de river, en dey wuz a man in dah, kivered up, en I went in en unkivered him and didn' let you come?" (229). Having interrupted the story and returned his listener's attention to an earlier moment in the story, Jim explains that, "Well, den, you kin git yo' money when you wants it, kase dat wuz him [Huck's Pap]" (229). Where the obituary pictures of Emmeline Grangerford and the seemingly but not really dead body of Jim had previously stirred Huck to "fantods" and to attempts to respond conventionally to the reality of death, here, Huck does not even seem to register this information. Instead, the narrative returns to the present before moving quickly to a future that is a final repudiation of the past: "I been there before." The promises of sentimentality—of continuity in the face of change and over time, of the strength of the bonds of affection to create and maintain family and society, of a shared basis for understanding and interpretation—have been fractured, leaving Huck still without a way to mourn and still without a home.

Converting Loss to Profit:
Collaborations of Sentiment and Speculation

It's the economy, stupid.

—James Carville

I've always been attracted to the standard model of American individualism and, at least sometimes, identified myself with it. What "real" American doesn't fantasize about being the isolato, the dissenter, the exceptional hero who flees into the territories and thereby, somehow, saves those left behind? This figure has drawn a lot of scholarly attention and is, without a doubt, key to the way that Americans imagine themselves and their country. But what happened to the isolatoes when their mission of escape turned into a mission of settlement, when the territories became states, when the Ishmaels returned home? And what about those from whom the American hero fled, those whom the American hero was supposed to save? Did they recognize themselves as needing salvation or did they, also, think of themselves as "real" Americans?

This book has been an attempt to recover this other model of American identity, which I see as based on a sense of collaborative individualism. If most books on the topic of American subjectivity have focused on the possessive individual, it would be fair to say that mine examines the collectively haunted individual: the individual who does not exist unless in an ongoing, reciprocal relationship with an other in which the boundaries between self and other, past and present, alive and dead are constantly being negotiated. The collaborative self is produced and perpetuated only through participation in an economy of emotions in which affections circulate in the form of gifts to bind disparate persons together into subjects able to recognize themselves and act on the world.

As I explained in part 1, I found the traces of this process in the amateur literary productions of rural, frontier America, where the exchange
of artifacts through a presentation economy not only marked, but created, boundaries of inclusion and exclusion. I wasn't looking for alternate
models of American selfhood when I began this project; rather, I was
just trying to figure out what these people were doing and what they
thought they were doing when they were writing and exchanging these
"tokens of affection."

What I came to see was that through the ostensibly personal processes
of converting private grief into collective mourning—the conversion of
anomie into socialization and the conversion of spiritual skepticism into
certainty—many individuals whose gender and economic status otherwise limited their claim to "Americanness" were able to define collaboratively the ground of their "American" subjectivity. What I have described
as the collaborative poetics of American sentimentality functioned positively to enable its users to reposition themselves from the margins to
the center of cultural authority. In this way, sentimentality had been instrumental in solving (or seeming to solve) the conundrum posed by
America's motto—E Pluribus Unum—as it helped to establish the outlines and content of the American middle class. The American self, like
the dollar, takes its value from the economy it operates in. It is only
worth whatever it can be exchanged for. America's motto is not, after
all, Contra Plures Unum, which, after all, would be more applicable to
the more commonly studied model of the self-reliant individual. This
is not to say that this "collaborative individual" is more American, but
rather to recognize that it has existed as the invisible complement to the
possessive individual.

Throughout this project I've been trying to stress the collaborative
nature of sentimentality not only because this term describes the way
that sentiment facilitates "joint intellectual efforts" but also because it
describes the way sentiment simultaneously coerces that other kind of
collaboration which may be defined as "treasonous cooperation." I would
like to expand briefly on this second meaning by continuing my discussion of Twain. For Twain's responses to a culture structured by sentiment
are both insightful and typical of the responses of the many who still
owe much to sentiment. His disdain and suspicion remain quite familiar

and continue to be shared because sentimentality continues to perform its important work.

This dual stance toward sentimentality is epitomized in his fictions, which suggest a critical apprehension of the dangers and faults of sentimentality; yet this understanding does not come from Twain himself having achieved a position outside of sentimentality's effect. Clemens's *Autobiography,* for example, details his sincere indebtedness to the sentimental ethos. The mode of sentimentality provided him with the structures through which he viewed the most important events of his life, including his relationships with his mother, his wife, and his daughters. The various fragmented narratives and lyrics that Clemens offers in his *Autobiography* as the story of Mark Twain's life are predominantly sentimental. As for so many who move themselves from the cultural margins to the cultural center of America, it is within, not in opposition to, the culture of sentiment that Samuel Clemens shaped himself into Mark Twain, into the husband of Olivia Langdon Clemens, into the Papa to his sainted daughter Susy, and into the protégé of William Dean Howells. His *Autobiography* details the way the economy of sentiment forges the relationships with others that define Clemens's sense of personal identity. And late in life, using these same strategies of sentimentality, Samuel Clemens also tried to assuage the challenge to this relational sense of personal integrity that was posed by the successive deaths of his daughter and his wife. The traces of these efforts exist in the extremely conventional and sentimental elegies he wrote on these occasions.

His early novels, also, document the debt owed by those members of the solidly middle class of Americans to what Shirley Samuels has so rightly called "the culture of sentiment." The critical commonplace (which has begun to be complicated since the feminist revision of American literary history) in regard to this is that Twain repudiated sentiment and all its works. But I've tried to suggest that these are actually testaments to his cynical disillusionment. Twain's disillusionment with America and with sentiment, like that of many other middle-class, white Americans, was driven by a sense of betrayed trust. Sentiment was both fulfilling its promise too well and not fulfilling it all. Sentiment, or as Abraham Lincoln put it, "the mystic chords of memory," had failed in its promise to touch "the better angels of our nature" and so to prevent the "bonds of our affection" from breaking. Having failed in this way, it was hard put to "bind up the nation's wounds" during the Reconstruction.

But it was also becoming clear that the utopian potential inherent in sentimentality could threaten its ideological effect of determining the parameters of the class identity on which white, Protestant "Americans" counted. I'm qualifying, of course, Fredric Jameson's argument in *The Political Unconscious* that "all ideology in the strongest sense, including the most exclusive forms of ruling-class consciousness just as much as that of oppositional or oppressed classes is in its very nature Utopian" (289). Until quite recently only the ideological nature of sentimentality had been explored. Following Jameson's lead, I have been arguing that what gives sentimentality its continuing ideological strength is that it formally establishes connections (allows for "the unity of the collective") among various people. But what I'm now suggesting is that part of the source of Twain's (and others') dis-ease with sentimentality came from the real-ization that the same mechanism that converted Clemens into a pillar of Hartford, Connecticut society (that is, the economy of love and affec-tion) might collapse beneath a flood of de-differentiating, though con-ditional, love. For the economy of sentiment is not a closed system avail-able only to those whose claim to participation is already patent. It could be, theoretically and practically, joined by anyone able to master and de-ploy its strategies. In other words, disdain arose as what might be called the ideological (or class-enforcing) functions of sentimentality became visible to those who had been, in part, created through its instrumen-tality. In part, this disdain came as reaction to the relatively successful efforts by disenfranchised groups, such as blacks, to deploy sentiment in their own efforts to claim the status of real "Americans." As Hazel Carby and Claudia Tate have convincingly argued, black women writers of the Reconstruction and post-Reconstruction era (such as Frances Harper and Pauline Hopkins) appropriated sentimentality as they tried to claim a place for black Americans within the middle class. This is even seen in the work of black male intellectuals during that era, as in W. E. B. DuBois's *Souls of Black Folk,* which depends on sympathy as well as rea-son to forward its project. The sentimental extension of the boundaries of inclusion around people of color and various Catholic, ethnic groups of Europe threatened to collapse the racial and class privilege of people like Clemens by working too well.

So what to do? It has been frequently noted that one of Twain's solutions to the problem of middle-class America is escape. To escape, that is, into the territories where the "ties that bind" have not yet been forged or to escape into a fantastic world where the rules governing human behavior seem not to hold. But, though Twain might imagine the desire to forgo the shaping bonds of affections (or at least the constraints of middle-class life), he was unable to imagine much of an alternative. Twain's alternative to a sentimental world is its binary opposite: a cynical world whose logic is a parallel inversion rather than a replacement of the sentimental. When Twain's characters do escape, they find themselves faced with a world dominated by the threats against which sentimentality had defined itself—loneliness, grief, arbitrary determinism, and meaninglessness—and from which Twain, himself, had fled. In Twain's personal life this escape took the form of withdrawing from the orbit of his wife and daughters into the homosocial world of men's clubs and dinners. As a carnivalesque paradise of would-be bachelors, this escape does not construct a corollary tartarus of maids but rather reinforces the ongoing sanctum of the angel of the home. In his early fictions and nonfictions Twain's escapees "light out for the territories" in which the worlds of love and ritual that have been left behind are re-created with a difference. I'm thinking, of course, of numerous scenes in Twain's works (for instance chapters 10 and 11 of *Roughing It,* which tell the tale of the outlaw Slade) in which his picaro wanders into a world of hate and ritual where gunshots circulate through an economy of hatred that, like the economy of sentiments, results not in the construction of an ongoing sense of self and society but in the destruction of self and society.

In Twain's later, darker fictions, such as *The Mysterious Stranger* or *Letters from the Earth,* Twain imagined and reimagined worlds of increasingly profound and uneasy familiarity where the difference between the world of escape and the world from which one escapes is small. Cynicism, then, was Twain's other answer to the problem of sentimental America, and this too remains a typical stance of those for whom sentimentality has already done its work. His cynicism was expressed not only conventionally through the modes of irony and parody but also in what has come to be celebrated as an innovative and distinctively American form of literary realism. One of his most deeply cynical works is the satiric social novel *The Gilded Age: A Tale of Today* (1873), on which Twain collaborated with Charles Dudley Warner. Yet, as the convoluted plot of the corrupted Reconstruction self and nation unfolds, it becomes clear that cynicism toward sentiment does not mean a rejection of its promise of providing a ground on which disparate individuals and interests can come together. Instead, Twain and Warner depict a version of the culture of sentiment where cultural status, won through the manipulation of the economy of affection, is brokered into economic wealth through the operation of what I would like to call "speculative collaboration." Twain's famous figure of Colonel Sellers, who constantly attempts to broker his cultural status into economic status, is only one example of many in this book. Sellers's failures in these ventures are the source of much of the comedy of the book. More important, however, these speculative ventures drive the plot, which ultimately supports the intrinsic value of the sentimental self and nation.

If sentimentality facilitates the construction of a collaborative individual from the predicate of loss, so does speculation. It doesn't matter whether one is cynically or sincerely participating in the economy. It doesn't matter whether memories (representations of what is imagined to have been lost) or hopes (representations of what is imagined to be desired) are being exchanged. Both economies, together, define the utopian notion of the American self, which admits to no essential qualifications (such as race, gender, or class) except that it love and it spend. Both economies allow for the creation of something (self, class, nation) from nothing while hiding the limits these economies impose on who can participate in these constitutive rituals. But they differ from and so complement each other in that while sentiment allows for the production of positive cultural capital out of loss, speculation allows for the conversion of cultural capital into economic capital through the replacement of memory by hope. The important difference is that if sentimental collaboration endows the self with subjectivity, speculation invests the collaborated individual with the economic capital it needs to act on the capitalist world. This American self, I have argued, can neither repudiate the circulation of affections through an emotional economy nor repudiate the circulation of money through a market economy.

Harriet Gould's Book

*The following poems have been transcribed from a manuscript album of verse origi-
nally owned by Harriet Gould of Dover, Vermont. The album came to its present
owners, Ralph and Verne Howe of Wilmington, Vermont, from the estate of
Florence Fox Howe also of Wilmington. While the poems are transcribed literatim
in the appendixes, when they are quoted in the body of this book spelling is standardized and errors are silently corrected.*

Harriet A. Gould's
Book Dover Vt
March 18th 1837

[page 1]

Through all thy life let virtue Shine,
And by the Lord be led.
Then shall his blessings all divine,
Still cluster round thy head.
Thy days shall glide along in peace
And Jesus be thy friend
Thy death shall be a sweet release
Thy days shall never end —
  Mansfield Bruce

[page 2]

Should dearest friends some kind memento trace,
Along the unwritten columns of this book
When distance or the grave hides form and face
Into this volume sweet t'will be to look.

Each fond remembrance oft will speak to you
In language which may never be forgot
Of those who ever constant were and true
And gently whisper O forget me not.
   Lois Gould

[page 3]

[3a]

New England's fruitful soil
Requires no culture from a servile toi;
No master's torturing lash offends the ear,
No slave is now or ever shall be here;
Whene'er he treads upon our sacred fields,
Their guardian genius an asylum yeilds;
His chains drop from him; and on Reason's plan
He claims the gift of God — the rights of man —
   Alvin Gould

[3b]

Who but a mother can so form and temper the infant mind, that
   theman, like the fabled demi-god, whom his mother plunged into
   theStyx, shall be invulnerable in every part. Blessed privelige! to
   train up the child of one's heart, in the way of truth andsoberness
   having the guarantee of heaven that when he is old hewill not
   depart from it.
   A. Gould

[3c]

I sigh not for beauty nor languish for wealth
But grant me kind Providence virtue and health

Then richer than kings, and more happy than they
My days shall pass sweetly and swiftly away
   A. Gould

[page 4]

How sweet to dwell where all is peace
Where calm delight ensues
How sweet to feel superior bliss
And have our souls renewed

Or should our path with thorns be strewed
And we by all forgot
How sweet in heaven a friend to view
That will forget us not
   Olive S. Gould

[page 5]

On the late Elder Jonathan Huntley

Thou lovely saint how calm thy sleep
Beneath the silent turf
Nor storms that o'er thy relics sweeps
Nor vain nor noisy mirth
Nor bitter strife or cares or woes
Nor aught below the sky
Can e'er disturb thy sweet repose
Or cause one gentle sigh
Now finished are thy works of love
Thy gospel labor o'er
No more thy tongue shall more
Thy voice be heard no more
And now on Jesus' loving breast
Thy weary soul reclines
And ther eternally shall rest
And feast on love devine
Nor shall thy flesh remain in night
But at the archangel's voice
Triumphant rise to worlds of light
To share in endless joys

[page 6]

Tis finished the conflict is past
The heaven born spirit is fled
Her wish is accomplished at last
And now she is entombed with the dead
The months of her affliction are o'er
The days and nights of distress
We see her in anguish no more
She has gained her happy release
No sickness or sorrow or pain
Shall ever disquiet her now
For death to her spirit was gain
Since Christ was her life when below
Her soul has now taken its flight
To mansions of glory above
To mingle with angels of light
And dwell in the kingdom of love
The victory now is obtain'd
She has gone her dear Savior to see
Her wishes she fully has gain'd
She is now where she longed to be
Then let us forbear to complain
That she is remov'd from our sight
We soon shall behold her again
With new and redoubled delight
    H A Gould

[page 7]

This world is all a fleeting show,
For man's illusion given;
The smiles of joy, the tears of wo,
Deceitful shine, deceitful flow —
There's nothing true but heaven!

And false the light on glory's plume,
As fading hues of even;

And love and hope and beauty's bloom
Are blossoms gathered for the tomb —
There's nothing bright but heaven!

Poor wanderers of a stormy day,
From wave to wave we're driven;
And fancy's flush, and reason's way —
Theres's nothing bright but heaven!
   John Howard

[page 8]

Hail lovely spring, thy balmy zephers hail!
Winter has yielded to thy soft control;
Thy melting eloqurnce subdued her power,
Thy smiles benignant cheer the drooping soul.

The tenants of the grove thy mildness hail,
With sweetest lays their grateful homage pay
To thee, who bids the changing seasons roll,
And holds o'er nature universal sway.

The verdant landscape stretches o'er the plain
The hills, they brighten with a lovely hue;
So faith, in long perspective, veiws above,
Those heavenly hills, with verdure ever new.

O! lovely Spring! emblems of heaven above —
When death's cold winter shall be pass'd away,
Then shall we veiw a bright, eternal spring,
And night shall yield to everlasting day.
   Lucy Howard
   Dover April 23 1837

[page 9]

Things That I Love
I love to see the beauteous form
With manly courage blended

The virtuous poor forsaken wretch
I love to see befriended
I love the man who scorns deceit
Nor stoops to guilty pleasure
I love the man who counts his word
The brightest of his treasure
I love the man who spurns the knave
And scorns to share his plunder
I love the Author who can read
And write without a blunder
I love the man so nobly proud
Misfortune cannot blight
The man who braves the jeering crowd
And sternly claims his right
I love the man who dares engage
In virtues noble cause
Tho fools deride and atheists rage
Against her sacred laws
    H A Gould

[page 10]

Ah! none but those who feel can tell
The sorrow which the bosum swells,
The pangs which rend the bursting heart
When called from those we love to part.

Yet kindness hides the rod beneath,
Whom Jesus loves he chasteneth;
Then raise to Heaven thy moistened eye,
Thy dearest Friend can never die.
He'll see thee in thy loneliness,
And closely to his side he'll press
The heart that rests on him alone,
When every other Friend is gone.
And soon, life's fleeting journey o'er,
He'll take thee to that deathless shore

Where friend with freind shall glory give,
To Him that died that we might live.
  Abigail M. Lazell

[page 11]

Melintha Lazell
Volume that signets of love art enshrining
Claimest thou mine on thy delicate breast
Take then the gift a plain flower entwining
Friendship as pure though less gay than the rest.
Mine is the seal of that real affection
Warm as the life-blood enduringly true
She would desire at whose gentle direction
Thou goest forth the fond pledge to renew.
Album! I trust to thy beautiful keeping
Wishes for her that my throbbing heart thrill
Holier love lingers o'er her unsleeping —
Would it were met while it waiteth there still.
Friendship must fail like the pledge of its tracing
Be there one page with a signet divine
Heart of my friend: prayrful wishes are placing
One worth adoring in thy living shrine.

[page 12]

At Parting
Sister quickly we must part
But still we will not mourn
For grief lies heavy on the heart
With grief already born

Although to us it seemeth hard
That severed we must be
Yet for our good afflictions come
As often do we see

If fate permit on earth once more
That we should meet again

O may we in that love confide
Which constantly has been

Farewell and when I'm far away
O thou will think of me
And let my image be effaced
Never from thy memory
    L. Curtis Lazell

[page 13]

The longest run of earthly bliss
Is short and hangs upon a breath
The strongest tie of nature is
But weak and soon disolv'd by death
    H. Gould

[page 14]

When evening spreads her shades around
And darkness fills the arch of heaven
When not a murmer not a sound
To fancy's sportive ear is given

When the broad orb of heaven is bright
And looks around with golden eye
When nature softened by her light
Seems calmly solemnly to lie

Then when our thoughts are raised above
This world and all this world can give
Oh Sister, sing the song I love
And tears of gratitude receive

When sleeping in my grass grown bed
Shouldst thou still linger here above
Wilt thou not kneel beside my head
And Sister sing the song I love
    Isaac M Lazell

[page 15]

How oft the tendrest ties are broken
How oft the parting tear must flow
The words of friendship scarce are spoken
Ere those are gone we love below
Like suns they rose and all was bright
Like suns they set and all is night
    Hannah F Gould

[page 16]

When Adam was created he dwelt in Eden's [shade]
As Moses has related and soon a bride was made
Ten thousand times, ten thousand creatures swarm'd around
Before a bride was form'd but yet no mate was found
He had no conversation but seem'd as if alone
Till to his admiration he found he'd lost a bone
Great was his admiration when first he saw his bride
Great was his exhaltation to find her by his side
He spake as in a rapture I know from whence you came

From my left side extracted and woman is your name
So Adam he rejoiced to see his lovely bride
A part of his own body the product of his side
The woman was not taken from Adam's head you know
So she must never rule him tis evidently so
The woman was not taken from Adam's feet you see.
So he must not abuse her, the meaning seems to be
The woman she was taken from under Adam's arm
So she must be protected from injury and harm
The woman she was taken from near to Adam's heart
By which you are directed that they must never part

[page 17]

My dearest friends in bonds of love
Whose hearts in sweetest union prove
Your friendship's like a drawing band

Yet we must take the parting hand
Your company's sweet, your union dear
Your words delightful to mine ear
And when I see that we must part
You [brant?] like cords around my heart
How sweet the hours have pass'd away
When we have met to sing and pray
How loth we've been to leave the place
Where Jesus shows his smiling face
O could I stay with friends so kind
How would it cheer my drooping mind
But duty must take the parting hand
Then since it is gods holy will
We must be parted for a while
In sweet submission all as one
We'll say our father's will be done

How oft I've seen your flowing tears
And heard you tell your hopes and fears
Your hearts with love e'en seem to flame
Which makes me think we'll meet again
Ye mourning souls in sad surprise
We seek for mansions in the skies
O trust his grace in all that land
We'll no more take the parting hand
Dear Christian friends both old and young
I hope in Christ you will go on
And if on earth we meet no more
O may we meet on Canaan's shore
I hope you'll all remember me
If you on earth no more I see
An interest in your prayers I crave
That we may meet beyond the grave
O glorious day O blessed hope
My heart leaps foraward at the thought
When on that happy happy land
We'll no more take the parting hand
    Lucy Lazell

[page 18]

Time is like a stream that hastens from the shore
Flies to an ocean where tis known no more;
All must be swalled in this endless deep
And motion rest in everlatsing sleep
The stars shall drop, the sun shall lose his flame
But thou, O God, forever shine the same.
  Edward Howe

[page 19]

Should sorrow o'er thy brow
Its darkerned shadow fling
And hopes that cheer thee now
Die in thier early spring
Should pleasure at its birth
Fade like the hues of even
Turn thou away from earth
There's rest for thee in heaven
If ever life should seem
To thee a toilsome way
And gladness cease to beam
Upon its clouded day
If like the wearied dove
O'er shoreless ocean driven
Raise thou thine eye above
Thy better rest is in heaven
But O! if thoughtless flowers
Throughout thy pathway bloom
And gaily fleet the hours
Unstained by earthly gloom
Still let not every thought
To this poor world be given
Not always be forgot
Thy better rest in heaven
When sickness pales thy cheek
Or dims thy lustrous eye

And pulses low and weak
Tell of a time to die
Sweet hope from earth shall whisper then
Tho' thou from earth be riven
There's bliss beyond thy ken
There's rest for thee in heaven
   J H Bright, Dover Apr. 29th 1838

[page 20]

A Happier Clime
When sailing on this troubled sea
Of pain, and tears, and agony,
Though wildly roar the waves around,
With restless and repeated sound,
'Tis sweet to think that on our eyes
A lovelier clime shall yet arise;
That we shall wake from sorrow's dream
Beside a pure and living stream.

Yet we must suffer here below
Unnumbered pangs of grief and wo
Nor must the trembling heart repine
But all unto its God resign
In weakness and in pain made known
His powerful mercy shall be shown
Until the fight of faith is o'er
And earth shall vex the soul no more
  HG
  Dover March 13th 1842

[page 21]

To a Friend
Remember Me
When morning beams with splender bright
In *western lands* doth rise
And sprinkle o'er with rosy light

The fair and tranquil skies
When musick's notes are chanted forth
And heard from ev'ry tree
In this gay hour of nature's mirth
My friend   remember me
And when the beauties of the day
Are past, and night have come
And curtained round the bright and gay
With sad and pensive gloom
Then as before the alters shrine
You humbly bend the knee
And supplicate for grace divine
O then   remember me
　　Elvira Burr

[page 22]

Selected

a.

"Who can find a virtuous Woman? for her price is far beyond rubies
The heart of her husband doth safely trust in her, so that he shall have
　　no need of spoil,
She will do him good and not evil all the days of her life,
She stretcheth out her hands to the poor; yea she reacheth forth her
　　hands to the needy.
Strength and honor are her clothing; and she shall rejoice intime to
　　come.
She openeth her mouth with wisdom, and in her tongue is the lawot
　　kindness."
　　Dover July 2, 1848   L. B.

b. Autumn
Sweet sabbath of the year,
While evening lights decay,
Thy parting steps methinks I hear
Steal from the world away
Amid thy silent flowers
Tis sad but sweet to dwell

Where falling leaves and drooping flowers
Around me breathe
Fare well
   L. B.

[page 23]

The Evening Hour
This is the hour when memory wakes
Visions of joy that could not last
This is the hour when fancy takes
A survey of the past
She brings before the pensive mind
The absent scenes of earlier years
And who long have been consigned
To silence and to tears
The few we liked the one we loved
A sacred hand came stealing on
And many a form far hence removed
And many a pleasure gone
This is the hour when fancy wreaths
Her spells round that could that could not last
This is the hour that memory breaths
A sigh to pleasures past
   Nathan Lazelle, Dover December 15. 1839

[page 24]

On Friendship
Selected
Friendship is a pleasure so refined
It serves to elevate the mind
I've loved it from my earliest youth
And more than once have felt its truth
Its strongly woven in this heart
The strings will break before they'll part
It boasts a noble growth on these our coasts
But how superior will it shine

Transplanted to its native clime
There in heaven may we meet
And an immortal friendship greet.
 Lydia C. Lazelle, Dover Dec. 15. 1839

[page 25]

To The Memory of Mrs. Lucy Howard who died Feb. 3rd 1841
Dear Sister I have left you and bade you adieu
I never on earth shall again see you
Your body is laid in the cold grave to rest
But I trust your soul is among the blest.
While I am journeying in this world of sin
you are singing the praises of your heavenly King
You are freed from the cares and sorrows of life
Your sufferings are over you have ended the strife

Rest sweetly my friend in your lowly abode
May nothing disturb you till awaken'd by God
When the Arch Angel shall sound your dust will arise
O then may I meet you above the skies.
 Harriet Gould
 Dover Feb. 7th 1841

[page 26]

Friendship to you while life remains
And may you land where glory reigns
May smiling mercy cheer each scene
And sorrow never intervene
 Abigail Sherman

[page 27]

How sweet when rests my weary head,
At twilight hour, on nature's pillow,
How sweet where tranquil scenery's spread,
To gaze upon the trembling willow.

To view a smiling landscape far,
Green fields, and forest trees in motion,
The sapphire arch, the twinkling star,
Inspire my heart with calm devotion.

Thus would I bid this world adieu,
My soul with holy hope collected,
And by the star of faith's bright view,
See heavenly mercy's face reflected.
    Esther A. Gould

[page 28]

The rambles of Death.
Selected
Death came to a beautiful boy at play
As he played 'mong the summer flowers,
But they seem'd to wither and die away
In their very sunniest hours.

"I have come," in a hollow voice said Death,
"To play on the grass with thee'
But the boy look'd frighten'd and held his breath
In the midst of his childish glee.

"Away, away from my flowers," he said,
"For I know, and love thee not."
Death look'd at the boy, and shook his head:
Then slowly he left the spot.

He met a maiden in girlhood's bloom,
And the rose on her cheek was bright,
And she shuddered as tho' a ghost from the tomb
Had risen before her sight.

She sood by the brink of a fountain clear —
In its waters her beauty view'd,
When Death with his haggard face, drew near,
And before the maiden stood.

"Fair damsel," he said, with a courtly pride,
"To thee I this goblet gaff,"
But she turned with a buoyant step aside,
And fled with a ringing laugh.
He journeyed on, where an old man sat
On the trunk of a worn-out tree —
A poor old man — for his held out hat
Was a symbol of beggary.

Death drew quite near, till the old mans eyes
Were rais'd to his wrinkled face;
With a frightened look of wild surprise,
He rose from his resting place.

"I come to succor" Death mildly said,
But the old man would depart —
Again he look'd and shook his head'
For he knew full well his mark.

"They all of them, shuddering, turn away —
The boy in his childish glee,
The maiden young, and the old man gray:
Yet they all shall come to me."

And he gather'd them all, for the boy was weak,
The old man yielded his breath —
And the rose grew pale on the maidens cheek,
As she sank in the arms of Death.
   Melvina Burr, Dover May 21st 1848

[page 29]

Reflections

When in childhood's sunny morning
Gaily bounds the heart and high
If the dark and stormy future
All were spread before the eye
Who would wish to live and meet it
Who would not sooner die

When the waves of disappointment
O'er hopes brightest scenery roll
When the loved in death are sleeping
When the anguish sinks the soul
Who without a friend to share it
Could drink all life's bitter bowl

It is meet that scorn and scandal
Toil and strife should wait us here
Cloud and storm will only fit us
For a holier happier sphere
Sorrow flings no poisoned arrow
Where affection wipes the tear
  H A Gould
  Dover May 20th

[page 30]

[30a]

If Jesus' smile I have
When I am call'd to die
How cheerfully I'll leave
This dull mortality
  Harriet Gould
  May 20th

[30b]

The sting of death will cease to be
If I by faith my Savior see
  H.A.Gould

[page 31]

Contemplate when the sun declines
Thy death with deep reflection
And when again he rising shines,
The day of resurrection
  H. A. G.

[page 32]

Farewell unto this wilderness
Of dismal foes and sad distress
Now from the top of Pisgah I
The heavenly Canaan do espy

1

I love that doth no limits know
That save me from eternal woe
And fed and doth'd me all my days
Inspire my soul to sing thy praise

2

Farwell my wife whom I do love
Thy better husband is above
When I am gone he will support
And be thy refuge and thy fort

3

I hope in heaven to see your face
When death shall and your mrtal race
When we shall reign with Christ our king
And everlasting praises sing

4

Farewell my children near and dear
May Jesus for your help appear
And be your father kind and just
When I am rotten in the dust

5

Farewell my parents now Farewell
I hope in heaven with you to dwell
Let not this worlds deceitful toyes
Disturb your peace and heavenly joys
Farewell my brothers sisters too
Ah many a time I've prayed for you
That God would fill you with his love
What I might meet you all above
Farewell my friends whom I do prize
Christ is your friend who never dies
Farewell my foes may Jesus shine

Into your hearts with light divine
Farewell vile body soon you must
Be meat for worms that breed in dust
Kind angel guards will bear my soul
Up where unbounded pleasures roll
My God will raise my scatter'd dust
At the revival of the just
And soul and body reunite
In perfect peace and sweet delight
And now dear Lord what have I more
To do upon this mortal shore
O raise me to thy courts above
To swim in seas of perfect love
     Dover Feb 25th 1838

[page 33]

When gathering clouds around I view
And days are dark and friends are few
On him I lean who not in vain
Experienced very human pain
He sees my wants allays my fears
And counts and treasures up my tears

If aught should tempt my soul to stray
From heavenly virtues narrow way
To fly the good I would pursue
Or do the sin I would not do
Still he who felt temtation's power
Shall guard me in that dangerous hour

If wounded love my bosom swell
Deceived by those I prized too well
He shall his pitying aid bestow
Who felt on earth severer wo
At once betrayed, denied, or fled
By all who shared his daily bread

When vexing thoughts within me rise
And sore dismayed my spirit dies
Yet he tho once vouchsafed to bear
The sickning anguish of despair
Shall sweetly sooth shall gently dry
The throbbing heart the streaming eye

When sorrowing o'er some stone I bend
Which covers all that wasa friend
And from his voice his hand, his smile,
Divides me for a little while
Thou Savior see'st the tears I shed
For thou didst weep o'er Lazarus dead

And O when I have safely past
Through every conflict but the last
Still still unchanging watch beside
My painfull bed — for thou hast died
Then point to realms of cloudless day
And wipe the latest tear away
   S. Curtis Lazell

[page 34]

Alone I walked the ocean strand
A pearly shell was in my hand
I stooped and wrote upon the sand
My name the year and day
As onward from the spot I passed
One lingering look behind I caste
A wave came rolling high and fast
And washed my lines away

And so methought 'twill shortly be
With every mark on earth from me
A wave of dark oblivion's sea
Will sweep across the place
Where I have trod the sandy shore
Of time and been to me no more

Of me my day the name I bore
To have mo track nor trace

And yet with him who counts the sands
And holds the waters in his hands
I know a lasting record stands
Inscrib'd against my name
Of all this mortal part has wrought
Of all this sinking soul has thought
And form there fleeting monents caught
For glory or for shame
   Dover June 18th 1837
   Harriet A Gould

[page 35]

Broken Ties
The broken ties of happier days
How often do they seem
To come before the mental gaze
Like a rembred dream

Around us each disseverd chain
In sparkling ruin lies
And earthly hands can ne'er again
Unite these broken ties

The parent of our infant home
The kindreds that we loved
And from our arms perchanse may roam
To distant scenes removed

Or we have watched their parting breath
And closed their weary eyes
And sighed to think how sadly death
Can sever human ties
   L C Burr

[page 36]

Lines Written on the Death of a Young Lady

Hark! Hark! my young friends 'tis a melancholy sound
The arrows of death they fly swiftly around
There was one of our number who was all in her bloom
She has been call'd away by death and laid in her tomb

Altho she is dead she is speaking unto you
And her language is this bid your follies all adieu
Prepare you to meet the last sorrows of life
That your souls may be launched in the mansions of light

But tho she is dead she will soon be forgot
Her friends and relations will soon her forget
Their sighs and their tears will all be wiped away
For there she lies moldering and turning into clay
And now she is buried she invites you to come
And read the inscription you will find on her tomb
Go look you in the churchyard and read you with care
Remember 'tis not long before your bodies will lie there
    HA Gould

[page 37]

For Mrs Harriet A. Gould

While over life's darkling plain
Unheeded as we roam,
Through many a path of hoy and pain,
God leads his children home.
And though sometimes in prospect viewed,
The winding way seems dark and rude;
Ah! who the backward scene hath scanned,
But blessed his Father's guiding hand.
    Hannah S. Jones.
    Dover June 11th 1838

[page 38]

This world with its glories and all we hold dear
Now shining in Beauty must soon disappear
But a moment they glitter then fade to the eye
Like meteors of night that flash o'er the sky
Home Home Sweet Home
There is no place like home There is no place like home

Though pleasures rich clusters now temptingly glow
In the frost of the grave no flowers shall blow
And home that we loved deserted become
And fond ones we cherished shall sleep in the tomb
. . . .
Then give me a home far up in the skies
Where hope never withers where hope never dies
The home of the christian where pilgrims are blest
And the exiles of earth forever shall rest
    Abby M Gould
    Belvidere March 22 1849

[page 39]

The flowers that bloomed around us,
Have drooped away and died,
And friends we loved who are now removed,
Have perished by our side.

The peace that once has known them,
Shall know them now no more,
And now with them life's fevered dream,
That cheered them on is o'er.

Thus all that's fair in nature,
To marked for stern decay,
In every place the human race,
By Death are nade a prey.

Then let us choose the path of life,
And well ourselves prepare,

And then we may when called away,
Go where our kindred are.
   L. G.
   March 25th 1841

[page 40]

This token of Friendship accept,
Though not clothed in an elegant style,
And oft, when you see it, reflect,
On the writer, your Friend, for awhile.

Oft think of my friendship for you,
And affection, which never shall fail,
Affection, which warm, yet is true,
Which often my bosom shall fill.

May the blast of misfortune ne'er rise,
To afflict you with sorrow, and woe,
Not a cloud to e'er darken your skies,
While on life's transcient journey you go.

May the sun of prosperity shine,
May Religion enliven your way,
And numberless blessings divine,
Still attend you through life's fleeting day.

[page 41]

There is something great in that person
against whom the world exclaims, at whom
every one throws a stone, and on whose
character all attempt to fix a thousand
crimes without being able to prove one
   Zimmerman

[page 42]

[42a]

If you never judge another till you have
calmly observed him, till you have heard him
heard him out, put him to the test, and
compared him with yourself and others, you
will never judge unjustly

    Lavater

[42b]

Riches do not consist in the possession of wealth
but in the use of it

    Socrates

[42c]

If thou wouldst be happy bring thy mind
to thy condition, and have an indifferance for more
than what is sufficient

    Wm Penn

[42d]

All that you see, judge not,
All that you hear believe not
All that you know tell not.
All that you can do, do not

    Alvin Gould

Addenda to *Harriet Gould's Book*

The following poems represent addenda to the manuscript, Harriet Gould's
Book. *Written on separate sheets, they had been kept together in an envelope
placed within the covers of the manuscript.*

I.
Lines on the Death of Warren S. Gould who died April 6th 1843

Oh can it be a year has fled
Its scenes of grief and joy
Since we were bending o'er the bed
Of thow my sainted boy?   4

Since almost with a broken heart
I watched each faint drawn breath
And felt I could not with thee part
To meet the embrace of death   8

My first born son — Oh what a tie,
Was that to rend apart
My lovely one that he must die
Thrust daggers to my heart   12

Ten thousand schemes of love and joy,
Which fathers always plan
And dream about a smiling boy,
When he shalt be a man.   16

Ten thousaand hopes that [fairly?/ early] work
And down the future smiled
All these would die beneath the stroke
That should destroy my child   20

Until I saw the closing gasp
And we were forced to part
I did not know how firm a grasp
He had upon my heart.   24

That fatal blow — that fatal blow,
That smote so fair a son,
I did not know I loved him so
Until the deed was done.   28

When one we love is born away
And we are left behind
How thick the beacons of memory play
And cluster round the mind.   32

The acts he did, the words he spake,
The pleasing smile he wore
From drear oblivion's dreams awake
As fresh as e'er before.   36

Alas my boy, though sundered far
Beyond those orbs that shine,
I look above those twinkling stars
And claim thee still as mine.   40

He's stepped within the peaceful tomb
As if he had gone to find
A quiet rest within his room
And left his friends behind   44

Oh it shall be a source of joy
That earth so near to heaven
That love can go and clasp my boy
And feel a welcome given   48

Oh thow that smitest but to beat?/[heal]
I have felt thy chastening rod
Assist me now to do thy will
And put my trust in God   52

That when I've trod life's journey o'er
And at death's portal stand
My Warren at the opening door
May wave his little hand   56

And cry fear not the threshold crossed
You'll find no thrill but joy
This is the better one you lost
He is now an angel boy   60
     Dover, Oct. 20th 1851

II. Lines Written on the death of Warren,
son of John, &, Harriet Gould.

Wake harp, assume again thy plaintive strains,
And sing, in pensive tones, while funeral numbers flow
A touching theme, of blighted youth, of hopes parental,
Blasted by the hand of death, now waits my lyre —
     Death, the despoiler of our earthly bliss, the marer
Of our joys, surveys with eager eye the young & fair
Passes, full of infirmity and age, — for sprightliness
And youth — breathes mildew o'er our brightest scenes,
And stamps *mortality,* on what we hold dear.
     It was a lovely boy, a child of promise fair.
     A bud just bursting into bloom, when, nipped by
Frosts of dire diseases, it drooped and fell, as if too fragile
To endure the damps of time, too tender long to grow on
Earth's hard soil, it fell, or rather by its heavenly Sire
Transplanted to more genial lands — to a far gentler clime —
To its own native soil, forever there to bloom, a fadeless flower.
     A favored one! as though it did disdain the fickle scenes
Of Time, it early closed its eyes on earth, and soared to
Realms of bliss — the Paradise of God, and now, at home,
Among the Spirits blest, of that sweet land, it tunes its
Little harp, and sings with Seraphs to the Lamb of God.
     Oh happy child! Who would recall thee back?
Though nature fond, that in parental bosums ever lives laments thy
     loss

Tho' sad thy vacant place amid the social band;
Tho' empty be thy seat, around thy Father's board;
Yet faith beholds thee now around thy other Father's throne,
Among the holy ones that gather there.

    We view thy glorious change, and sinking out of self,
Adore that God, who cleansed thee by his own dear blood
From foul stains of native guilt, and took thee
To himself.   His ways are equal, just, and good.
We bow in humble awe, and fain would say,
His will be done.   But should fond memory,
Reaching back to what thou *wast,* call up sad feelings
For thy early fate, we'll take an eye of faith, and
See thee as thou *art,* all holy — heavenly — pure; then
Will sweet resignation say — "sure all is well."
We rest assured, that when each angel's trump shall
Sound, commanding the drear grave to yield her charge,
Then shall thy sleeping dust awake and stamped with
Immortality, reunite forever with thy happy soul, in
Union all divine, eternally to live in realms above, enrapt
In visions beatific,

    Sweet Child, thou art gone to the regions of day,
The breath of the morning hath borne thee away;
To Christ, who redeemed thee thy happy souls flown,
Forever to be with thy Savior, at home.

We will not lament, for *our* loss is *thy* gain;
We wish not thy return to this region of pain;
For we feel, thou hast entered a permanent rest,
In that happy Country — the land of the blest.

These lines were written merely to beguile a lonely hour, without a design of presenting them to the eyes of any. However, trusting you will forbear to *critisize* them, or at least, will be indulgent enough to pass by their imperfections, I take the liberty of sending them to you, as a token of respect.

    Your &c
    Mrs. Gould   Sarah A. Sparks

III.

Oh can it be that Wayland's dead
My lovely darling son
Oh can it be his soul has fled
To its eternal home.   4
How sad how very sad the hour
That bore him far away
Oh ne'er while memory holds her seat
Shall I forget that day.   8
But deeper sadder is the gloom
That rests on all around
As one by one the days move on
In their appointed rounds,   12
And still my babe returns no more
To cheer my aching heart
The silken ties that bound him there
Have all been torn apart.   16
How can I check the falling tear
How can I hush the sigh
Dear Savior let me ever feel
Thy grace and presence nigh   20
I know my boy though lost to me
Has reached the blissful shore
The soul divested of its clay
Can sing its suffering o'er   24
He's safely housed from every storm,
Secure on Jesus' breast.
O may we strive to meet him there
And share his blissful rest.   28
And while we tread the toilsome way,
Which oft is dark and drear
We know that both our darling boys
Are safe from grief and fear.   32
And if to God we faithful prove,
And act the Christians part
We'll join them in that world above
Where we shall never part.   36

IV.

He sleeps beneath this fir tree bough
Our darling and our joy
The angels came and took from us
Our little cherub boy.   4

His little feet, no more we hear,
Nor see his smiling face;
He's gone from us to Jesus' arms,
We've none to fill his place.   8

His playthings all lay on the shelf,
There's none to use them now;
These little hands we used to chafe,
We'll clasp no more below.   12

His pleasant smile we now do miss,
Which once our hearts did cheer;
His "good night, pa, and mamma too",
On earth no more we'll hear.   16

For that dear Savior who on earth,
Bid children come to him,
Has taken our dear little boy
Up from this world of sin.   20

To dwell in that delightful land,
Where sorrow ne'er can come;
And where all those who love the Lord
May find a "welcome home".   24

V.

Weeping Mother; what can feeble friendship say
To sooth the anguish of this mournful day
They, they alone, whose hearts like thine have bled
Know how the living sorrow for the dead   4
Each tutored voice that seeks such grief to cheer
Strikes cold upon the weeping parent's ear

I've felt it all alas too well I know
How vain all earthly power to hush thy wo   8
God cheer the childless Mother, tis not given
For man to ward the blow that falls from heaven
I've felt it all as thou art feeling now
Like thee with stricken heart and aching brow   12
I've sat and watch'd by dying beauty's bed
and burning tears of hopeless, anguish shed
I've gazed upon the sweet but pallid face
And vainly tried some comfort there to trace   16
I've listen'd to the short and struggling breaths
I've seen the cherub's eye grow dim in death
Alas I've veiled my head in speechless gloom
And laid my little ones to rest in the cold and silent   20
tomb.
   Mother

VI. Lines on the death of Lucien P. Howe who died
June 19th 1865; by his mother (Abigail Gould Howe)

Death has been here and borne away
The idol of our home,
The joy and pride of parents hearts
Now sleeps within the tomb.   4
Our hearts are bowed with heavy grief
Our dwelling lone and sad
It seems that earth has not the power
Again to make us glad.   8
There's not a place within our home
Or scene to which we turn
But speaks unto our bleeding hearts
Lucien will not return.   12
Thrice death has come within our fold
Three lovely boys ar gone
Their little graves are side by side
How can we cease to mourn   16
Our first sweet bud was called away

He filled our home with bliss
That was a heavy blow to bear
But not a blow like this   20
At dawn of day we miss the voice
That once our hearts did cheer
"Good morning father" mother too
On earth no more we'll hear.   24
We miss him through the weary day
And when our work is done
We still can see his vacant place
Alas, Alas, he's gone.   28
We love to think of all he said
The pleasing smile he wore
And memory brings him back again
Just as he was before.   32
He was too fair for this cold earth
Too lovely long to stay
We loved him Oh could love have saved
He had been ours to day.   36
But still amid the deepest gloom
There shines a light from far
Our lovely little flowers now bloom
In heaven where angels are,   40
The woes of time, the blight of sin
The tempters fearful snare
Sickness and pain earth's partings too
Will not be theirs to share.   44
Then let us as we journey on
Through lifes dark rugged way
Strive so to live that we may meet
In Heaven's eternal day.   48
We'll look beyond the bounds of time
Since earth has lost its charm
And seek for our poor hearts to find
In faith a healing balm   52
We'll go to Him who once had trod

Afflictions thorny way
A man of sorrows used to grief
He'll not turn us away. 56

VII. Lines occasioned by the death of Little Irwin. — Who died
Dover, April 2nd. 1854. [by Marian, sister of Abigail]

"Death loves a shining mark."
Oh Death, how solemn is thy coming; Thy stern mandate is felt and acknowledged by all the world. The weeds of mourning, we so often see
tell too well the loss of friends. A few short days ago I saw a lovely babe,
sleeping in death's cold arms. It was a sweet budern trusted to fond parents and all their hopes were centered in their child — The flowers of
summer had bloomed and died; the wild winds of winter had chanted
their last sad requiem; and Spring with her purling brooks and fragrant
flowers, were once more coming to greet the child of beauty; and diffuse
into his soul a greater love for his Creator. But death came also; and the
cold inanimate formof a dear child of scarce a year told where he had
done his work.

How my heart bled for that mother as she bent for the last time over
the remains of the lovely sleeper, beautiful even in death. Thy sorrow is
great dear mother and it well becomes thee to weep for the departed.
The hand of affliction has been laid heavily upon thee; "But perhaps it is
good that you have been afflicted" A child as dear as your own life you
have seen consigned to the cold and silent tomb. But there is a balm for
every wound and the same hand that afflicts can heal. The loved of earth
has been called away but a little while before. Soon you will join him in
that star-lit home on high, never more to part.
The Father's hopes have been crushed and the Mother's heart left bleeding in early life; for the loss of their first born and only child. But grieve
not mourning friends for we trust he is far beyond the pains of this world
of sorrow and death in the bright abodes of Heaven.

His little voice breathes forth the tone,
To soothe a mothers aching heart;
It points you from this world so lone,
To act a *Christian's noble* part.

Father if thy heart is sad,
Look to God for he is good;
"For his mercies they endure,
Ever faithful, ever sure."

Mother if thy sad heart pains thee.
God's kind hand wil e'er sustain thee;
Bowed by grief and sorrow here,
Lift thy aching heart in prayer.

Then come dear parents dry your tears,
And think its for the best;
For Christ has called him from your side
With Angels now to rest.

The turf is green above the mound,
Neath which the floweret lies;
But come fond parents *hope* and *trust,*
His home is in the skies.

Though the silent sods now press,
Above thy "Little Irwin's" breast;
Though in the grave the casket lies,
The gem still sparkles in the skies.

A little while you linger here,
And freely shed the mourners tear;
Then on light wings so bright and pure,
You'll meet him in his glory there.

His little hands clasp on the throne,
Singing "Father, Mother come;
And stay with me in my bright home,
Where sorrow cannot enter in.

Think dear friends he had no sins to be forgiven. He only blossomed here on earth then soared away to Heaven I think could he but speak to you from yonder fair bright world He'd whisper to the parents dear weep not for Winni *now*

Farewell dear Irwin now farewell,
A long and last adieu;
You never can come back to us,
But we must go to you.
/ / / / / / / / / / / / / / / / / /
These kind words to parents dear
Will I present to you;
Hoping and trusting you may find,
A home in Heaven, "Adieu."
 From Marian —

VIII. Some Time

Some time, when all life's lessons have been learned,
And sun and stars forevermore have set,
The things which our weak judgement here has spurned —
The things o'er which we grieved with lashes wet —   4

Will flash before us out of life's dark night,
As stars shine most in deeper tints of blue;
And we shall see how all God's plans were right,
And how what seemed reproof was love most true.   8

And we shall see, that, while we frown and sigh,
God's plans go on as best for you and me;
How when we called, he heeded not our cry,
Because his wisdom to the end could see;   12

And, e'en as prudent parents disallow
Too much of sweet to craving babyhood,
So God, perhaps, is keeping from us now
Life's sweetest things because it seemeth good.   16

And if, some time coming led with life's wine,
We find the wormwood, and rebel and shrink,
Be sure a wiser hand than yours or mine
Pours out this potion for our lips to drink;   20

And if some friend we love is lying low,
Where human kisses cannot reach his face,

Oh! do not blame the loving Father so,
But bear your sorrow with obedient grace.   24

And you shall shortly know that lengthened breath
Is not the sweetest gift God sends his friend,
And that sometimes the sable pall of death
Conceals the fairest boon his love can send.   28

If we could push ajar the gates of life,
And stand within, and all God's working see,
We could interpret all this doubt and strife,
And for each mystery find a key.   32

But not to-day. Then be content, poor heart:
God's plans, like lilies pure and white, unfold;
We must not tear the close shut leaves apart:
Time will reveal the calyxes of gold.   36

And if through patient toil we reach the land
Where tired feet, with sandals loose, may rest,
When we shall clearly know and understand,
I think that we shall say that "God knew best."   40

Introduction: The Forgotten Language of Sentimentality

1 See in particular Sigourney's "The Unspoken Language," in which she lays out the superiority of this language of sentiment to later, learned, verbal languages. (For a full discussion of this poem see chapter 6.) This is one of several poems in which Sigourney articulates a theory of sentimental communication. Another is "Eve," in which Sigourney engages in a critique of sentimentality's limitations even as she deploys them. The work of Sigourney suggests a greater consciousness of the cultural and literary ramifications of her aesthetic choices than has been conventionally granted to sentimentalists. (Quotations here follow the 1860 edition of her *Illustrated Poems* cited by poem title and line number.)

2 In this study I am interested in producing what Clifford Geertz in *The Interpretation of Cultures* calls a "thick description," one that will foreground what the "symbolic action" of sentimentality "has to say about itself" (27).

3 As I discuss more fully later, it has been a characteristic of twentieth-century approaches to American sentimentality to focus on narrative rather than poetry. This is not to say that sentimental poetry was not considered an embarrassment to the American literary tradition, but that the ground of the debate over the role of sentimentality in American culture was established in discussions of the American novel such as Herbert Ross Brown's 1940 *The Sentimental Novel in America* and James Baldwin's 1949 essay on *Uncle Tom's Cabin* entitled "Everybody's Protest Novel."

4 At the same time as describing nineteenth-century poetry as "inconsequential" to the development of later American poetry, Lawrence Buell's survey of New England literary history calls for the kind of aesthetic and cultural reevaluation that the nineteenth-century sentimental or domestic novel has been receiving since the late 1970s. I am indebted to Professor Buell for his encouragement on this project. Recent revisions of major teaching anthologies such as the *Heath Anthology of American Literature* or the *Norton Anthology of American Literature* contain larger selections of the "fireside" poets as well as more selections from the women poets of the last century. This trend suggests that the perception of the place, or rather non-place, of popular nineteenth-century American poetry is beginning to change as the repercussions of the

feminist revision of American literary history begin to be felt on more and more branches of the discipline.

5 See Hans Jauss's *Towards an Aesthetic of Reception* for a description of the importance of understanding what he calls the "horizons of literary expectations": "The reconstruction of the horizon of expectations, in the face of which the work was created and received in the past, enables one on the one hand to pose questions that the text gave an answer to, and thereby to discover how the contemporary reader would have viewed and understood the work" (171).

6 Benedict Anderson's concept of imagined communities laid out in his book of the same name has greatly influenced me here. I am also indebted to Fredric Jameson's call for the unpacking of the utopian aspects of patently ideological constructs in *The Political Unconscious.* This has allowed me to break down what I have come to feel is an unprofitable schism between arguments about sentimentality that attempt to position it as either progressive or regressive. The profound ideological work done through sentimentality relies on it offering its users a sense of utopian belonging and community at the same time that it provides for the production of class-defining boundaries and expressions of power. In a contemporary context, Vice President Albert Gore has been speaking on the need to exercise sympathy and empathy in the service of maintaining and perpetuating what he calls the community of Americans.

7 Thus, while I agree with David S. Reynolds's statement in *Beneath the American Renaissance* "that during the American Renaissance literariness resulted not from a *rejection* of socio-literary context but rather from a full *assimilation* and *transformation* of key images and devices from this context" (7), I cannot agree that antebellum literature is so easily divided between conventional and subversive modes. American sentimentality, as I define it, can be deployed in the service of the status quo or against it.

8 Poems in *Harriet Gould's Book* are cited herein by author and page number (and line number); full transcriptions appear in appendix 1 below. The poem quoted here is one of a group of eight mourning poems kept together in an envelope placed within the album; these poems (transcribed in appendix 2) are cited by author and roman numeral I–VIII (with line numbers as appropriate). While the poems are transcribed literatim in the appendixes, when they are quoted in the body of this book spelling is standardized and errors are silently corrected.

9 See part II for a more detailed discussion of the distinction I would like to make between these poems as redundant reproductions of what is lost rather than as replacements for what is lost.

Part One The "Language Which May Never Be Forgot"

1 Haight is best known for his important work on George Eliot, which did much toward establishing Eliot's twentieth-century reputation and much toward making the novel available to New Critical readings. Haight is not the only important modernist critic who began his career by looking at the women writers of the nineteenth century. F. O. Matthiessen, who was most firmly to revise the meaning of the American Renaissance, began his career with a biography of Sarah Orne Jewett (1969). The uneasy relationship on the part of both the New Critics and those who established the field of American studies to the sentimental tradition has been much noticed in the years since feminist revisions of literary and cultural studies began in the 1960s. The best discussions can be found in Susan K. Harris's *Nineteenth-Century American Women's Novel: Interpretative Strategies* and Suzanne Clark's *Sentimental Modernism: Women Writers and the Revolution of the Word.*

2 Newton Arvin, for example, in his 1962 literary biography of Longfellow, took great pains to dissociate himself from what he understood as the feminine contamination of his subject's work. The issue of gender in the formation of the modernist aesthetic has increasingly been noticed. Frank Lentricchia's entry on modernism for the *Cambridge History of American Literature* provides a good starting place for examining the way that gender inflected the anxieties that influenced the high modernists. The best book-length study of this is Suzanne Clark's *Sentimental Modernism.* But see Jerome McGann's *The Poetics of Sensibility,* which begins with a similar discussion but moves to attempt to recover just what it was that the modernists so feared.

3 I am agreeing here with McGann, whose *The Poetics of Sensibility* is premised on the belief that "the twentieth-century reader's access to this kind of writing was short-circuited from the start" (1). James Baldwin's anxieties about the powers of sentimentality (anxieties about its ability to incite mob violence, about its complicated role in a rational political world), which he expresses in "Everybody's Protest Novel" (1949), should be taken seriously. Writing in the shadow of totalitarianism, Baldwin, like Hemingway's Frederick Henry, has a visceral knowledge of the dangerous residue of nineteenth-century culture.

4 To say that the poetics of sentiment has been elided is not to say that it has not continued to perform important work in American culture. Though an abstract understanding of the language has been lost (to academics in particular), Americans have continued to speak it and to be shaped by this speaking. I take up this subject in the epilogue to this book, in which I discuss some important instances of contemporary sentimental collaborations from several different cultural registers. As Joanne Dobson notes in "Reclaiming

Sentimental Literature" no other literary discourse illustrates so well the constructed nature of literary histories.

5   The mid-twentieth-century view of women's contribution to American literary culture is best represented by two publications of 1940: Herbert Ross Brown's *The Sentimental Novel in America* and Fred Lewis Pattee's *The Feminine Fifties*. By the time the war was over and the G.I. Bill had flooded universities it was no longer even necessary to dismiss the importance of women's work. This war, too, was over. Special cases could now be made for a few kinds of women's literature (as can be seen in Helen Papashvily's *All the Happy Endings* [1956]) and for the literature of a few women (as can be seen in the work during these years on Emily Dickinson).

6   Barbara Welter's 1966 article in *American Quarterly* proved to be a turning point in scholarly treatments of women's literary work, for it began the important challenge to the literary histories of the twentieth-century that had shaped the field in such a way as to exclude women.

7   I am indebted to the models provided by Richard Bushman, Mary Kelly, and Robert Gross for ways to expand our understanding of literary culture in nineteenth-century America. It is my contention that Longfellow, Sigourney, and Stowe are only the most prominent exponents of a cultural poetics of sentiment and that their prominence depended on, rather than drove, a widespread literary practice of writing that was part of an even wider spread practice of literary and extraliterary expression.

8   In her recent essay "Reclaiming Sentimental Literature" Dobson also sees "bonding" as one of the "principal theme[s] of the sentimental text" (265). She also, later in her essay, remarks on the representations of the "keepsake" tradition of presenting memorial gifts. Dobson's essay is one of the best attempts (along with McGann's) of describing the literary conventions of sentimentality. Dobson, McGann, and myself seem to be among the few who have come to realize the importance of verse in the sentimental tradition. My own work differs significantly from these since I am using the literary texts (and our rich vocabulary for describing the operation of literary texts) as keys to understanding a larger set of cultural practices.

1 Harriet Gould's Book: *Description and Provenance*

1   Lois Gould's epigraph transforms the limitless potential of this book into what it is: a keepsake album. Similar books were used for ledgers, daybooks, and so forth. Specialized books with elaborate engravings also became fashionable in some circles. Cindy Dickinson's "Creating a World of Books, Friends and Flowers: Gift Books and Inscriptions, 1825–60," provides a terrific introduction to this practice. Any thorough investigation of this practice

begins with Ralph Thompson's still unsurpassed study of 1936, *American Literary Annuals and Gift Books, 1825–1865.* These commercial publications were precursors to the vogue for commercially produced greeting cards later in the century.

These fancy editions have been the object of interest for collectors of prints and books and have, therefore, tended to pass into archives such as the American Antiquarian Society and the Vermont Historical Society. Dickinson stresses, without analyzing, the importance of personalized inscriptions in investing these texts with special meaning. The plainer versions are easily found in local historical societies throughout New England.

2   I would like to express my appreciation for the help given to me by two late relatives of Harriet Gould and her sister-in-law Abigail Gould Howe (whose work figures largely in the chapter 2). Mrs. Ruby Howe Jones and Mrs. Helen Gould Upton. Both women were in their nineties when I interviewed them about the people named in this album. Mrs. Upton had been town clerk of Dover for most of this century. Both she and Mrs. Jones were generous in their recollections of how these earlier generations of women figured in their family histories.

3   See William Gilmore's *Reading Becomes a Necessity of Life: Material and Cultural Life in Rural New England, 1780–1835* for a detailed study of the reading practices of this area. Inspired by Pierre Bourdieu, Gilmore examines the traces of literate behavior in order to discriminate the set of different "habitus" of reading in the upper Connecticut River valley. One of the local papers, *Spooner's Vermont Journal* of Windsor, Vermont, in 1825 featured Mrs. Hemans's "Stranger to the Ivy," "The Consumptive" by W , and "Oh There Is a Dream of Early Youth" with no author but attributed to *Blackwood's Magazine.* This selection reminds us that, as scholars of British Romanticism such as Anne Mellor and Jerome McGann have noted, the parameters of the Romantic movement looked quite different to those who were participating in it.

4   The American Antiquarian Society, for example, has a relatively large collection of New England keepsake books. Only a few of these, such as the "Album of Eugenia" and the "Album of Elizabeth," are as thoroughly completed as Harriet Gould's.

5   As we shall see later, the writers in Harriet Gould's album had a distinctly non-modernist relation to the concept of authoriality: most of the poems are signed by the person who copied them into the album rather than labeled with a particular author's name. This is common to most albums and keepsake books, which are interested less in originality than in authenticity. "Authentic" experience seems often to be expressed in the language of another.

6   Derek Pearsall in conversation pointed out to me the marked similarities between what I am describing here and medieval practices. The Findern Manu-

script from the late fourteenth and early fifteenth centuries provides an interesting parallel since it contains many rare examples of medieval women's private writings and was owned, apparently, by a woman. Most of the extant versions of Chaucer, for example, are found in miscellanies in company with works of much lesser quality and bearing the name of the most famous wonder, rather than any of the authors of the individual works.

7   I am indebted for this information to Ruby Howe Jones and Helen Gould Upton, as explained in note 2 above. Since the recollections of these women went back to the late nineteenth century, they were able to provide some insight into the practice of poetry in these families and into the personalities and relationship among the individuals who signed *Harriet Gould's Book*.

8   This tendency has been elaborated by Sacvan Bercovitch in his important study *The American Jeremiad*. Contemporary Vermont politics is much inflected by this nostalgic sense of the nineteenth century, despite much evidence indicating that actual nineteenth-century Vermonters were not conscious of their Edenic privilege.

9   This sense of "sentimental" comes both from dictionary definitions and a review of the evolution of the connotations of the term as an aesthetic signifier.

10 Wendy Simonds and Barbara Katz Rothman in *Centuries of Solace: Expressions of Maternal Grief in Popular Literature* specifically take on the puzzle posed by the high visibility of dead-baby poems and stories in the nineteenth-century popular press versus the current dearth of literary representations of child death. They mention that exceptions are found within anti-abortion literature, which features the confessions, in verse or prose, of women who have sought abortions. See Barbara Johnson's pathbreaking "Apostrophe, Animation, and Abortion" from 1986 for a formalist explanation of the function of apostrophe in women's poems on children and childbearing.

For an excellent overview of the distinctive role played by death and grief in nineteenth-century America, see Martha Pike and Janice Armstrong's collection of essays entitled *A Time to Mourn: Expressions of Grief in Nineteenth-Century America*. Increasingly, literary scholars such as Pamela Boker in *The Grief Taboo in American Literature* and Sharon Cameron in her discussion of Emerson's essay "Experience" have begun to take seriously the force of grief in nineteenth-century America.

11 It was as part of the rural cemetery movement of the early part of the century that Americans first began to sanction the dedication of capital to works of art such as sculpture and painting. Art historians of early American portraiture have shown that many portraits are of the dead.

12 I have been particularly fortunate that the area from which this manuscript album derives has been the subject of many in-depth studies from different disciplines. Nell Kull's *History of Dover, Vermont: Two Hundred Years in a Hill*

Town is a good local history of the area. Gilmore's *Reading Becomes a Necessity* is a thorough analysis of the reading in Windham County (including Dover, Vermont) from the Revolutionary War through the 1830s. The present-day owners of *Harriet Gould's Book,* Ralph Wesley Howe Jr. and his wife, Verne Bass Howe, helped greatly by opening their extensive collection of archival and secondary works on New England to me. In their collection, I had access to family records such as the *Howe Genealogy* and town memorabilia such as programs for the Wilmington and Dover Old Home celebrations. These programs contain accounts of the town, its families, and their experiences of change. My luck was in having such a wide variety of perspectives to draw on, from the interested and personal to the academic. Standard histories of Vermont include Walter Crockett, *Vermont: The Green Mountain State* and David Ludlum, *Social Ferment in Vermont, 1791–1850.* See also Muller and Duffy, *An Anxious Democracy: Aspects of the 1830s.*

13   In early 1877, Vermont published a separate declaration of independence from Great Britain as New Connecticut and later that year "petitioned Congress to be 'ranked among the free and independent states; and delegates therefrom, be admitted to the seat in Congress' " (Doyle 18). Its name was changed later that year to Vermont (Doyle 20). Vermont claims with Texas the distinction of having been a separate "Republic" before joining the United States of America.

14   See Gilmore's study of reading in New England for an analysis of the degree of literacy and the meaning of reading in Windham County. For in-depth studies of the differences between the two major valleys, see Benjamin Hall's 1858 *History of Eastern Vermont* and Chilton Williamson's 1949 *Vermont in Quandary, 1763–1825.*

15   See Kull chap. 7. This pattern of settlement was consistent with that of lower New England. Richard Bushman in *Refinement in America* provides a thorough historical survey and analysis of this process.

16   Although Vermont does contain some stands of old growth forest, most of the current forest is regrowth that occurred in this century or replanting directed by state and federal forestry services.

17   Joan Hedrick provides a vivid discussion of the Brattleboro water cure in chap. 16 of her biography of *Harriet Beecher Stowe.*

18   See the first five chapters of William Doyle's *The Vermont Political Tradition: And Those Who Helped Make It,* for a discussion of Bennington's key role in revolutionary activism. See also Williamson's *Vermont in Quandary, 1763–1825* for an illustration of how Vermont's mythic role as the seat of Yankee virtue begins to be established as early as Royall Tyler's satirical 1787 drama *The Contrast.* It is furthered by Stowe in *Uncle Tom's Cabin:* Ophelia, St. Clare, and Legree are all from Vermont, and it is the orderly Vermont households that

show up the moral laxness of the slave-holding household. Vermont maintains this position through the end of the century, as shown by Owen Wister's use of Bennington in *The Virginian* as the original home of Miss Molly Wood.

19   This distinction is established and supported by Gilmore in *Reading Becomes a Necessity.*

20   According to Doyle, somewhere between ten and fifteen thousand people heard Daniel Webster speak on July 8, 1840, on Stratton Mountain several miles from the town of Dover where Harriet and her family lived.

21   Only recently have historians of the book, sociologists, and literary historians (led by Mary Kelly, Cathy Davidson, William Gilmore, and Robert Gross) returned to the questions opened by William Charvat in his posthumously published study *The Profession of Authorship in America, 1800–1870.*

22   See part IV below for a full discussion of Twain and sentimentality.

23   Lawrence Levine's argument in *Highbrow/Lowbrow* holds for poetry as well as for theater. The status of poetry was perhaps even more vexed because of the cross-coding of gender and class valences in the practice of what was a private genre.

24   See Cathy Davidson on the vexed role of the novel in early America.

25   As Joan Hedrick and Mary Kelly have shown, the "parlor" was an important site of cultural production and consumption and is, therefore, one of the most crucial of the spaces of signification in the new bourgeois home of the nineteenth century.

26   The main conduit of the new aesthetic, which comes to be recognized as Romanticism, is the first Great Awakening, in which a spontaneous outpouring of fervent emotion is celebrated and enacted in the hymns sung communally by congregations. The other conduit in the colonial period was the secular poetry of Young, Gray, and More and, in the postrevolutionary period, that of women poets such as Felicia Hemans. The lead of revisionist scholars of the British Romantic era, such as Colin Campbell, Jerome McGann, and Anne Mellor, deserves to be followed by Americanists.

27   Ann Douglas in her path-breaking work, *The Feminization of American Culture,* attributes this process to many causes but cites particularly the effect of disestablishment on the ministry. For another account, one that pays more attention to the force of the Second Great Awakening, see David Reynolds's *Faith in Fiction.*

28   For a full description of this schism, see Sidney Ahlstrom's *A Religious History of the American People.* In chap. 40, "Slavery, Disunion, and the Churches," he explains that the "experience of the Baptists in the schisms brought on by sectional strife differed from that of other denominations primarily because its polity was so distinctly congregational that the chief national agency was in theory no more than a cooperative agency of churches" (663).

29   Linda Kerber in *Women of the Republic: Intellect and Ideology in Revolutionary America* describes this construction of femininity as addressing the gap made by the discourse of rights and the actual economic and political powerlessness of women. Though it addressed this gap, it did not erase it. This construct blends into and nourishes the construct of the cult of true womanhood, which also depended upon the ideological separation between the domestic and the political/economic spheres. Barbara Welter's essay "The Cult of True Womanhood" remains the best description of this phenomenon.

30   See my forthcoming article "Gendered Transcendentalisms: Elizabeth Oakes Smith and the *Sinless Child*," which provides a full reading of this important poem as part of a demonstration that our current understanding of the parameters of Transcendentalism will change under the burden of the new Americanist and recent feminist scholarship.

31   Baptists, for example, were the first of the organized American churches to take a formal stand against slavery (1833, in the New Hampshire Confession). This promoted the schism that created a separate Southern Baptist Church in the 1840s. See Ahlstrom 664–65 on Baptists and slavery and Baptists and spiritual emotionalism. See also Ann Douglas 36–37. The emotional anti-intellectualism that was already part of the Baptist value system from its founding was reinforced by the eighteenth century's Great Awakening and by the nineteenth century's Second Great Awakening.

32   In fact, the fourth school district of Dover was called the Canaan district.

33   For a full discussion of how this transformation occurs in narrative, see Reynolds, *Faith in Fiction*. Verse allows us to see how the nonprofessional people who may have been the consumers of the fiction Reynolds discusses acted on their world. Unlike Reynolds and Douglas, I attribute a greater degree of agency to the ordinary non-elite people of the time.

2   "We Shore These Fragments against Our Ruin"

1   See my introduction for a review of attempts to define sentimentality. As recently as 1993 the American Studies Association devoted a panel to the problem of defining sentimentality. Robert Sayre, while continuing the trend toward thematic definition, defines it by the presence of "four key values": "benevolence, sincerity, refinement and discipline" ("Redefining Sentimentality" 3).

2   Examples of the topoi of loss and bonding are legion in the popular poetry of the antebellum era; see the poetry of Longfellow, Whittier, Oakes Smith, and Sigourney. Of the many writers on sentimentality only Joanne Dobson in "Reclaiming Sentimental Literature" has taken extensive notice of loss as a formal trope. Unlike Dobson, I connect this thematic concern with the rhe-

torical characteristics of sentimentality as a mode. See part II of this study for discussion of the function of loss in the creation of the sentimental subject.

3   My next chapter deals extensively with the nature of these gift economies. While conventionally gift economies have been seen in contrast to (preceding or opposing) capitalist economies, anthropologists and sociologists have begun to pay increasing attention to the role that they play in contemporary capitalist economies. The classic descriptions are, of course, provided by Marcel Mauss and Mary Douglas. The best of the recent revisions is David Cheal's *The Gift Economy.* It was, not surprisingly, Lewis Hyde's lovely book of essays on poetry as a gift that pointed me in this direction.

4   The question of sentimental masculinity has begun to be noticed, as shown by the work of Gregg Camfield, Eric Haralson, and others. I take up the question in part III, where I contrast the use of sentimentality by two prominent sentimental poets: Sigourney and Longfellow.

5   Karen Halttunen makes a similar point in *Confidence Men and Painted Women.*

6   Several studies, including Carroll Smith-Rosenberg's important 1975 essay "The Female World of Love and Ritual: Relations between Women in Nineteenth-Century America," and Nancy Cott's 1977 *The Bonds of Womanhood: "Woman's Sphere" in New England, 1780–1835,* stress the importance and structure of affectionate relationships among women. My efforts are devoted to understanding the mechanisms of this affection.

7   *The Gates Ajar* is one of the main subjects of part II of this study.

8   I have been unable to discover if this Hannah F. Gould is one and the same as the published poet Hannah Flag Gould. Hannah Flag Gould was from southern Vermont, according to Rufus Griswold (*Female Poets*) but it is more than possible that the Hannah in Harriet's book is a local woman. A grave for a Hannah F. Gould exists in the same cemetery as Harriet Gould. Toward the conclusion Harriet Gould did copy one of the Hannah Flag Gould's poems into her *Book* (page 34).

9   Another word for the goal and action of sentimentalism, which links it more closely than is conventional with that other American exponent of Romanticism, is transcendence.

10 This definition is from the 1969 edition of the *American Heritage Dictionary of the English Language.*

11 The best argument for this construction is laid out by Fisher in his discussion of "making a thing a man" (*Hard Facts* chap. 4). See also Warhol, *Gendered Interventions,* for a persuasive argument that the breakdown between fiction and reality, represented and representor is one of the primary effects of the narrative interventions within nineteenth-century women's didactic fiction. I would argue that the frequency of direct address in the sentimental novel bespeaks an appropriation of traditionally lyric devices to the service

of prayer, linking the prayer-like power of verse to the more pedestrian mode of prose.

12 The exception, of course, would be the Quaker and Mennonite communities, who continue to employ the second-person informal pronouns.

13 Osgood published several volumes of poetry during her lifetime and was noted especially for her wit. Rufus Griswold's *The Female Poets of America* includes a number of her poems, including "'Ashes of Roses,'" an exemplary dead-baby poem. See Emily Stipes Watts's *The Poetry of American Women from 1632 to 1945* for a thorough discussion of Osgood's contribution to American poetics. Joanne Dobson has begun a useful revision of Osgood's reputation in *Strategies of Reticence*.

14 See Emerson's essay "The Poet," quoted in the epigraph to my introduction.

15 See Elaine Showalter, "Piecing and Writing." Showalter's use of the quilting metaphor seems particularly apt, but my research has shown that Showalter's understanding of this as gendered practice is unwarranted.

16 As Halttunen argues, authenticity was the most highly valued characteristic of the American middle-class person while hypocrisy was the most feared.

Part Two Sentimental Collaborations: Mourning and the American Self

1 See Lewis Stilwell's *Migration from Vermont* as well as Nell Kull's *History of Dover* or William Gilmore's *Reading Becomes a Necessity* for detailed descriptions of emigration from this area. Some of the famous people to have left Vermont include Brigham Young (from the same region as Dover) and Stephen Douglas. See also Philip Fisher's "Democratic Social Space."

2 Eric Hobsbawm's introduction to *The Invention of Tradition* suggests that family rituals, such as, I would argue, the exchange of mortuary poetry that becomes so prevalent during the nineteenth century, highlight the "contrast between the constant change and innovation of the modern world and the attempt to structure at least part some parts of social life within it as unchanging and invariant" (2).

3 The quoted passage appears in Theodor Adorno's critique of Thorstein Veblen's discussion of gift-giving as an extension of conspicuous consumption in the service solely of status. David Cheal argues throughout his *The Gift Economy* that this is the goal of gift economies in late capitalist cultures. Cheal concludes his study by asserting that the "dominant social definitions in the gift economy today are derived from a feminized ideology of love" (183).

4 Like Gillian Brown and Elizabeth Barnes, I, too, see sentimentalism as key to understanding the development of American individualism. While both of these authors provide insightful demonstrations of places where sentimentalism is reflected or modeled in various discourses, I am interested in how

sentimentality operates rhetorically to intervene in the construction of a new sense of subjectivity that can more adequately meet the needs of the non-traditional, non-European person. My own understanding of this process draws heavily on recent anthropologists' attempts to understand and describe the function and operation of gift economies within capitalist and modern cultures. See, for example, Weiner, *Inalienable Possessions.*

5 Sentimental collaboration would be a good example of what Hobsbawm describes as an "invented tradition," which comes into being as an attempt to "structure at least some parts of the social life" within the "constant change and innovation" of the modern world. An invented tradition seems as if it always has existed but in fact has a history that has been forgotten.

6 These articles can be the material items associated with the lost person, as in Gillian Brown and Lynn Wardley's discussions, or articles that have been created as vehicles or vessels for some aspect of the person. Marcel Mauss's discussion of gift economies explores the way that such an article or artifact exercises its force (the force of binding the possessor in a relationship of obligation with all of the previous donors) across distances of time and space (see "The Spirit of the Thing Given," *The Gift* 8–10). For interesting revisions of gift economies which take issue with Mauss's assumption that gift economies are characteristic only of non- or pre-market economies, see Weiner and Cheal.

7 I am indebted to James Carrier's "Gifts in a World of Commodities: The Ideology of the Perfect Gift in American Society" for pointing me to this passage in Emerson. Carrier's essay discusses "the way that [gifts] can be used to generate and define personal identity" (19). Carrier uses Emerson to voice the American ideology of the perfect gift that bears "the identity of the giver" (21).

8 The necessary predicate to the sentimental mode, like the elegiac mode, is loss. The gift of affection embodied in these products of the imagination is an attempt to counteract the experientially perceived fact of loss.

9 In discussing the operation of systems of total prestation ("anything or series of things given fully or obligatorily as a gift or in exchange, *The Gift* xi), Mauss says that such "institutions seem to us to be best represented in the alliance of pairs of phratries in Australian and North American tribes, where ritual, marriages, succession to wealth, community of right and interest, military and religious rank and even games all form part of one system and presuppose the *collaboration* of the two moieties of the tribe" (6; emphasis added). Although most of this statement is not to the matter here, my thinking about the relation between sentimental exchange and collaboration stems from this presupposition of Mauss's.

10 Gillian Brown's provocative study *Domestic Individualism: Imagining Self in*

Nineteenth-Century America also takes on the relationship between sentimentality and the liberal ideology of possessive individualism. I am much indebted to her analysis for the provocative idea of seeing the sentimental artifact as the object of fetishistic attachment on the part of its owner. Using *Uncle Tom's Cabin* as an exemplary case, Brown sees "Stowe's sentimental fetishism" as an investment of "domestic possessions with this sense of empathy between the object and its owner" (51). She goes on to argue that "sentimentalism images an elevated and sanctified fetishism, a fetishism that transforms commodities" by removing them from the market (51). Lynn Wardley also sees a "belief that some spirit inhabits all things" as a "familiar element of the nineteenth-century domestic ideology" (205). Wardley notes that the "uncanny power of Victorian material culture to elicit emotion, to provoke somatic response, bewitch, heal, or avenge wrong, resonates not only with the Catholic faith in the power of relics, but also with the Pan-African religions of the antebellum South" (205). The theories of the fetish that both Wardley and Brown seem to be adhering to suggest a parallel between sentimental cultures and so-called traditional or non market economies. Following the work of Cheal and Carrier, who study gift economies in twentieth-century Western cultures, I see the circulation of fetishized gifts (in this case poems or other symbolic containers of one's affections) as reinforcing and interrelating with the market economy of commodities. When, later in the century, the production and marketing of commercial greeting cards makes it possible to buy something that expresses one's sentiments at a moment of loss or transition, this bought object is able to perform the same kind of work that these homemade poems do.

11   According to Karen Halttunen in *Confidence Men and Painted Women* this anxiety generated Victorian America's binary of authenticity versus hypocrisy. The middle-class belief in the ability to conform oneself to sincerity had a necessary corollary belief in the ability to pretend to be sincere. I argue that the economy of emotions encouraged by the sentimental mode provides the creation and perpetuation of memories of transitory states. One's selfhood then seems to be dependent on being converted and circulated as a memory.

12   In other words, the literary and discursive features of American sentimentality are tied to its role in a "gift economy." For the purposes of this study, Cheal's definition of gift economy is probably the most applicable: "a system of *redundant* transactions within a moral economy, which makes possible the extended reproduction of social relations" (19; emphasis added).

*3   "And Sister Sing the Song I Love": Circulation of the Self
and Other Within the Stasis of Lyric*

1   See Mitchell Breitwieser's study of Mary Rowlandson's captivity narrative for
    a discussion of the stresses placed on Puritan ideology by the experience of
    grief.

2   A paradigm for the elegy as celebration of the poet's art, is, of course, Milton's
    "Lycidas." The loss of Lycidas to the "shepherd's ear" becomes the shepherd's
    gain; and the poem, "Lycidas," is the powerful proof of Milton's own genius if
    not proof of the transformation of lost Edward King into "the genius of the
    shore" (49, 183). In sonnet 55, Shakespeare's persona brags that "Not marble,
    nor the gilded monuments / Of princes, shall outlive this powerful rhyme."
    But the scarcity of poems that convey a greater sense of the eulogized than
    of the eulogizer belies this claim. The self-contradicting claim made on be-
    half of poetry is that it can provide a kind of immortality for the object of
    representation that is second only to the immortality of spiritual salvation.

3   See David Stannard's *The Puritan Way of Death* and "Where All Our Steps
    Are Tending: Death in the American Context" for discussions of the change
    from colonial to nineteenth-century mourning practices in New England.
    See also Anita Schorsch's *Mourning Becomes America* and two of Lawrence
    Stone's articles on the subject: "Death and Its History" and "Death in New
    England."

4   Phoebe Lloyd, in "Posthumous Mourning Portraiture," begins her essay on
    this once "flourishing industry" in this way: "Among the most engaging nine-
    teenth-century American paintings are portraits of children. It may be dis-
    turbing to discover, therefore, that often such likenesses were taken from the
    corpse." She goes on to argue that what "motivated this seemingly unusual
    practice was the desire to maintain family continuity; for if death took one
    member, the gap could be bridged through art" (71). Where Lloyd sees such
    practices as contradictions of Tocqueville's description of American individu-
    alism, I see them as efforts to reinforce and make viable such an individual as
    Tocqueville describes.

5   This is similar to the practice of quilting, which often made use of "found"
    materials and appropriated designs into a useful and beautiful object. Unlike
    quilting, which Elaine Showalter in "Piecing and Writing" sets up as a meta-
    phor for "an American poetics of gender" (222), men as well as women (as
    we shall see) practiced the art of sentimental mourning poetry. The death of
    children seems to have been as apt to be memorialized by men as by women.
    The death of Emerson's son, Waldo, inspired his efforts in different genres:
    lyric and essay. In addition, Emerson took care to move his son's grave to the
    new Forest Cemetery of Concord and to see to an adequate stone marker.

6   Reflecting the sociological bent of the mid–nineteenth century, Simonds opens with a set of statistics on childhood death: "According to a recent medical authority, twenty-two per cent. of our race die before they are one year old; thirty-seven per cent. before they are five years old; and nine-twentieths of the whole number born, die before reaching their fifteenth year" (preface). He does not comment on whether there was a perceived increase or decrease in child mortality since the previous era. The authors of a comprehensive study of "expressions of maternal grief in parlor literature," Wendy Simonds and Barbara Katz Rothman, disclaim connections made between degrees of affection for children and fertility or mortality rates.

7   In the medieval era, marriage often served as an analogy for the Trinity as well as an analogy for the relation between God and man. To collapse these analogies and to make one's spouse the object of an almost sacred veneration was to fall into uxoriousness, to risk cheating God of the love that was meant for him. Marriage with its hierarchical yet reciprocal responsibilities reinforced a particular model of secular and spiritual authority.

8   Unconditional love within a family, which such a model claims must be free and voluntary on both sides, reinforces a lateral, rather than hierarchical, model of spiritual and secular authority.

9   See part I for a full description of the provenance of this manuscript.

10   Harriet and John Gould had only one other living child, Frank Gould. I wish to thank the town clerk of Dover, Mary Lou Raymo, and the town clerk of Wardsboro, Vermont, Jackie Bedard, for their kind help during the winter of 1989.

11   Like the album, *Harriet Gould's Book,* this hair picture is from the private collection of Ralph Wesley Howe Jr. and Verne Bass Howe of Wilmington, Vermont. Both items were inherited from Mrs. Florence Howe, also of Wilmington. From the same source are two other albums from later in the century.

12   Although written in Harriet Gould's hand, "Lines Written on the Death of Warren" contains internal evidence that it was written by John Gould. This and the fact that at least one other poem of this set, poem V, was written by a man but entered into circulation by a woman, undercuts much of the conventional wisdom as to the gender valences carried by antebellum poetry.

13   The speaker of the poem uses the first-person singular pronoun and then refers to the plans for the future "Which fathers always plan." Since the majority of the remaining seven pieces in this set refer to or are written in the hand of Abigail Gould Howe, I have inferred that this poem may have been a gift from Harriet Gould to her younger sister-in-law and that the shared bond created by this exchange of poems accounts for the provenance of the manuscript in the Howe family collections rather than with the Gould family.

14   The juxtaposition of grief and joy established so early on in this poem becomes both a structural and a thematic key for understanding not only this poem but much of the other poetry of *Harriet Gould's Book*. This uneasy amalgamation of grief *and joy* becomes in the work of a later New England poet, Emily Dickinson, more fully assimilated to become elation or joy through grief.

15   I am thinking here in particular of Bradstreet's "In Memory of my Dear Grand-child Anne Bradstreet. Who deceased June 20 1669 being three years and seven months old," where she chastises herself in this way for immoderate grief: "More fool then I to look on that was lent, / As if my own, when thus impermanent." But I do not want to make too great a contrast between Bradstreet's Puritan practice and the Goulds' because they are clearly related, the one growing out of the other.

16   Warren Gould's cemetery is in an older, more open, cemetery on the Dover Common. The East Dover Cemetery in which Abigail Howe's children are buried, with its shading trees and intimate size, is much closer to the newer ideal of a rural cemetery promoted by the rural cemetery movement.

17   Tessellation, according to the *American Heritage Dictionary,* means "to form into a mosaic pattern, as by using small squares of stone or glass. M. C. Escher's elaborate and eye-bending graphics provide a good example (though in one dimension) of what I mean, in that ever more complicated patterns are formed by the accumulation and repetition of a simple pattern.

18   According to the *Howe Genealogy,* Abigail and Lorenzo Howe had a total of eleven children, including the four buried near each other in the East Dover Cemetery.

19   That both Gould and Howe use the occasion of the deaths of their children to engage in scrutinizing their own relationships with God suggests that the Protestant tradition of rigorous self-examination does not completely disappear from the expressions of the sentimental Christian ethos.

20   A figure of an eagle with outspread wings is imprinted on upper right-hand corner of the lined paper. The right-hand border of the page has been cut, slightly irregularly. Marian Sherman's poem (VII) is on a double sheet of what is apparently the same brand paper. The handwriting does not match Marian's but it is quite similar to Abigail Gould Howe's in "Lines on the Death of Wayland."

21   Sharon Cameron elucidates this concept in her discussion of Emily Dickinson's poetry entitled *Lyric Time.*

4 *The Circulation of the Dead and the Making of the Self in the Novel*

1 Numerous other examples of sentimental collaboration can be found including Susan Warner's *The Wide, Wide World* and Nathaniel Hawthorne's *House of the Seven Gables.*

2 Note, for instance, Harry's declaration that it is on behalf of his wife and child that he seeks the status of a freeman, and the many, many times it is a memento of a child that pushes Tom to heroic action: George's dollar, Eva's angelic visitation, the haunting of Legree by the token of Eva's hair that he perceives as a piece of his "sainted" mother's hair.

3 The relationship between speculation and sentiment is treated more fully in the Epilogue.

4 The tale of Midas is only one example.

5 See also the discussion of chapter 22, below. Integral to Eva's death scene is the book of Revelation, which structures her experience of dying to the extent that the world of summer villas on Lake Pontchartrain blends with the world described by the biblical writer called the Evangelist. The lake becomes the "sea of glass, mingled with fire," while the clouds become "great gates of pearl," through which Eva evidently expects to enter in the train of the 144,000 virgins of the lord (226–27).

6 Cassy is Eliza's mother; Emmeline is George's sister.

7 Stowe describes the contents of Mrs. Bird's drawer as "memorials gathered with many a tear and many a heart-break!" (73).

8 See Stowe 298. See pages 172–73 for the full text of George's verbal declaration of independence and page 332 for the narrator's reinterpretation of this: "To him, it is the right of a man to be a man, and not a brute; the right to call the wife of his bosom his wife, and to protect her from lawless violence; the right to protect and educate his child; the right to have a home of his own, a religion of his own, a character of his own, unsubject to the will of another."

9 Although it is conventional to consider *Uncle Tom's Cabin* as a sentimental novel, sentimentality is only the most important of several literary modes deployed by Stowe. Like *Moby-Dick,* the novel depends upon several modes, including allegory, realism, irony, and comedy. Also like *Moby-Dick,* it binds several genres, including poetry, hymns, drama, and ethnography, together into its narrative. At key points in the book the sentimental mode corrals these disparate modes and genres and redirects their energies toward the denial of all that makes this book a novel: that is, time and difference.

10 See Sharon Cameron's *Lyric Time: Dickinson and the Limits of Genre* for a fuller discussion of this.

11 Ann Douglas, in her introduction to the 1981 Penguin edition of *Uncle Tom's*

Cabin, describes Lincoln as "not being altogether facetious when he greeted Stowe in 1863 as 'the little lady who made this big war'" (19).

12   The abolitionist sentiments of the characters are assumed and gestured to throughout the story.

13   Up to Roy's death they had continued to call each other by pet names, which for the protagonist is a sign of their unique or model intimacy: "I wonder if all brothers and sisters keep up the baby-names as we did. I wonder if I shall ever become used to living without them" (3).

14   The narrator goes on to explain that "that was settled so long ago for me that it makes it very different. Roy was all there was" (8). Mary acknowledges throughout these early pages that the affection between the siblings was unusually strong and herself suggests that she and Roy have a mutual self-sufficiency that marriage could only disrupt. That she and her aunt accept that they are in analogous situations, having lost a brother and a husband respectively, further reinforces this idea. Is it possible that Phelps as a spiritualist is suggesting that Roy (short for Royal) and Mary are like the mythical Egyptian siblings Isis and Osiris?

15   Mary's aunt Winifred calls such poems the "work of Satan" (57).

Part Three The Competition of Sentimental Nationalisms: Lydia Sigourney and Henry Wadsworth Longfellow

1   My jumping-off place for much of the discussion that follows is Anderson's provocative *Imagined Communities,* which examines the paradox that it is the very sense of communal "fraternity that makes it possible, over the past two centuries, for so many millions of people, not so much to kill, as willingly to die for such limited imaginings" (7). The poems of Sigourney and Longfellow seem to offer some insight into what Anderson calls the important differences in the "style in which they [national communities] are imagined," since they seem to lie close to the "cultural roots" of American nationalism (6, 7). While the following discussion will flesh out this argument, it will also suggest a qualification of Anderson's characterization of these imaginings as "limited." For while they are no doubt limiting and no doubt (as I treat more fully in part IV's discussion of Twain and the betrayal of the promise of sentiment) fatal, the more interesting question is, why would a person, a people, choose to imagine in quite this way? In other words, what nonlimiting function could these imaginings have played? In what way could they have been liberating or problem-solving? Here of course I am merely following Fredric Jameson's lead that the key to understanding ideological power is to reveal its utopian promise as well as to unmask its oppressive mechanisms.

But I also been influenced by the work of one of Anderson's critics, Partha Chatterjee, whose *Nationalist Thought and the Colonial World* provided a useful summary of the political theories informing Anderson. But more important, Chatterjee insists on and more systematically than Anderson explains the irrational, extrarational nature of nationalistic thought. He underscores what the poetry of Longfellow and Sigourney seems to be pointing to—that nineteenth-century nationalism was in a perverse relationship to the Enlightenment that had spawned the nations: "If nationalism expresses itself in a frenzy of irrational passion, it does so *because* it seeks to represent itself in the image of the Enlightenment and *fails* to do so. For Enlightenment itself, to assert its sovereignty as the universal ideal, needs its Other; if it could ever actualize itself in the real world as the truly universal, it would in fact destroy itself" (17; emphasis in original). The nationalist poems of Sigourney and Longfellow give a pretty complete picture of what that "Other" of Enlightenment is: sentiment. The culture of sentiment, I argue, is the way in America that the promises of the Enlightenment have been able to be sustained.

2   As Werner Sollors notes in *Beyond Ethnicity*, the process of becoming American is related by Crèvecoeur to "images of continental sexual procreation and birth" so that these latent qualities are brought out in the almost sexual relationship with the new land and then passed on to later generations in an almost Lamarckian system of inheritance (76).

3   Crèvecoeur states this dilemma more fully in this way: "If I attach myself to the mother country, which is 3,000 miles from me, I become what is called an enemy to my own region; if I follow the rest of my countrymen, I become opposed to our ancient masters: both extremes appear equally dangerous to a person of so little weight and consequence as I am, whose energy and example are of no avail" (letter 12, "Distresses of a Frontier Man").

4   Elizabeth Barnes's *States of Sympathy: Seduction and Democracy in the American Novel*, one of the best discussions of the "political significance" of "sentimental identification," owes much to her canny and lucid reading of Paine's *Common Sense*. Barnes makes two crucial points about Paine's treatise. On the one hand, it provides a good example of the argument for why sympathy is "fundamental to the creation of a distinctly 'American' character" (3). On the other, Paine shows "the political expediency of setting limits on the sympathetic imagination" (3). Barnes's argument and mine complement each other greatly, but where we differ is in our understanding of the way that sympathy performs the work we agree it does. Barnes, because she focuses on narrative, sees the main mechanism of sentiment to be the representation of familial structures. While these representations are significant elements of the mode

of sentiment, I have argued that they only do the work of constructing affective identities when in conjunction with the rhetorical tropes of apostrophe and the heteroglossic diction of sentiment.

5   See *Literary History of the United States* (Spiller et al. 166); also Leon Howard's *The Connecticut Wits* and Carla Mulford's essay in *Deism, Masonry, and the Enlightenment*.

6   Barlow lays out his theory of the epic in the preface to the *Columbiad,* where he is careful to claim Lucan rather than Virgil as his model. In fact, Barlow considered Virgil a dangerous exemplar even while he aspired to performing a similar function for his own country.

7   I'm using Jameson's term "the political unconscious" in a slightly different way than he uses it in his book of the same name, since I am suggesting that Barlow was consciously trying to impress a hermeneutic frame on the unconscious of his readers via the symbolism of his narrative. Barlow seems peculiarly conscious of what Louis Althusser calls the power of calling or naming to arrest and make real subjectivity.

8   In maps from the early years of the nineteenth century, most of the continent between the Atlantic and Pacific was represented by empty space. This cartographic blankness was violated only by the thin traces of exploratory missions such as Lewis and Clark's 1805 journey and the tenuously placed markers of the larger geomorphic aspects of the regions. Political boundaries with the European colonies and Amerindian peoples were only vaguely agreed upon. The boundary with the northern British colony was not even fixed until the Webster-Ashburton Treaty of 1842. Large sections of what is now the state of Maine were contested through the War of 1812 and first came under U.S. jurisdiction as part of greater Massachusetts. Just as the efforts to fill in the graphic picture of America were oddly spasmodic, only paradoxical efforts had been made fully to define and claim the term "America."

9   Lauren Berlant uses this term in her excavation of Hawthorne's problematic and problematizing relation to it in *The Scarlet Letter* and "The Custom House." My argument takes issue with hers in that I resist the ahistoricism implicit in her claim that Hawthorne in the 1840s is wrestling with a construct that always already existed and always already served the interests of the politically elite. Instead, the poetry of Sigourney and Longfellow (Hawthorne's classmate at Bowdoin) shows that the Jacksonian era witnessed the creation of the national symbolic through an ideological competition of similar but significantly different symbols.

10   In contrast to Timothy Dwight's *Conquest of Canaan* (another attempt at an American epic), Barlow's choice of tenor and vehicle bypasses the Bible and conventional Protestant typology in favor of a classical mythology that has been carefully purged of aristocratic tendencies.

11   Note that Whitman differs from his Enlightenment predecessors in that his descriptions of Americans do try to make a place for both genders and in that the epic form he devises is qualified by the contrary influences of the sentimental mode. A further discussion of Whitman's debt to sentimentality would be warranted. See Mary Louise Kete, "Sentimentality" in *Walt Whitman, an Encyclopedia*, ed. J. R. LeMaster and Donald Kummings (New York: Garland Publishing, 1998).

12   In the ensuing discussion I have chosen to use the anthropological term "Amerindians," rather than "Native American" to refer to the indigenous peoples of the Americas, because during the Jacksonian era the term "Native American" explicitly was used by white Americans of Anglo descent who sought to exclude more recent immigrants to America, such as the Irish or Eastern Europeans, as well as people of color, from the category of American. For a compelling discussion of the ironies surrounding the use of this term during the Jacksonian era, see Timothy Powell's forthcoming book, *The Beautiful Absurdity of the Beautiful Identity: Conflicting Constructions of the Nation in Nineteenth-Century America* (1994).

13   Of course, the discovery of gold within Cherokee domains and the needs of the expanding cotton industry greatly inflamed this anxiety.

14   Part of Jackson's fame derived from his role in the wars against the Creeks and the Seminoles. See Arthur Schlesinger's *The Age of Jackson*, Edward Pessen's *Jacksonian America: Society, Personality, and Politics*, and Daniel Boorstin's *The Americans: The National Experience*. See Philip Fisher's "Democratic Social Space: Whitman, Melville, and the Promise of American Transparency" for an insightful discussion of the some of the cartographic solutions to the problems arising from the adoption of European and Romantic notions of nationalism in America.

15   See Berlant's *Anatomy of a National Fantasy*, which gives a reading of Hawthorne's registration of resistance to what she calls the dominance of the national symbolic.

5   The Competition of Sentimental Nationalisms

1   Although some work has begun to be published on Sigourney's contributions to the Romantic ethos, more needs to be done, for her efforts in refashioning the American landscape rightly stand alongside William Cullen Bryant's and Thomas Cole's. See Nina Baym's "Reinventing Lydia Sigourney" for the most recent take on this question. Baym builds on work of the 1980s, such as Mary DeJong's "Profile" and Sandra Zagerall's "Expanding 'America': Lydia Sigourney's *Sketch of Connecticut*, Catherine Sedgwick's *Hope Leslie*." Perhaps

the best of this work from the 1980s is Annie Finch's useful and provocative essay, which takes seriously Sigourney as an American Romantic.

2   See, for example, the engraving by Thomas Moran of the opening of *The Song of Hiawatha* in the Houghton, Mifflin "household edition" of Longfellow's complete works. See also the engraving to Sigourney's "Oriska" by G. H. Cushman in Carey and Hart's 1849 *Illustrated Poems by Mrs. L. H. Sigourney.* Quotations from Longfellow's poems in this chapter and the next follow the 1940 *Complete Poetical Works;* Sigourney's are quoted from the 1860 Philadelphia edition of *Illustrated Poems by Mrs. L. H. Sigourney.*

3   Both Freud and Lacan describe the rebellion of the spirit which arises from the alienation of subjectivity as a drive to return to a presymbolic state of un-differentiation with the world of nature. But my understanding of the force of sentimental practice draws more heavily on anthropological understandings of grief such as Renato Rosaldo's in *Culture and Truth.* See Mitchell Breitwieser's study of Mary Rowlandson's *captivity narrative* as an example of the kind of insights that an anthropological and psychoanalytical account of grief and mourning can shed on our understanding of literature as a social act.

4   My understanding of the importance of apostrophe to the mode of sentimentality is greatly indebted to Barbara Johnson's essay "Apostrophe, Animation, and Abortion," which deals explicitly with this form in relation to pregnancy and pregnancy loss. But the classic definitions, of course, recur to Quintilian and Longinus.

5   The ship celebrated here, with "graceful curve and slow degrees / That she might be docile to the helm," and built both "for freight, and yet for speed," is, of course, the *Yankee Clipper,* which outclassed all its competitors until replaced by steam.

6   "Sail forth into the sea of life, / O gentle, loving, trusting wife" (367–8).

7   John L. Sullivan, writing for the *U.S. Magazine and Democratic Review,* coined this term in 1845. See *Macropolitics of Nineteenth-Century Literature: Nationalism, Exoticism, Imperialism* (ed. Arac and Ritvo) for a helpful set of essays which reexamine the problem of constructing national identity in America during this period. My point is that while it was manifest that America had a destiny, it was not obvious at all what that destiny would be. To say its destiny would follow the template of the family was not to say much when the structure of the family, itself, was in flux.

8   I am indebted to the members of the Doctoral Conference on American Literature and Culture at Harvard University for aspects of the ensuing reading and for the encouragement they have given me over the last several years. I would especially like to thank Anita Goldman, Laura Korobkin, Lynn Wardley, and Meredith McGill for encouraging me to flesh out this argument.

9 See Bourdieu's *The Field of Cultural Production* for a general discussion of the relationships and values of different "capitals," and Walter Benn Michaels's study of American realism in *The Gold Standard*. Bourdieu's concept of the nature of the "habitus" of cultures, structured by antagonisms as well as agreement, lies just beneath much of my argument here.

10 See parts I and II above, in which I use the description of the nature and function of gift economies to understand the circulation of manuscript verse in rural New England. My model is also influenced by Carroll Smith-Rosenberg's "The Female World of Love and Ritual: Relations between Women in Nineteenth-Century America" and Nancy Cott's description of New England culture. It is here that my understanding of the rhetorical power of sentiment differs most significantly from others.

11 Lacan, in his essay "The Mirror Stage," denotes the set of symbolic structures that constitute the individual subject as the Law of the Father.

12 See "Eve" as another example of Sigourney's use of the mode of sentimentality as a means to examine critically its own rhetorical and ideological implications. Harriet Beecher Stowe's definitively sentimental *Uncle Tom's Cabin* also contains a critique of laissez-faire capitalism as well as an exposé of false sentimentalism in which a celebration of the emotions causes increased selfishness (cf. Marie St. Clare).

13 See Johnson's essay on animating power of the lyric apostrophe.

14 Werner Sollors's *Beyond Ethnicity* has an interesting discussion of the use of the image of the alma mater within constructions of American ethnicity. He persuasively suggests that this term, as when used by Crèvecoeur ("He becomes an American by being received in the broad lap of our great *alma mater*") should be read as the "antitype" to the melting pot as the model for the generation of Americanness. See also Annette Kolodny's *The Lay of the Land: Metaphor as Experience and History in American Life and Letters* for a discussion of the symbolic collapse of woman and land in the American tradition. Sigourney's poetry, as well as Oakes Smith's, suggests interesting ways in which Kolodny's thesis could be qualified by looking at early nineteenth-century American women poets' efforts. Anne Mellor's claim that our definitions of Romanticism will have to change now that we have a chance to take seriously the contributions of women is even more true for the study of American Romanticism.

15 The term "republican mother" derives from Linda Kerber's *Women and the Republic: Intellect and Ideology in Revolutionary America*. The concept of the republican mother arose in the effort, she explains, to define a political role for women. The paradigm of the cult of true womanhood (described by Barbara Welter in "The Cult of True Womanhood: 1820–1860") is generally seen as successfully eliding the political force of the republican mother. But it is also

possible to see the irrationally and emotionally structured concept of the "true woman" as a way that the Enlightenment goal of the republican citizen could be achieved.

6 The Other American Poets

1   Longfellow, like Whittier and Lowell, belonged to the set of New England poets variously known as the "schoolroom" or "fireside" poets. These are the same group described by Poe as presiding over the province of "Frogpondia." Their poetry, like that of Lydia Sigourney, most often operates within what I prefer to call the "mode" of sentimentality—appealing to the feelings above reason and addressing the subject of the family as the primary metaphor for all other important subjects. Perry Westbrook's studies of New England literature and culture provide interesting readings of Sigourney and her contemporaries which avoid the conventional trap of automatically discounting them.

2   Lewis recounts that when "his cordial letter welcoming *Leaves of Grass* in 1855 was published in the *New York Tribune,* Emerson muttered in some dismay that had he intended it for publication he 'should have enlarged the *but* very much.'

3   In my introduction and chapter 1, I argue that sentimentality as a discursive mode was instrumental in the construction of middle-class identity. See also Lori Ginzberg's *Women and the Work of Benevolence,* Cecile Dauphin's essay "Women's Culture and Women's Power: An Attempt at Historiography," and Nancy Cott's *The Bonds of Womanhood: "Woman's Sphere" in New England, 1780–1835.*

4   Joseph Butler in his 1726 sermon "On Compassion" uses this text as the basis for an attack against Hobbesian pessimism. Butler's sermon is a brief encapsulation of the tenets of Hume's more thorough *Enquiry Concerning Morals.*

5   The shortest sentence of the New Testament, "Jesus wept" (John 11.35), was often invoked by sentimentalists, who put Jesus' susceptibility to the power of grief on a level almost at a par with his act of redemption. In response to his own grief over the loss of his friend, Lazarus, and his sympathy for Lazarus's sisters' grief, Jesus violates the boundaries between death and life to restore his friend to himself.

6   See the introduction to part 1, above, for a fuller discussion of Sigourney's fate in the twentieth century. Longfellow's reputation has not been significantly revised since the 1960s, when, as in Newton Arvin's critical biography, his aesthetic currency was at its nadir. Edward Wagenknecht's biography provides a slightly more sympathetic reading of Longfellow as an "American

humanist." Kenneth Cameron's *Longfellow among His Contemporaries* provides an excellent, non–Emerson-centered, description of literary New England.

7 See Cathy Davidson's *Reading in America* and her *Revolution and the Word* for discussions of the role of the book as cultural artifact in America and the role of the author. William Charvat's *The Profession of Authorship in America* is, of course, the starting point for any discussion of the struggles of American authors to define a role for themselves in America.

8 This view has begun to be superseded, as in Karen Halttunen's *Confidence Men and Painted Women,* but it continues to operate in many studies and anthologies. The entries for Lydia Sigourney in standard reference books such as *American Women Writers* (ed. Faust 1979, 1983) or the standard work on American women poets, Emily Stipes Watts's important *Poetry of American Women* (1977) unproblematically reiterate this view. This is not to discount the construct of separate spheres (best articulated in Mary Kelly's *Private Women, Public Stage: Literary Domesticity in Nineteenth-Century America*) but to develop a more complex understanding of the various kinds of work this enabled and disabled. See Linda Kerber in "Separate Spheres, Female Worlds, Women's Place: The Rhetoric of Women's History" for a good discussion of this situation.

9 The editors of the *Literary History of America* (revised repeated since its first publication in 1946) thoroughly dismiss Sigourney as a poet despite their puzzled admission "until Longfellow came into his own in the fifties, the most widely read American poet [she published sixty-seven volumes] was the 'Sweet Singer of Hartford'" (ed. Spillers et al. 289).

10 See also Alan Shucard's *American Poetry: The Puritans through Walt Whitman* on Bryant as the first American Romantic poet.

11 Felicia Hemans, like Sigourney, has come to be known as predominantly a writer of occasional mortuary verse despite the evidence of her complete works and her fame in her own time. She is only now beginning to be the subject of some critical attention. Sigourney was largely responsible for the publication of Hemans's *Complete Works* in America. Sigourney provided a critical introduction ("An Essay on Her Genius") for this posthumous edition.

12 A recent article on nineteenth-century Welsh women poets and the rise of Welsh nationalism stresses that English prejudice against the Welsh through the late nineteenth century judged Welsh women to be more "licentious than their English sisters" (Aaron 33). Hemans, though a resident of Wales for most of her life, considered herself and was perceived as only marginally Welsh, being more closely associated with English culture and writing in English. See also Anne Mellor's *Romanticism and Gender* and Jerome McGann's *The Poetics of Sensibility* for extended and theoretical treatments of Hemans's contribution to British Romanticism.

13   Sigourney's posthumously published autobiography, *Letters of Life* (1866), indicates that this was one of the most rewarding periods of her life. Her school focused less on "finishing" her young lady pupils and more on providing them with a rigorous intellectual education. This pedagogical experiment also allowed her, as an orphan, to participate in a large, artificially created "family" of sisters in which she herself had the prominent role.

14   See Gordon Haight's *Mrs. Sigourney* and Sigourney's *Life*.

15   Sarah Josepha Hale paid Sigourney a great deal of money for the right to use Sigourney's name on the masthead of the *Godey's Ladies Book* between the years 1840 and 1842 (Haight, n.p.).

16   The contrast between Haight's treatment of this practice and Sigourney's own explanation is quite telling of the differences between their assumptions about the proper work of poetry.

17   Carroll Smith-Rosenberg's important "The Female World of Love and Ritual: Relations between Women in Nineteenth-Century America" is a good starting place for understanding this mechanism. See also Ralph Thompson's study of the annual and gift book phenomenon, which, I contend, was one way in which these two economies were bridged.

18   This demotion occurred in the dual wake of F. O. Matthiessen and the New Criticism.

19   See Charvat.

20   Longfellow's academic career as one of the first professors of modern languages and literature in America began at his alma mater, Bowdoin College, and continued at Harvard College.

21   See Samuel Longfellow's three-volume biography.

22   In his recent introduction to a Penguin edition of Longfellow, Lawrence Buell has noted that Longfellow's poetics has hardly been given serious attention recently. As a result, I would argue, his poetics has been misunderstood. Arvin, for example, in his 1962 study, cannot understand how Longfellow "could fall victim to the bad sentimental taste of his age—there is of course a good sentimental taste—and there were subjects that normally betrayed him into the sort of false and misplaced feelings that one finds in Lydia Hunt[*sic*] Sigourney" (79). I am indebted to Professor Buell for his sustained enthusiasm for this project and for his having thrown down the gauntlet, in *New England Literary Culture,* which this book, in part, takes up.

23   The new edition of the *Heath Anthology of American Literature* is probably the best example of how this treatment of Sigourney is changing, for it actively seeks to redress this problem by including Sigourney as well as other popular women poets.

24   See Nina Baym's "Reinventing Lydia Sigourney" for a contrasting view of Sigourney's project.

25 Note that Karen Halttunen in her *Confidence Men and Painted Women* describes a cultural anxiety over the claim of authenticity made by the culture of sentiment.

Part Four Mourning Sentimentality in Reconstruction-Era America: Mark Twain's Nostalgic Realism

1 Twain's sentimentality has been a problem for critics since his own time. Twain himself was most deeply offended by expressions of "sham sentiment," but true sentiment (feelings felt and expressed by himself or by those closest to him) was both honorable and effective. For example, in reaction to the deaths of close family members, Twain wrote highly formal and sentimentalized letters and poems that he shared among the survivors. What have been seen as lapses into sentimentality from realism have been accounted for by critics as either capitulations to the corrupting, feminizing influence of Twain's wife, Livy (see Van Wyck Brooks in *The Ordeal of Mark Twain* and Bernard DeVoto in *Mark Twain at Work* for the outlines of this argument), or as oscillations between two modes of consciousness (see Justin Kaplan's *Mr. Clemens and Mark Twain*). More recently, Peter Stonely has recast Twain's use of sentimentality as a more or less controlled appropriation of feminine discourse in *Mark Twain and the Feminine Aesthetic*. Gregg Camfield, in his essay "Sentimental Liberalism and the Problem of Race in *Huckleberry Finn*," undertakes to show that "the book's advocacy of racial equality, though buried in irony, is almost completely sentimental, and that fact may well account for both the spirited attacks on and equally spirited defenses of Twain's attitudes toward race as manifested in his depiction of Jim" (102).

2 See chapter 2 above for a full discussion of sentimental collaboration and gift economies.

3 This phrase "the culture of sentiment" is the title of a collection of essays about sentimentality in America edited by Shirley Samuels.

4 For example, black writers of the Reconstruction and post-Reconstruction era such as Frances Harper and W. E. B. DuBois appropriate sentimentality as they try to claim a place for black Americans within the middle class on the basis of shared gentility. See *Iola Leroy* but also Harper's magazine poetry, and compare DuBois's prose elegy "Of the Passing of the First-Born" in *The Souls of Black Folk*. See Claudia Tate's *Domestic Allegories of Political Desire: The Black Heroine's Text at the Turn of the Century* and Hazel Carby's *Reconstructing Womanhood: The Emergence of the Afro-American Woman Novelist* for discussions of black appropriations of sentimentality.

5 In the concluding chapter of *The Political Unconscious*, Fredric Jameson argues that "all ideology in the strongest sense, including the most exclusive forms

of ruling-class consciousness just as much as that of oppositional or oppressed
classes is in its very nature Utopian" (289). Until quite recently only the ideological nature of sentimentality had been explored. I have been arguing that
what gave sentimentality its continuing ideological strength is that it formally establishes connections (allows for "the unity of the collective") among
various people. The threat was that extending the boundaries of inclusion
around people of color, and various Catholic ethnic groups of Europe, on
the basis of shared sentiment alone would challenge the simultaneously held
group or class identity that was essentially racist. See also Fisher and Tompkins.

6   See Stonely's *Mark Twain and the Feminine Aesthetic* for a good discussion of
Twain and gender. Stonely's emphasis on gender obscures his attention on
issues of class.

7   See chapter 2 above for a full discussion of how I see the circulation of fetishized objects working to promote sentimental collaboration. See also Lynn
Wardley's "Relic, Fetish, Femmage" and Gillian Brown's *Domestic Individualism,* which I discuss in notes to that chapter.

8   Most accounts of gift economies stress the importance of the accumulation
of symbolic capital to the maintenance of social status. See notes to chapter 2
for my critique of this position.

9   In other words the sentimental subject was one defined by relations to goods
and objects. But, following Gillian Brown, I see this relation as one of owner-
ship and mastery.

10   And is thus linked to the Emersonian or Transcendentalist project laid out in
"*Nature*" or in "The Poet." See my introduction and chapter 1 for a full argument for associating Emerson's Transcendentalist call for the poet with the
practice of large numbers of ordinary Americans who had neither the pre-
tensions to philosophy nor Emerson's unique qualifications yet nevertheless
participated with him in this work.

11   As I describe in chapter 2, sentimental collaboration also helps to establish
diachronic continuity by linking the present moment to the past and to the
future.

12   In *Confidence Men and Painted Women* Halttunen persuasively argues this point
as a means of accounting for and interpretating the repeated figures of the con
man in nineteenth-century fiction. Twain's best such figure, Colonel Sellers
of *The Gilded Age,* would be another way of tracing the shift in the role of
sentiment, since Sellers, while clearly a confidence man, is also an important
and benevolent stimulus to the actions of the characters. This is discussed
more fully in the Epilogue.

13   This is not to suggest that these stresses had not already been present or that
they were not in some way inherent to sentimentality. Rather, with Hal-

tunnen, I would argue that these pressures were not only already present in antebellum culture but are an inherent tension within the logic of sentimentality.

14   I am most indebted for this outlook to Alan Trachtenberg's *Reading American Photographs*. A collection of essays edited by Martha Sandweiss provides a wide range of studies that share Trachtenberg's methodical emphasis. These recent efforts supplement the foundational work done by Robert Taft in his 1938 *Photography and the American Scene: A Social History*. Good studies that emphasize either the technological trajectories of the field or the biographical histories of the photographers include William Welling's *Photography in America: The Formative Years, 1939–1990,* Stephen B. Jarekie's catalogue of the extensive show at the Worcester Art Museum in *American Photography: 1840–1900,* and Roy Meredith's *Mathew Brady's Portrait of America* and *Mr. Lincoln's Camera Man.*

15   Oliver Wendell Holmes, an early and prominent theorist and promoter of photography, called photographic visiting cards "the social currency, the sentimental 'greenbacks' of civilization" (qtd. in Taft n.p.). Keith Davis in his essay "'A Terrible Distinctness" quotes Coleman Sellers's 1862 rhetorical question concerning the popularity of photoportraits among the Union troops: "What countless numbers of sun-pictures have been exchanged at the anxious partings of friends from those whom the chances of battle may keep from ever meeting again on earth!" (142–43). But as Davis goes on to argue, and Trachtenberg supports, field photography during the war gave rise to images that only with difficulty served the sentimental goal of healing feelings of loss. Photographers had to pose their subjects in order to achieve aesthetic expectations of "reality" and, as an 1862 review of an exhibit of war photographs at Brady's studio describes it, the "weird copies of carnage" had begun to exert a shift in these aesthetic expectations (qtd. in Davis n.p.). Davis argues persuasively that, "with mouths agape and limbs crumpled in strange, un-idealized positions, these corpses did not conform to contemporary notions of honorable or heroic sacrifice. The brutal inertness of death challenged ideological and political abstractions" (152). I would argue that there is a parallel between what happens in narrative and visual aesthetics around this time. The ambition of photography had been to fix reality, to repudiate the loss of the moment that the photograph seems to be able to capture. The result of the conscious application of this technology to the subject of war produced representations of moments that many might have preferred to repress or forget.

16   Oliver Wendell Holmes, "The Stereoscope and the Stereograph," *Atlantic Monthly* 3 (June 1859): 748.

17   Quoted in Barbara Chandless's essay "The Portrait Studio and the Celebrity."

18   And it did; photographs of the dead took over the established role of paint-

ings of the dead as household icons which were available to a broader range of people. See Michael Lesy's *Wisconsin Death Trip,* which documents this practice in late-nineteenth- and early-twentieth-century America.

19   I am indebted here to Trachtenberg's essay "Albums of War" in *Reading American Photographs.* Trachtenberg documents the expectation that photography would be the "Clio of the War" and the disappointment or disequilibrium that ensued when "Clio often found herself at odds with the indiscriminateness of the camera" (80, 83).

20   How much more difficult would it have been for Mary Cabot of *The Gates Ajar* to believe that her brother Roy was actively enjoying a pleasant afterlife and still with her and helping push aside the "gates of life." See Trachtenberg's discussion of the history and reception of documentary albums of Civil War photographs produced by the major photographic firms of the mid–nineteenth century. Trachtenberg argues persuasively that it is not until sufficient time elapses, until the end of the Reconstruction era, that these images are able to be read as "beautiful" and not horrible.

21   I quote Lincoln's speeches from *The People Shall Judge: Readings in the Formation of American Policy.* At the time of this speech, March 4, 1861, a stalemate had begun at Fort Sumter, which was held by federal troops but besieged by troops of the newly declared Confederacy. The Confederate convention had met just one month before. See Gary Wills's *Lincoln at Gettysburg* for a full and insightful reading of the Gettysburg Address that highlights Lincoln's sentimental rhetoric.

22   In *The Gilded Age,* Dilworthy's "sham sentiment" is unmasked and, though the needs of the freedmen are not served, despite its own corruption neither is the federal government imposed upon.

23   See chapter 3 above for a discussion of sentimentality's contribution to the idea of nationhood in America during the prewar years.

24   Philip Fisher in "Democratic Social Space: Whitman, Melville, and the Promise of American Transparency" describes how "without a single environment or climate, without a culture, and without, in the deep romantic sense, a language, the national fact of America meant that somehow the problem of identity had been solved by other, unprecedented means" than had been employed in Europe.

25   See chapter 3 above for examples from the poetry of Sigourney and Longfellow.

26   Reconstruction was first proposed in 1863, and the provisional terms Lincoln proposed at that early date immediately became fuel for the continuation of hostilities. According to the *Oxford English Dictionary,* the word "reconstruction" was first used in the sense Lincoln does in the eighteenth century.

27 See chapter 1 above for a discussion of the role of apostrophe in the operation of the mode of sentimentality.

28 They continued to be devoted to the extension of rights on the basis of a common humanity. The sentimental mode allowed the extension of full liberal subjectivity to others by eliding what had previously been seen as impassable differences. Within sentimental rhetoric around this issue, expanding suffrage to black men was the way that the nation could return to its previous state of wholeness.

29 But perhaps the failure of sentimentality on the political front was paralleled or foreshadowed by events within the Lincoln home; for Mrs. Lincoln's belief in Willie's presence was one of several symptoms of an increasing dissociation of personality that became worse throughout her lifetime.

30 The collaboratively written *The Gilded Age* is too complex to deal with in this chapter, but I would like to suggest that it expresses both Twain's stances toward the sentimental while also suggesting a provisional, if qualified, solution. If mourning cannot hold the country together and provide a means for it to move forward, then perhaps hope or speculation could.

7 *Invoking the Bonds of Affection:* Tom Sawyer *and America's Morning*

1 As recently as 1986, a critic of *Huckleberry Finn* defined sentimentality as "a self-satisfied basking in various emotions, copious weeping for no good reason, pseudo-feelings replacing real ones, and a consequent loss of touch with life's authentic tragedies" that had a "profoundly warping" effect on "the crucial issues of the period" (Heath 62).

2 I am indebted to Phillip Kete for directing me to Orwell's 1943 review for the *Tribune*. Orwell's opinion of Twain (an opinion that some passages of the *Autobiography* suggest that Twain may have sometimes shared) was that Twain "had in him an iconoclastic, even revolutionary vein which he obviously wanted to follow up and yet somehow never did follow up. He might have been a destroyer of humbugs and a prophet of democracy more valuable than Whitman, because healthier and more humorous. Instead, he became that dubious thing a 'public figure' flattered by passport officials and entertained by royalty, and his career reflects the deterioration in American life that set in after the Civil War" (371).

3 Justin Kaplan makes the point in *Mr. Clemens and Mark Twain* that "*The Gilded Age* was the antecedent of *Tom Sawyer, Huckleberry Finn, The Mysterious Stranger* —a beginning, not a dead end" (170).

4 As T. S. Eliot noted in his 1950 introduction to *Huckleberry Finn*, "the fact that he has a father only emphasizes his loneliness; and he views his father with a terrifying detachment" (322).

5 In most American states through the antebellum era, a child would be considered legally orphaned only after the death of the father.

6 The plot of Huck's transformation from wild boy to adopted boy thematically underscores and reinforces Tom's plot.

7 By the end of the novel, the actions of the plot will have operated as carnival in the sense outlined by Bakhtin, since Tom's apparent rebellion and antisocial behavior will have provided the opportunity for society to affirm its ties to him and for Tom to affirm his commitment to society.

8 See Gregg Camfield in "Sentimental Liberalism and the Problem of Race in *Huckleberry Finn*" for a discussion of Twain's problematic and complex use in the novel of the strategy of sentimentality to ameliorate the line of color, to take on the problem of race.

9 I use the qualifier *seems* here because the close of the *Tom Sawyer* in which Huck enthusiastically proposes to "stick to the widder till I rot" and to make her proud that "she snaked" him "in out of wet" is undermined by the opening segments of *Huck Finn*.

10 Philip Fisher in *Hard Facts* has persuasively argued that the aim of sentimentality was to enable a "dangerous" extension of subjectivity.

11 "Huck Finn's wealth and the fact that he was now under the Widow Douglas's protection, introduced him into society—no, dragged him into it, hurled him into it—and his sufferings were almost more than he could bear" (211).

8 *Mourning America's Morning:* The Adventures of Huckleberry Finn

1 See Fisher, *Hard Facts.*

2 In fact, Twain himself tells a sentimental anecdote that parallels the story Jim tells concerning his deaf daughter. The story concerns Sandy, "a little slave boy" who gets on Clemens's nerves on account of his constant singing. When young Clemens asks his mother to "shut him up": "The tears came into her eyes and her lip trembled" as she explains that "he sings to show that he is not remembering" his lost mother and home and that "if you were older, you would understand me; then that friendless child's noise would make you glad" (*Autobiography* 1.102). In the context of the *Autobiography,* this is an example of Twain's mother's native goodness that parallels Huck's.

3 Gregg Camfield makes a similar argument in "Sentimental Liberalism and the Problem of Race in *Huckleberry Finn.*"

4 For examples, see Michael Egan in *Mark Twain's* Huckleberry Finn: *Race, Class, and Society,* William Heath in "Tears and Flapdoodle: Sentimentality in *Huckleberry Finn,*" and Marden Clark's "No Time to Be Sentimentering."

5 See Lucille M. Schultz's "Parlor Talk in Mark Twain: The Grangerford Parlor

and the House Beautiful" for a full exploration of the contrast in treatment of these two parallel settings.

6   This, too, has its parallel in *Huck Finn:* "Cold corn-pone, cold corn-beef, butter and butter-milk — that is what they had for me down there, and there ain't nothing better that I've ever come across yet" (82).

7   This practice was not uncommon and had been well established in America since at least the late eighteenth century. American portrait painter Charles Willson Peale had painted a portrait of his dead daughter and his mourning wife. It hung in his studio "behind a curtain to which he attached a note: 'Before you draw this curtain consider whether you will afflict a Mother or a Father that has lost a Child'" (catalog of Pike and Armstrong, *A Time to Mourn*).

8   Important because she is the prime agent of the circulation of mourning sentiments, inadequate because even when she was alive this only paralleled, rather than interfered with, the progress of the feud.

9   Some recent articles that address the meaning of Huck's lonesomeness include Paul Schacht's "The Lonesomeness of Huckleberry Finn," Carol Strickland's "Of Love and Loneliness: Society and Self in *Huckleberry Finn*," and Randall Knoper's "'Away from Home and amongst Strangers': Domestic Sphere, Public Arena, and *Huckleberry Finn*."

SELECTED BIBLIOGRAPHY

Aaron, Jane. "Daughters of Dissent: Women's Poetry and Welsh Methodism, 1780–1830." *Planet: The Welsh Internationalist* 994 (Aug./Sept. 1992).

Abel, Elizabeth, and Emily K. Abel, eds. *The Signs Reader: Women, Gender, and Scholarship.* Chicago: Univ. of Chicago Press, 1983.

Adams, Hazard, and Leroy Searl, eds. *Critical Theory Since 1965.* Tallahassee: Univ. Press of Florida, 1986.

Adorno, T. *Prisms.* Cambridge: MIT Press, 1981.

Ahlstrom, Sidney E. *A Religious History of the American People.* New Haven: Yale Univ. Press, 1972.

"Album of Elizabeth." Ms. album, circa 1840s. American Antiquarian Soc., Worcester, Mass.

"Album of Eugenia." Ms. album from North Adams area. American Antiquarian Soc., Worcester, Mass.

Alcott, Louisa May. *Little Women.* New York: Bantam, 1983.

Alger, William Rounseville. *The Friendships of Women.* Boston: Roberts, 1868.

Anderson, Benedict. *Imagined Communities: Reflections on the Origin and Spread of Nationalism.* London: Verso, 1991.

Arac, Jonathan, and Harriet Ritvo, eds. *Macropolitics of Nineteenth-Century Literature: Nationalism, Exoticism, Imperialism.* Philadelphia: Univ. of Pennsylvania Press, 1991.

Arendt, Hannah. *On Revolution.* New York: Viking, 1965.

Ariès, Philippe. *The Hour of Our Death.* New York: Knopf, 1981.

Arvin, Newton. *Longfellow: His Life and Work.* Boston: Little, Brown, 1962.

Baker, Houston A., Jr. *Blues, Ideology, and Afro-American Literature: A Vernacular Theory.* Chicago: Univ. of Chicago Press, 1984.

Baldwin, James. "Everybody's Protest Novel." *Partisan Review* 16 (June 1949): 578–85.

Banner, Louis W. *Elizabeth Cady Stanton: A Radical for Women's Rights.* Glenview, Ill.: Scott, 1980.

Barlow, Joel. *The Works of Joel Barlow in Two Volumes.* Gainesville, Fla.: Scholars' Facsimiles, 1970.

Barnes, Elizabeth. *States of Sympathy: Seduction and Democracy in the American Novel.* New York: Columbia Univ. Press, 1997.

Baym, Nina. "Reinventing Lydia Sigourney." *American Literature* 62 (1990): 385–404.

———. *Woman's Fiction: A Guide to Novels by and about Women in America, 1820–1870.* Ithaca: Cornell Univ. Press, 1978.

Bender, Thomas. *Community and Social Change in America.* Baltimore: Johns Hopkins Univ. Press, 1982.

Bercovitch, Sacvan. *The American Jeremiad.* Madison: Univ. of Wisconsin Press, 1978.

———. *The Office of the Scarlet Letter.* Baltimore: Johns Hopkins Univ. Press, 1991.

———, ed. *Reconstructing American Literary History.* Cambridge: Harvard Univ. Press, 1986.

Bercovitch, Sacvan, and Myra Jehlen, eds. *Ideology and Classic American Literature.* Cambridge: Cambridge Univ. Press, 1987.

Berg, Barbara J. *The Remembered Gate: Origins of American Feminism: The Woman and the City, 1800–1860.* New York: Oxford Univ. Press, 1978.

Berlant, Lauren. *The Anatomy of National Fantasy: Hawthorne, Utopia, and Everyday Life.* Chicago: University of Chicago Press, 1991.

Berry, Thomas E., ed. *Readings in American Criticism.* New York: Odyssey, 1970.

Boker, Pamela. *The Grief Taboo in American Literature: Loss and Prolonged Adolescence in Twain, Melville, and Hemingway.* New York: New York University Press, 1996.

Boorstin, Daniel J. *The Americans: The National Experience.* New York: Vintage, 1967.

Bourdieu, Pierre. *Distinction: A Social Critique of the Judgement of Taste.* Trans. Richard Nice. Cambridge: Harvard Univ. Press, 1984.

———. *The Field of Cultural Production: Essays on Art and Production.* New York: Columbia Univ. Press, 1993.

Boynton, Miss Catherine E. Ms. album, circa 1836. American Antiquarian Soc., Worcester, Mass.

Bradstreet, Anne. *Works.* Ed. John Harvard Ellis. New York: Peter Smith, 1932.

Bredvold, Louis I. *The Natural History of Sensibility.* Detroit: Wayne State Univ. Press, 1962.

Breitwieser, Mitchell R. *American Puritanism and the Defense of Mourning: Religion, Grief, and Ethnology in Mary White Rowlandson's Captivity Narrative.* Madison: Univ. of Wisconsin Press, 1990.

Brooks, Van Wyck. *The Ordeal of Mark Twain.* Rev. ed. New York: Dutton, 1933.

Brown, Gillian. *Domestic Individualism: Imagining Self in Nineteenth-Century America.* Berkeley: Univ. of California Press, 1990.

Brown, Herbert Ross. *The Sentimental Novel in America, 1789–1860.* Durham: Duke Univ. Press, 1940.

Buel, Joy Day, and Richard Buel Jr. *The Way of Duty: A Woman and Her Family in Revolutionary America.* New York: Norton, 1984.

Buell, Lawrence. "Introduction." *Henry Wadsworth Longfellow: Selected Poems*. New York: Viking-Penguin, 1988.

———. *Literary Transcendentalism: Style and Vision in the American Renaissance*. Ithaca: Cornell Univ. Press, 1973.

———. *New England Literary Culture: From Revolution to Renaissance*. Cambridge: Cambridge Univ. Press, 1986.

Butler, Joseph. *Fifteen Sermons Preached at the Rolls Chapel*. London: Printed for W. Botham, 1726. London: W. R. Mathews, G. Bell, 1914.

Cameron, Kenneth. *Longfellow among his Contemporaries: A Harvest of Estimates, Insights and Anecdotes from the Victorian Literary World and an Index*. Hartford: Transcendental Books, 1978.

Cameron, Sharon. *Lyric Time: Dickinson and the Limits of Genre*. Baltimore: Johns Hopkins Univ. Press, 1981.

———. "Representing Grief: Emerson's 'Experience.'" *Representations* 15, (summer 1986): 15–41.

Camfield, Gregg. "Sentimental Liberalism and the Problem of Race in *Huckleberry Finn*." *Nineteenth-Century Literature* 46 (1991): 96–113.

Campbell, Colin. *The Romantic Ethic and the Spirit of Modern Consumerism*. Oxford: Blackwell, 1987.

Carby, Hazel. *Reconstructing Womanhood: The Emergence of the Afro-American Woman Novelist*. Oxford: Oxford Univ. Press, 1987.

Carrier, James. "Gifts in the World of Commodities: The Ideology of the Perfect Gift in American Society." *Social Analysis* 29 (1990): 19–37.

Chai, Leon. *The Romantic Foundations of the American Renaissance*. Ithaca: Cornell Univ. Press, 1987.

Chandless, Barbara. "The Portrait Studio and the Celebrity." Sandweiss 48 75.

Charvat, William. *The Profession of Authorship in America, 1800–1870*. Ed. Matthew J. Bruccoli. Columbus: Ohio State Univ. Press, 1968.

Chatterjee, Partha. *The Nation and Its Fragments: Colonial and Postcolonial Histories*. Princeton: Princeton Univ. Press, 1993.

———. *Nationalist Thought and the Colonial World: A Derivative Discourse?* London: Zed, 1986.

Cheal, David. *The Gift Economy*. London: Routledge, 1988.

Clark, Christopher. *The Diary of an Apprentice Cabinetmaker: Edward Jenner Carpenter's 'Journal' 1844–1845*. Worcester, Mass.: American Antiquarian Society, 1988 303–94

Clark, Marden J. "No Time to Be Sentimentering." *Mark Twain Journal* 21.3 (spring 1983): 21–23.

Clark, Suzanne. *Sentimental Modernism: Women Writers and the Revolution of the Word*. Bloomington: Indiana Univ. Press, 1991.

Clemens, Samuel L. *The Adventures of Huckleberry Finn.* 2d ed. New York: Norton, 1961.

Clifford, James, and George E. Marcus, eds. *Writing Culture: The Poetics and Politics of Ethnography.* Berkeley: Univ. of California Press, 1986.

Cole, Donald B. *Handbook of American History.* New York: Harcourt, Brace, 1968.

Colesworthy, S. H. Ms. album, circa 1841. American Antiquarian Soc., Worcester, Mass.

Cott, Nancy F. *The Bonds of Womanhood: "Woman's Sphere" in New England, 1780–1835.* New Haven: Yale Univ. Press, 1977.

Crockett, Walter H. *Vermont: The Green Mountain State.* New York: Century History, 1921–23.

Culler, Jonathan. *On Deconstruction: Theory and Criticism after Structuralism.* Ithaca: Cornell Univ. Press, 1982.

————. *The Pursuit of Signs: Semiotics, Literature, Deconstruction.* Ithaca, N.Y.: Cornell Univ. Press, 1981.

Dauphin, Cecile. *Correspondence: Models of Letter Writing from the Middle Ages to the Nineteenth Century.* Princeton, N.J.: Princeton Univ. Press, 1997.

Dauphin, Cecile, et al. "Women's Culture and Women's Power: An Attempt at Historiography." *Journal of Women's History* 1.1 (spring 1989): 63–88.

Davidson, Cathy N. *Revolution and the Word: The Rise of the Novel in America.* New York: Oxford Univ. Press, 1986.

————, ed. *Reading in America: Literature and Social History.* Baltimore: Johns Hopkins Univ. Press, 1989.

Davis, Keith. "'A Terrible Distinctness.'" *Photography in the Nineteenth Century.* Sandweiss 48–75.

Declaration of the Faith and Practice of East Dover Baptist Church. 1899. Ts. East Dover Baptist Church, East Dover, Vt.

Deetz, James. "Death's Heads, Cherubs, and Willow Trees." *Passing: The Vision of Death in America.* Jackson, 48–59.

DeJong, Mary. "Legacy Profile: Lydia Howard Huntley Sigourney (1791–1865)." *Legacy: A Journal of American Women Writers* 5, no. 1 (spring 1988): 35–43.

DeVoto, Bernard. *Mark Twain at Work.* Cambridge: Harvard Univ. Press, 1942.

Dickinson, Emily. *The Complete Poems of Emily Dickinson.* Ed. Thomas H. Johnson. Boston: Little, Brown, 1960.

DiMaggio, Paul. *Audience Studies of the Performing Arts and Museums: A Critical Review.* Washington, D.C.: National Endowment for the Arts, 1978.

Dinnerstein, Dorothy. *The Mermaid and the Minotaur: Sexual Arrangements and Human Malaise.* New York: Harper, 1976.

Dobson, Joanne. "Reclaiming Sentimental Literature." *American Literature: A Journal of Literary History, Criticism, and Bibliography* 69.2 (June 1997).

————. *Strategies of Reticence.* Bloomington: Indiana Univ. Press, 1989.

Donovan, Josephine. *Feminist Theory: The Intellectual Traditions of American Feminism.* New York: Ungar, 1985.

Dorfles, Gillo. *Kitsch: The World of Bad Taste.* New York: Bell, 1968.

Douglas, Ann. *The Feminization of American Culture.* New York: Anchor, 1988.

Douglas, Mary. *Natural Symbols: Explorations in Cosmology.* New York: Pantheon Books, 1970.

———, ed. *Rules and Meanings: The Anthropology of Everyday Life.* Harmondsworth: Penguin, 1973.

Doyle, William. *The Vermont Political Tradition: And Those Who Helped to Make It.* Barre, Vt.: Northlight Studio, 1984.

Draper, John W. *The Funeral Elegy and the Rise of English Romanticism.* New York: New York Univ. Press, 1929.

Dublin, Thomas, ed. *Farm to Factory: Women's Letters, 1830–1860.* New York: Columbia Univ. Press, 1981.

DuBois, Ellen Carol, ed. *Elizabeth Cady Stanton; Susan B. Anthony: Correspondence, Writings, Speeches.* New York: Schocken, 1981.

DuBois, W. E. B. *The Souls of Black Folk.* New York: Bantam, 1989.

Dwight, Timothy. *The Conquest of Canaan: A Poem, in Eleven Books.* (1785) Westport, Conn.: Greenwood, 1970.

Eagleton, Terry. *The Ideology of the Aesthetic.* Oxford: Blackwell, 1990.

———. *Literary Theory: An Introduction.* Minneapolis: Univ. of Minnesota Press, 1983.

Egan, Michael. *Mark Twain's Huckleberry Finn: Race, Class and Society.* Atlantic Highlands, N.J.: Humanities Press, 1977.

Eliot, T. S. "An Introduction to *Huckleberry Finn*." Clemens, *The Adventures of Huckleberry Finn.* 2d ed. New York: Norton, 1961.

———. *Selected Prose.* New York: Harcourt, 1975.

Emerson, Ralph Waldo. *Selections from Ralph Waldo Emerson: An Organic Anthology.* Ed. Stephen E. Whicher. Boston: Houghton Mifflin, 1960.

Epstein, Barbara Leslie. *The Politics of Domesticity: Women, Evangelism, and Temperance in Nineteenth-Century America.* Middletown, Conn.: Wesleyan Univ. Press, 1981.

Faust, Langdon Lynne. *American Women Writers.* 2 vols. New York: Ungar, 1983.

Fiedler, Leslie. *Love and Death in the American Novel.* New York: Dell, 1966.

Finch, Annie. *The Ghost of Meter: Culture and Prosody in American Free Verse.* Ann Arbor: Univ. of Michigan Press, 1993.

———. "The Sentimental Poetess in the World: Metaphor and Subjectivity in Lydia Sigourney's Nature Poetry." *Legacy: A Journal of American Women Writers* 5.2 (fall 1988): 3–18.

Fisher, Philip. "Democratic Social Space: Whitman, Melville, and the Promise of American Transparency." *The New American Studies.* Ed. Fisher.

————. *Hard Facts: Setting and Form in the American Novel.* New York: Oxford Univ. Press, 1987.

————, ed. *The New American Studies: Essays from* Representations. Berkeley: Univ. of California Press, 1991, 60–101.

Fletcher, Angus. "Whitman and Longfellow: Two Types of the American Poet." *Raritan: A Quarterly Review* 10.4 (spring 1991): 131–45.

Flexner, Eleanor. *Centuries of Struggle: The Women's Rights Movement in the United States.* Cambridge: Harvard Univ. Press, 1959.

Foster, Charles I. *An Errand of Mercy: The Evangelical United Front, 1790–1837.* Chapel Hill: Univ. of North Carolina Press, 1960.

Foucault, Michel. *The Archaeology of Knowledge and the Discourse on Language.* New York: Pantheon, 1972.

————. *Discipline and Punish: The Birth of the Prison.* New York: Vintage, 1979.

Freud, Sigmund. "Mourning and Melancholia." 1917. *The Standard Edition of the Complete Psychological Works.* Ed. James Strachey. London: Hogarth, 1953–74. Vol. 14.

Gates, Henry Louis, Jr., ed. *Black Literature and Literary Theory.* New York: Methuen, 1984.

Geertz, Clifford. *The Interpretation of Cultures: Selected Essays.* New York: Basic, 1973.

Gilbert, Sandra M., and Susan Gubar. *The Madwoman in the Attic: The Woman Writer and the Nineteenth-Century Literary Imagination.* New Haven: Yale Univ. Press, 1984.

Gilmore, Michael T. *American Romanticism and the Marketplace.* Chicago: Univ. of Chicago Press, 1985.

Gilmore, William J. *Reading Becomes a Necessity of Life: Material and Cultural Life in Rural New England, 1780–1835.* Knoxville: Univ. of Tennessee Press, 1989.

Ginzberg, Lori D. *Women and the Work of Benevolence: Morality, Politics, and Class in the Nineteenth-Century United States.* New Haven: Yale Univ. Press, 1990.

Gore, Albert. "The Cynics Are Wrong." Harvard Commencement Address, 1994. *Harvard Magazine* 96.6 (July–August 1994): 28–32.

Gould, Harriet. *Harriet Gould's Book.* Ms. album. Collection of Ralph W. Howe Jr., Wilmington, Vt.

Griswold, Rufus Wilmot. *The Female Poets of America.* 2d ed. Philadelphia: Henry C. Baird, 1852.

H. Sarah. Ms. album: "A Birthday Gift," circa 1828. American Antiquarian Soc., Worcester, Mass.

Haight, Gordon. *George Eliot: A Biography.* New York: Oxford Univ. Press, 1968.

————. *Mrs. Sigourney: The Sweet Singer of Hartford.* New York: Yale UP, 1930.

Hall, Benjamin H. *History of Eastern Vermont.* New York: Appleton, 1858.

Halttunen, Karen. *Confidence Men and Painted Women: A Study of Middle-Class Culture in America, 1830–1870.* New Haven: Yale Univ. Press, 1982.

Harris, Susan K. *Nineteenth-Century American Women's Novels: Interpretative Strategies.* Cambridge: Cambridge Univ. Press, 1990.

Hawthorne, Nathaniel. *The House of Seven Gables.* Columbus: Ohio Univ. Press, 1965.

———. *The Blithedale Romance.* Ed. Seymour Gross and Rosalie Murphy. New York: Norton, 1978.

———. *The Scarlet Letter.* New York: Bantam, 1989.

Heath, William. "Tears and Flapdoodle: Sentimentality in *Huckleberry Finn.*" *South Carolina Review* 19.1 (fall 1986): 60–79.

Hedrick, Joan D. *Harriet Beecher Stowe: A Life.* New York: Oxford Univ. Press, 1994.

Hegel, G. W. F. *On Art, Religion, Philosophy: Introductory Lectures to the Realm of the Absolute Spirit.* Ed. J. Glenn Gray. New York: Harper Torchbooks, 1970.

Hemans, Felicia. *The Works of Mrs. Hemans, with A Memoir by Her Sister and An Essay on Her Genius, by Mrs. Sigourney.* Philadelphia: Lea & Blanchard, 1842.

Hemingway, Ernest. *A Farewell to Arms.* New York: Scribner, 1969.

Hewitt, Nancy A. "Beyond the Search for Sisterhood. American Women's History in the 1980s." *Social History* 10 (October 1985): 299–321.

———. *Women's Activism and Social Change: Rochester, New York, 1822–1872.* Ithaca: Cornell Univ. Press, 1984.

Hobsbawm, E., and T. Ranger, eds. *The Invention of Tradition.* Cambridge: Cambridge Univ. Press, 1983.

Hofstadter, Richard. *Anti-Intellectualism in American Life.* New York: Knopf, 1963.

Horton, James O., and Lois E. Horton. *Black Bostonians: Family Life and the Community Struggle in the Antebellum North.* New York: Holmes & Meier, 1979.

Howard, Leon. *The Connecticut Wits.* Chicago: Chicago Univ. Press, 1983.

Howe, Florence. Ms. album, circa 1920. Collection of Ralph W. Howe Jr., Wilmington, Vt.

Howe, Julia Ward. *Reminiscences: 1819–1899.* Boston: Houghton, 1900.

Hume, David *An Enquiry Concerning the Principles of Moral.* Indianapolis: Hackett, 1983.

Hyde, Lewis. *The Gift: Imagination and the Erotic Life of Property.* New York: Vintage, 1983.

Jackson, Charles O., ed. *Passing: The Vision of Death in America.* Westport, Conn.: Greenwood, 1977.

Jacobs, Harriet A. *Incidents in the Life of a Slave Girl: Written by Herself.* Ed. L. Maria Child. Cambridge: Harvard Univ. Press, 1987.

James, Henry. *Roderick Hudson.* New York: Scribner's, 1907.

James, William. *The Varieties of Religious Experience: A Study in Human Nature.* New York: Longmans, Green, 1902.

Jameson, Fredric. *The Political Unconscious: Narrative as a Socially Symbolic Act.* Ithaca: Cornell Univ. Press, 1981.

Jarekie, Stephen B. *American Photography: 1840–1900.* Catalogue of the Worcester Art Museum. Worcester, Mass., n.d.

Jarvis, James Jackson. *The Art Idea: Sculpture, Painting and Architecture in America.* New York: Hurd and Houghton, 1877.

Jauss, Hans Robert. *Towards an Aesthetic of Reception.* Trans. Timothy Bahti. Minneapolis: Univ. of Minnesota Press, 1982.

Johnson, Barbara. "Apostrophe, Animation, and Abortion." *Diacritics* 16 (1986): 29–39.

Johnson, Paul E. *A Shopkeeper's Millennium: Society and Revivals in Rochester, New York, 1815–1837.* New York: Hill & Wang, 1978.

Jones, Jacqueline. *Labor of Love, Labor of Sorrow: Black Women, Work, and the Family from Slavery to the Present.* New York: Vintage, 1985.

Jones, Ruby. Telephone conversations with author, Claremont, N.H., January 4 and 7, 1989.

———. Letter to author, January 5, 1989.

Kacandes, Irene, et al., eds. *A User's Guide to German Cultural Studies.* Ann Arbor, Mich.: Univ. of Michigan Press, 1997.

Kafka, Franz. *Amerika.* Trans. Edwin Muir. New York: New Directions, 1962.

Kant, Immanuel. *Critique of Judgement.* Trans. J. H. Bernard. New York: Hafner, 1951.

Kaplan, Justin. *Mr. Clemens and Mark Twain.* New York: Simon & Schuster, 1966.

Kelley, Mary. *Private Women, Public Stage: Literary Domesticity in Nineteenth Century America.* New York: Oxford Univ. Press, 1984.

———. "The Sentimentalists: Promise and Betrayal in the Home." *Signs: Journal of Women in Culture and Society.* Chicago: Univ. of Chicago Press, 1979, 434–46.

Kerber, Linda K. "Separate Spheres, Female Worlds, Woman's Place: The Rhetoric of Women's History." *Journal of American History* 75(June 1988): 9–39.

———. *Women of the Republic: Intellect and Ideology in Revolutionary America.* New York: Norton, 1986.

Kete, Mary Louise. "Sentimentality." *Walt Whitman: An Encyclopedia.* Ed. J. R. LeMaster and Donald Kummings. New York: Garland Publishing, 1998.

Knoper, Randall. " 'Away from Home and amongst Strangers': Domestic Sphere, Public Arena, and *Huckleberry Finn.*" *Prospects: An Annual of American Cultural Studies* 14 (1984): 125–40.

Kolodny, Annette. *The Land before Her: Fantasy and Experience of the American Frontiers, 1630–1860.* Chapel Hill: Univ. of North Carolina Press, 1984.

———. *The Lay of the Land: Metaphor as Experience and History in American Life and Letters.* Chapel Hill: Univ. of North Carolina Press, 1975.

Kull, Nell M. *History of Dover, Vermont: Two Hundred Years in a Hill Town.* Brattleboro: Book Cellar, 1961.

Lacan, Jacques. *Écrits: A Selection.* Trans. Alan Sheridan. New York: Norton, 1977.

Lang, Amy Schrager. "Class and the Strategies of Sympathy." Samuels 128–42.

Lauter, Paul, et al., eds. *The Heath Anthology of American Literature.* Lexington, Mass.: D. C. Heath and Company, 1994.

Leach, William. *True Love and Perfect Union: The Feminist Reform of Sex and Society.* Middletown, Conn.: Wesleyan Univ. Press, 1989.

LeMay, J. A. Leo, ed. *Deism, Masonry, and the Enlightenment: Essays Honoring Alfred Owen Aldridge.* Newark: Univ. of Delaware Press, 1987.

Lesy, Michael. *Wisconsin Death Trip.* New York: Pantheon, 1973.

Levine, Lawrence W. *Highbrow/Lowbrow: The Emergence of Cultural Hierarchy in America.* Cambridge: Harvard Univ. Press, 1988.

Lewis, R. W. B. *The American Adam: Innocence, Tragedy, and Tradition in the Nineteenth Century.* Chicago: Univ. of Chicago Press, 1955.

Lloyd, Phoebe. "Posthumous Mourning Portraiture." Pike and Armstrong.

Longfellow, Henry Wadsworth. *The Complete Poetical Works.* Boston: Houghton, 1940.

———. *The Complete Poetical Works of Henry Wadsworth Longfellow: Household Edition with Two Hundred and Seventy Illustrations.* Boston: Houghton Mifflin, 1902.

Longfellow, Samuel, ed. *Life of Henry Wadsworth Longfellow with Extracts from his Journals and Correspondence.* Boston: Ticknor, 1886.

Ludlum, David M. *Social Ferment in Vermont, 1791–1850.* New York: Columbia Univ. Press, 1939.

MacKinnon, Catherine A. *Towards a Feminist Theory of the State.* Cambridge: Harvard Univ. Press, 1989.

Mainiero, Lina. *American Women Writers: A Critical Reference Guide From Colonial Times to the Present.* New York: Ungar, 1979.

Matthiessen, F. O. *The American Renaissance.* London: Oxford Univ. Press, 1941.

———. *Sarah Orne Jewett.* 1929. Gloucester, Mass.: P. Smith, 1965.

Mauss, Marcel. *The Gift: Forms and Functions of Exchange in Archaic Societies.* Trans. Ian Cunnison. New York: Norton, 1967.

McGann, Jerome J. *The Poetics of Sensibility: A Revolution in Literary Style.* Oxford: Clarendon; New York: Oxford Univ. Press, 1996.

———. *The Romantic Ideology: A Critical Investigation.* Chicago: Univ. of Chicago Press, 1983.

Mellor, Anne. *Romanticism and Gender.* New York: Routledge, 1993.

Melville, Herman. *Billy Budd, Sailor (An Inside Narrative).* Ed. Harrison Hayford and Merton M. Sealts Jr. Chicago: Univ. of Chicago Press, 1962.

———. *The Confidence-Man: His Masquerade.* Oxford: Oxford Univ. Press, 1989.

———. *Moby-Dick.* New York: Norton, 1967.

Meredith, Roy. *Mathew Brady's Portrait of America.* New York: Norton, 1982.

———. *Mr. Lincoln's Camera Man: Mathew B. Brady: 350 Brady Photographs.* 2d rev. ed. New York: Dover, 1974.

Michaels, Walter Benn. *The Gold Standard and the Logic of Naturalism: American Literature at the Turn of the Century.* Berkeley: Univ. of California Press, 1987.

Miller, Nancy K., and Carolyn G. Heilbrun, eds. *The Poetics of Gender.* New York: Columbia Univ. Press, 1986.

Miller, Perry. *The Life of the Mind in America from the Revolution to the Civil War.* New York: Harcourt, Brace & World, 1965.

Milton, John. *John Milton: Complete Poems and Major Prose.* Ed. Merret Y. Hughes. New York: Macmillan, 1957.

Mitchell, Juliet, and Ann Oakley, eds. *What Is Feminism: A Re-Examination.* New York: Pantheon, 1986.

Mitchell, W. J. T., ed. *The Politics of Interpretation.* Chicago: Univ. of Chicago Press, 1983.

Morgan, Robin, ed. *Sisterhood Is Powerful: An Anthology of Writings from the Women's Liberation Movement.* New York: Vintage, 1970.

Mulford, Carla. "Radicalism in Joel Barlow's 'The Conspiracy of Kings' (1792)." LeMay 137–57.

Muller, H. Nichols, III and John J. Duffy. *An Anxious Democracy: Aspects of the 1830s.* Westport, Conn.: Greenwood, 1982.

Nancy's Album. Ms. album, circa 1830s. American Antiquarian Soc., Worcester, Mass.

Newton, Ephraim H. *The History of the Town of Marlborough, Windham County, Vermont.* Montpelier: Vermont Historical Soc., 1930.

Oakes Smith, Elizabeth. *The Poetical Writings of Elizabeth Oakes Smith.* New York: J. S. Redfield, Clinton Hall, 1845.

———. *The Poetical Writings of Elizabeth Oakes Smith.* New York: J. S. Redfield, Clinton Hall, 1846.

———. *The Sinless Child and Other Poems.* New York: Wiley & Putnam, 1843.

———. *Woman and Her Needs.* New York: Fowlers & Wells, 1851. Micropublished in "History of Women." New Haven, Conn.: Research Publications, 1975.

Ortner, Sherry B., and Harriet Whitehead, eds. *Sexual Meanings: The Cultural Construction of Gender and Sexuality.* Cambridge: Cambridge Univ. Press, 1981.

Orwell, George. "Mark Twain—Licensed Jester." *The Collected Essays, Journalism, and Letters of George Orwell.* Vol. 2. Ed. Sonia Orwell and Ian Angus. New York: Harcourt, Brace & World, 1968.

Osgood, Frances S. *Poems by Frances S. Osgood.* New York: Clark & Austin, 1846.

Ossoli, Margaret Fuller. *Woman in the Nineteenth Century, and Kindred Papers Relating to the Sphere, Condition, and Duties of Woman.* Westport, Conn.: Greenwood, 1968.

P. M. P. Ms. album, circa 1827. American Antiquarian Soc., Worcester, Mass.

Paine, Albert B. *Mark Twain: A Biography.* New York: Harper, 1912.

———. *Mark Twain's Letters,* 2 vols. New York: Harper and Brothers, 1917.

Papashvily, Helen Waite. *All the Happy Endings: A Study of the Domestic Novel in America, the Women Who Wrote It, the Women Who Read It, in the Nineteenth Century.* 1956. Port Washington, N.Y.: Kennikat, 1972.

Parker, Gail, ed. *The Oven Birds: American Women on Womanhood, 1820–1920.* Garden City: Doubleday, 1972.

Parrington, Vernon Louis. *Main Currents in American Thought: An Interpretation of American Literature from the Beginnings to 1920.* New York: Harcourt, Brace and World, 1958.

Pattee, Fred Lewis. *The Feminine Fifties.* 1940. Port Washington, N.Y.: Kennikat, 1966.

People Shall Judge, The: Readings in the Formation of American Policy, vol. 1. Ed. Staff, Social Science, College of University of Chicago. Chicago: Univ. of Chicago Press, 1967.

Pessen, Edward. *Jacksonian America: Society, Personality, and Politics.* Homewood, Ill.: Dorsey, 1969.

———. *The Many-Faceted Jacksonian Era: New Interpretations.* Westport, Conn.: Greenwood, 1977.

Phelps, Elizabeth Stuart. *The Gates Ajar.* 1868. Cambridge: Harvard Univ. Press, 1964.

Pike, Martha, and Nancy Armstrong, eds. *A Time to Mourn: Expressions of Grief in Nineteenth-Century America.* New York: Museums at Stony Brook, 1980.

Poovey, Mary. *The Proper Lady and the Woman Writer: Ideology as Style in the Works of Mary Wollstonecraft, Mary Shelley, and Jane Austin.* Chicago: Univ. of Chicago Press, 1984.

Powell, Timothy. *The Beautiful Absurdity of American Identity: Conflicting Constructions of the Nation in Nineteenth Century American Literature.* Ph.D. dissertation, Brandeis University, 1995.

Rabinow, Paul, ed. *The Foucault Reader.* New York: Pantheon, 1984.

Rabinowitz, Richard. *The Spiritual Self in Everyday Life: The Transformation of Personal Religious Experience in Nineteenth-Century New England.* Boston: Northeastern Univ. Press, 1989.

Radway, Janice A. *Reading the Romance: Women, Patriarchy, and Popular Literature.* Chapel Hill: Univ. of North Carolina Press, 1984.

Ramazani, Jahan. *Poetry of Mourning: The Modern Elegy from Hardy to Heaney.* Chicago: Univ. of Chicago Press, 1994.

Reynolds, David S. *Beneath the American Renaissance: The Subversive Imagination in the Age of Emerson and Melville.* Cambridge: Harvard Univ. Press, 1989.

———. *Faith in Fiction: The Emergence of Religious Literature in America.* Cambridge: Harvard Univ. Press, 1981.

Rosaldo, Michelle Zimbalist, and Louise Lamphere, eds. *Woman, Culture, and Society.* Stanford: Stanford Univ. Press, 1974.

Rosaldo, Renato. *Culture and Truth: The Remaking of Social Analysis.* Boston: Beacon, 1989.

Rosenberg, Bernard, and David Manning White, eds. *Mass Culture: The Popular Arts in America.* Glencoe, Ill.: Free Press, 1957.

Rossi, Alice S., ed. *The Feminist Papers: From Adams to de Beauvoir.* Boston: Northeastern Univ. Press, 1973.

Ryan, Mary P. *Cradle of the Middle Class: The Family in Oneida County, New York, 1790–1865.* New York: Cambridge Univ. Press, 1981.

————. *Womanhood in America: From Colonial Times to the Present.* New York: Franklin Watts, 1983.

————. "A Woman's Awakening: Evangelical Religion and the Families of Utica, N.Y., 1800–1842." *Women and American Religion.* Ed. Janet Wilson James. Philadelphia: Univ. of Pennsylvania Press, 1980.

Sacks, Peter M. *The English Elegy: Studies in the Genre from Spenser to Yeats.* Baltimore: Johns Hopkins Univ. Press, 1985.

Samuels, Shirley, ed. *The Culture of Sentiment: Race, Gender, and Sentimentality in Nineteenth-Century America.* New York: Oxford Univ. Press, 1992.

Sandweiss, Martha. *Photography in Nineteenth-Century America.* New York: Abrams, 1991.

Sartre, Jean-Paul. *"What Is Literature?" and Other Essays.* Cambridge: Harvard Univ. Press, 1988.

Sayre, Robert. "Redefining Sentimentality." Paper given at the 1993 American Studies Assoc. Conference, Boston, Mass.

Scarry, Elaine. *The Body in Pain: The Making and Un-Making of the World.* New York: Oxford Univ. Press, 1985.

Schacht, Paul. "The Lonesomeness of Huckleberry Finn." *American Literature* 53 (1981): 189–201.

Schlesinger, Arthur M., Jr. *The Age of Jackson.* Boston: Little, Brown, 1945.

Schorsch, Anita. *Mourning Becomes America: Mourning Art in the New Nation.* New Jersey: Main Street, 1976.

Schultz, Lucille M. "Parlor Talk in Mark Twain: The Grangerford Parlor and the House Beautiful." *Mark Twain Journal* 19.4 (summer 1979): 14–19.

Schweitzer, Ivy. *The Work of Self-Representation: Lyric Poetry in Colonial New England.* Chapel Hill: Univ. of North Carolina Press, 1991.

Scott, Arthur L. *On the Poetry of Mark Twain with a Selection from His Verse.* Urbana: Univ. of Illinois Press, 1966.

Shakespeare, William. *The Riverside Shakespeare.* Ed. G. Blakemore Evans. Boston: Houghton Mifflin, 1974.

Showalter, Elaine. *The Female Malady: Woman, Madness, and English Culture, 1830–1980.* New York: Pantheon, 1985.

————. "Piecing and Writing." Miller and Heilbrun. New York: Columbia Univ. Press, 1986, 222–47.

Shucard, Alan. *American Poetry: The Puritans through Walt Whitman*. Boston: Twayne, 1988.

Sigourney, Lydia Howard Huntley. *Illustrated Poems by Mrs. L. H. Sigourney*. Philadelphia: Carey & Hart, 1849.

———. *Illustrated Poems by Mrs. L. H. Sigourney*. Philadelphia: Lindsay & Blakiston, 1860.

———. "Introduction." *The Works of Mrs. Hemans, with A Memoir by Her Sister and An Essay on Her Genius, by Mrs. Sigourney*. Philadelphia: Lea & Blanchard, 1842.

———. *Letters of Life*. New York: Appleton, 1866.

———. *Traits of the Aborigines of America*. Cambridge, 1822.

Simonds, Wendy, and Barbara Katz Rothman. *Centuries of Solace: Expressions of Maternal Grief in Popular Literature*. Philadelphia: Temple Univ. Press, 1992.

Simonds, William. *Our Little Ones in Heaven*. Boston: Gould & Lincoln, 1858.

Sklar, Kathryn Kish. *Catherine Beecher: A Study in American Domesticity*. New York: Norton, 1976.

Smith-Rosenberg, Carroll. "Beauty, the Beast, and the Militant Woman: A Case Study of Sex Roles and Social Stress in Jacksonian America." *American Quarterly* 23 (October 1971): 562–84.

———. "The Female World of Love and Ritual: Relations between Women in Nineteenth-Century America." *Signs* 1 (fall 1975): 1–29.

———. *Religion and the Rise of the American City: The New York City Mission Movement, 1812–1870*. Ithaca: Cornell Univ. Press, 1971.

Sollors, Werner. *Beyond Ethnicity: Consent and Descent in American Culture*. New York: Oxford Univ. Press, 1986.

Spillers, Hortense J., ed. *Comparative American Identities: Race, Sex, and Nationality in the Modern Text*. New York: Routledge, 1991.

Spillers, Robert, et al. *Literary History of the United States*. 3d ed. New York: Macmillan, 1963.

St. Armand, Barton Levi. *Emily Dickinson and Her Culture: The Soul's Society*. Cambridge: Cambridge Univ. Press, 1984.

St. John de Crèvecoeur, J. Hector. *Letters from an American Farmer and Sketches of Eighteenth-Century America*. New York: Penguin, 1981.

Stannard, David E. *The Puritan Way of Death: A Study in Religion, Culture, and Social Change*. Oxford: Oxford Univ. Press, 1977.

———. "Where All Our Steps Are Tending: Death in the American Context." Pike and Armstrong.

———, ed. *Death in America*. Philadelphia: Univ. of Pennsylvania Press, 1975.

Stilwell, Lewis D. *Migration from Vermont*. Montpelier: Vermont Historical Soc., 1948.

Stoddard, Elizabeth. *The Morgesons and Other Writings, Published and Unpublished*. Philadelphia: Univ. of Pennsylvania Press, 1984.

Stolnitz, Jerome, ed. *Aesthetics.* New York: Macmillan, 1965.

Stone, Lawrence. "Death and Its History." *New York Review of Books,* Oct. 12, 1978.

———. "Death in New England." *New York Review of Books,* Oct. 26, 1978.

Stonely, Peter. *Mark Twain and the Feminine Aesthetic.* Cambridge: Cambridge Univ. Press, 1992.

Stowe, Harriet Beecher. *Dred: A Tale of the Great Dismal Swamp.* Boston: Houghton Mifflin, 1886.

———. *Uncle Tom's Cabin: or, Life among the Lowly.* New York: Penguin, 1986.

Strickland, Carol C. "Of Love and Loneliness: Society and Self in *Huckleberry Finn.*" *Mark Twain Journal* 21.4 (fall 1983): 50–52.

Suleiman, Susan Rubin. *Authoritarian Fictions: The Ideological Novel as a Literary Genre.* New York: Columbia Univ. Press, 1983.

Taft, Robert. *Photography and the American Scene: A Social History.* 1938. New York: Dover, 1964.

Tate, Claudia. *Domestic Allegories of Political Desire: The Black Heroine's Text at the Turn of the Century.* London: Oxford Univ. Press, 1992.

Tenney, Lucy Maria. Ms. album, circa 1820. American Antiquarian Soc., Worcester, Mass.

Thompson, Ralph. *American Literary Annuals and Gift Books: 1825–1865.* New York: Wilson, 1936.

Thoreau, Henry David. *Walden and Civil Disobedience.* New York: Norton, 1966.

Tocqueville, Alexis de. *Democracy in America.* New York: Perennial Library, 1988.

Tompkins, Jane. *Sensational Designs: The Cultural Work of American Fiction, 1760–1860.* New York: Oxford Univ. Press, 1985.

Trachtenberg, Alan. *Reading American Photographs: Images as History, Mathew Brady to Walker Evans.* New York: Hill & Wang, 1989.

Twain, Mark. *The Adventures of Huckleberry Finn: Norton Critical Edition,* 2d ed. New York: W. W. Norton, 1961.

———. *Adventures of Tom Sawyer.* New York: Vintage/Library of America, 1991.

———. *Mark Twain's Autobiography.* 2 vols. New York: Collier, 1925.

———. *The Mysterious Stranger and Other Stories.* New York: Harper and Brothers, 1922.

Twain, Mark, and Charles Dudley Warner. *The Gilded Age.* New York: Oxford Univ. Press, 1996.

Upton, Helen. Telephone conversation with author, Dover, Vt., November 25, 1988.

Veblen, Thorstein. *The Theory of the Leisure Class.* New York: Penguin, 1979.

Wagenknecht, Edward. *Henry Wadsworth Longfellow: Portrait of an American Humanist.* New York: Oxford Univ. Press, 1966.

Walker, Cheryl. *The Nightingale's Burden: Women Poets and American Culture before 1900.* Bloomington: Indiana Univ. Press, 1982.

Wallis, Brian, ed. *Art after Modernism: Rethinking Representation.* New York: New Museum of Contemporary Art, 1988.

Wardley, Lynn. "Relic, Fetish, Femmage: The Aesthetics of Sentiment in the Work of Stowe." Samuels, 165–91.

Warhol, Robyn R. *Gendered Interventions: Narrative Discourse in the Victorian Novel.* New Brunswick: Rutgers Univ. Press, 1989.

Warner, Miss Jane R. Ms. album, dated 1833. American Antiquarian Soc., Worcester, Mass.

Watts, Emily Stipes. *The Poetry of American Women from 1632 to 1945.* Austin: Univ. of Texas Press, 1977.

Webb, Sarah E. Ms. album of Sarah E. Webb, 1841–43. American Antiquarian Soc., Worcester, Mass.

Weiner, Annette B. *Inalienable Possessions: The Paradox of Keeping While-Giving.* Berkeley: Univ. of California Press, 1992.

Welling, William. *Photography in America: The Formative Years, 1839–1900.* New York: Cromwell, 1978.

Welter, Barbara. "The Cult of True Womanhood." *American Quarterly* 18 (1966). Rpt. in *The American Family in Social-Historical Perspective.* Ed. Michael Gordon New York: St. Martin's, 1973.

———. *The Mind of America, 1820–1860.* New York: Columbia Univ. Press, 1975.

Westbrook, Perry D. *Acres of Flint: Writers of Rural New England, 1870–1900.* Washington, D.C.: Scarecrow Press, 1951.

———. *A Literary History of New England.* Bethlehem: Lehigh Univ. Press, 1988.

———, ed. *The Writing Women of New England, 1830–1900: An Anthology.* Metuchen, N.J.: Scarecrow Press, 1982.

Whitman, Walt. *Leaves of Grass.* New York: Signet, 1980.

———. "Preface." *Walt Whitman's Leaves of Grass: The First (1855) Edition.* Ed. Malcolm Cowley. New York, 1959.

Whittier, John Greenleaf. *The Complete Poetical Works.* Boston: Houghton, 1881.

Williams, Raymond. *Culture and Society: 1780–1950.* New York: Columbia Univ. Press, 1983.

Williamson, Chilton. *Vermont in Quandary, 1763–1825.* Montpelier: Vermont Historical Soc., 1949.

Wills, Gary. *Inventing America: Jefferson's Declaration of Independence.* New York: Vintage, 1979.

———. *Lincoln at Gettysburg: The Words That Remade America.* New York: Simon & Schuster, 1992.

Wister, Owen. *The Virginian: A Horseman of the Plains.* New York: Penguin, 1988.

Zagarell, Sandra. "Expanding 'America': Lydia Sigourney's Sketch of Connecticut, Catherine Sedgwick's Hope Leslie." *Tulsa Studies in Women's Literature* 6:2 (fall 1987): 225–45.

INDEX

Abolition, 27

Adorno, Theodor, 52, 235 n.3

Aesthetics, xi–xii, 2, 8, 12–15, 25–26, 49

Ahlstrom, Sidney, 29, 232 n.28

Alcott, Louisa May, 137

Allegory, 100, 117–121, 131, 166

American Adam, 115–116, 135, 142–143

American poet, 113, 133–143

American sentimental tradition, 1

Anderson, Benedict, 105, 122, 226 n.6, 242 n.1

Anthropology, xiii, 7

Apostrophe, 39–47, 67–78, 91–92, 117, 121–129, 155–156, 165

Ariès, Phillipe, 22

Aristotle, 89

Armstrong, Janice, 22

Arvin, Newton, 227 n.2

Bakhtin, M. M., 89. *See also* Genre; Heteroglossia; Monologia

Baldwin, James, 161, 225 n.3, 227 n.3

Baptist church, 20, 27–29, 232 n.28, 233 n.31

Barlow, Joel, 8, 108–113, 123, 135

Barnes, Elizabeth, 243 n.4

Baym, Nina, 14

Bennington, Vermont, 22–23

Bercovitch, Sacvan, 230 n.8

Berlant, Lauren, 244 n.9

Boethius, 55

Bonds, 6–9, 17, 31–39, 42, 52–55, 62, 72–77, 84–86, 90–95, 104, 115, 121,

126–138, 146, 153–159, 162, 165, 176, 181–184

Bourdieu, Pierre, 25, 247 n.9

Bradstreet, Anne, 70–73

Brattleboro, Vermont, 22–23

Breitwieser, Mitchell, 238 n.1

Bricolage, 48, 105, 174. *See also* Lévi-Strauss, Claude

Bright, J. H., 42

Brown, Gillian, 236 n.6, 236 n.10

Bryant, William Cullen, 135

Buell, Laurence, 225 n.4, 250 n.22

Burr, Lucy, 38

Byron, Lord, 25–26

Carpenter, Edward, 24

Carrier, James, 236 n.7

Carville, James, 181

Channing, William Ellery, 142

Cheal, David, 234 n.3, 235 n.3, 236 n.10, 237 n.12

Cherokee, 112

Child, Lydia Maria, 123–124

Civil War, 52–57, 94, 129, 139, 147–161

Clark, Suzanne, 227 n.1

Class, xii, 16, 34–35, 55–59, 66, 74, 82, 104, 123, 133–143, 146–151, 161–167, 181–186. *See also* Middle class

Coleridge, Samuel Taylor, 26, 135

Collaboration, 3, 79–80, 83–95, 105, 131–137, 142–143, 148–149, 181–182; and nation, 8, 105–106, 131, 148–155; and self, 4–8, 21–22, 32–37, 52–55, 77

Mary Louise Kete is Assistant Professor of English,
University of Vermont

Library of Congress Cataloging-in-Publication Data
Kete, Mary Louise.
Sentimental collaborations : mourning and middle-class identity
in nineteenth-century America / Mary Louise Kete.
p.   cm. — (New Americanists)
Includes bibliographical references (p.   ) and index.
ISBN 0-8223-2435-0 (cloth : alk. paper). —
ISBN 0-8223-2471-7 (paper : alk. paper)
1. American literature—19th century—History and criticism.
2. Mourning customs in literature.   3. Mourning customs—United
States—History—19th century.   4. Middle class—United States—
History—19th century.   5. Sentimentalism in literature.   6. Group
identity in literature.   7. Middle class in literature.   I. Title.
II. Series.
PS217.M67K48   2000
810.9'355—dc21   99-29366   CIP